DIGITAL EFFECTS ANIMATION USING MAYA

Kian Bee Ng

Publisher: Jenifer L. Niles
Interior Design/Comp: PageMasters
Cover Design: Sherry Stinson
Printer: InterCity Press, Rockland, Ma

CHARLES RIVER MEDIA, Inc.
P.O. Box 417, 403 VFW Drive
Rockland, MA 02370
781-871-4184
781-871-4376(FAX)
chrivmedia@aol.com
http://www.charlesriver.com

This book is printed on acid-free paper

DIGITAL EFFECTS ANIMATION USING MAYA

by Kian Bee Ng
    ISBN 1-886801-37-1
    Printed in the United States of America

99 00 01 02 7 6 5 4 3 2

CHARLES RIVER MEDIA titles are available for site license or bulk purchase by institutions, user groups, corporations, etc. For additional information, please contact the Special Sales Department at 781-871-4184.

CONTENTS

ABOUT THE AUTHOR

Kian received his bachelor degree in computer engineering in 1994 specializing in advanced computer graphics. However, his interest in computer graphics dates back to 1989 when he first owned an Amiga machine. Since then, his interest has been wide-ranging: from drawing, to modeling, animating, developing real-time virtual reality applications, writing plug-ins, and developing his own animation library system.

In 1996, he was certified as an Alias | Wavefront Instructor (Animation). He moved on to be certified as an Alias | Wavefront Principal Instructor (Animation) in 1997. He has worked on various projects, including console game animation, multimedia, video, real-time visualization, and feature film projects. His work has been short-listed for screening in the Computer Animation Festival in SIGGRAPH.

As a well-rounded CG artist, he received his Master of Business Administration degree in 1997. He is currently working as a Technical Director in a production company in Japan.

DEDICATION

I dedicate this book to my mother, Yong Lai Hua, who has taught me, in her many special ways, the art of perseverance and dedication.

TRADEMARK ACKNOWLEDGMENTS

All brand names and product names mentioned in this book are trademarks or registered trademarks of their respective companies.

ACKNOWLEDGMENTS

This book would remain on my to-do list if not for the support of the many wonderful individuals and organizations, among them:

My wife, Seki KeJia, for her patience, optimism, and above all, her love.

Alias | Wavefront, for sponsoring Maya, including me as a beta tester, and allowing me to capture and include all the Maya screenshots in this book. In particular, I would like to offer my sincere thanks to Marc Su, Alex Kelley, and the various support staff and engineers from both the Toronto and Tokyo offices for their patience and support.

Arete Image Software, in particular Reid Nicol and the support staff, for sponsoring the wonderful piece of software, Digital Nature Tools.

3D Café, in particular Carolyn Lueders, for the generous support of the models and textures given in the CD.

My publisher, Charles River Media, in particular Jenifer Niles, for giving me the opportunity to share my knowledge and ideas.

Pastor Jerry Jantzen of International Christian Fellowship, Sapporo, and all its members for their prayers and blessings.

My sisters, especially Stephanie Yeat Leng Ng, for her time dedicated to help settle all my mail and administrative work while I have been away from home.

And last but not least, my warmest thanks to my many students, colleagues, and friends, whom I am privileged to know over the years, both professionally and personally. This book would not exist without all your questions and ideas. Thank you.

1

INTRODUCTION

There are several books that provide insights into modeling, character animation, lighting, and rendering. However, few books are dedicated to digital effects animation. This is not surprising as effects animation often employs the use of particle systems, which is considered advanced animation in many contexts.

Traditionally, due to the complex nature of particle systems, digital effects were the domain of graphics programmers, mathematically inclined individuals, or production houses with big budgets to invest in state-of-the-art hardware and particle systems software. However, as software continues to evolve with more powerful functions, improved user interfaces, and better workflow, and while hardware continues to break new ground with higher computing power, many digital effects that were attainable only in high-budget feature films are now within reach of many production houses and animators.

CHALLENGE OF EFFECTS ANIMATION

Unlike models where objects and characters are defined geometrically using, say, a polygonal or NURBS system, the challenge facing most effects animators and technical directors is that effects cannot always be modeled or described using such systems. Effects animation often employs the use of particle systems, which is computationally expensive and less flexible. For example, character animators often can simplify and test their character animation through the use of simple skeleton structures or bounding boxes. However, with the use of particle systems, effects animators often need to test-render individual key frames to obtain a visual feedback of their animation. The challenge of creating effects animation is both technical as well as aesthetic: from problem-solving analysis to generating believable animation.

ROLE OF EFFECTS ANIMATOR

To be called an *effects animator* or *effects technical director (TD)*, you must have sufficient knowledge of what constitutes a particle system, the technical aspects of it, as well as the aesthetic ability to use the system to fulfill your desired animation. Based on the concepts in Betty Edwards' book, *Drawing on the Right Side of the Brain*, this would imply that both your left and right brains must be fully utilized. Lacking either technical or aesthetic skills, would be like using just one side of your brain—literally.

So, what does it take to be a good effects animator? The key to being a successful effects animator lies in a love of nature. Though technical understanding can bring you to a high level of competency, without a passion for nature and a keen desire to observe it, you will find it hard to excel in this field. It is analogous to learning to swim by studying the theory and physics of water dynamics in relation to the movement of various strokes, without physically going into the water. While you cannot transform yourself into the elements of nature, you can still be part of it by observing and integrating your aesthetic observation with your technical knowledge.

WHY MAYA?

Many books on animation either do not specify a particular software tool or cover all kind of software tools in the course of their tutorials. One of the good points of this approach is that you are likely to be able to apply the general techniques to several different software packages of your choice. However, at times you may find this approach too general because it does not allow you to explore the process in depth. This is analogous to learning programming using all pseudo codes and never applying theory to any particular programming language. Pseudo codes are great for generalizing ideas and teaching common techniques. However, that is as far as it can go. Without specifying a particular language, you will find that a lot depends on your own understanding and ability to apply the same techniques to a language of your choice.

Usually the books that teach programming techniques will focus on a particular programming language. And the techniques that you learn in such books, for example a C++ programming guide, are often applicable to other languages that are similar in structure and nature. Likewise, it is a better option for you to learn effects animation using a particular application than to generalize the method, and hope that you will be able to apply it later to the software of your choice. And in this case, the language of effects animation is Maya.

Maya is a complete, production-ready animation software package. The integrated nature of Maya's particle effects system with all the modeling functions make it one of the best off-the-shelf tools available for tackling challenging effects animation. Its revolutionary workflow allows complex animation to be created with much ease. In addition, the open architecture of Maya allows artists as well as programmers to easily add functions into the program. This feature is particularly useful in creating custom effects to meet your production goals. Unfortunately, many traditional software packages do not have such flexibility and instead bury their flexibility deep in the program code.

Having said that, it is not the intention of this book to replace the standard Maya tutorials or manuals. It simply uses Maya as the main tool to assist you in creating various examples of effects animation. The principles and practices discussed here are applicable to most other effects animation software. However, you will gain the most if Maya is also your language of choice for effects animation.

THE KEY FEATURES OF THIS BOOK

As an effects animator or technical director, one of the most crucial skills is your problem-solving ability. In a typical production environment, everything is in a state of flux. Unexpected changes often occur. Therefore, it is of paramount importance that your problem-solving skills enable you to meet the new requirements, modifications, and challenges. The importance of such skills cannot be overemphasized. Surprisingly, most 3D tutorial books do not even mention it.

The key features of this book are the problem-solving analysis and simulated production environment tutorials. In other words, instead of providing you with a series of steps eventually ending with the final results, I have created a simulated production scenario for each tutorial. As you begin each tutorial, a new scenario will be given to you. Along with these simulated scenarios, you will be given solutions that explain the instructions and at the same time different tasks that prompt you for further thinking. Hopefully, this approach will build your problem-solving skills.

In addition, though the emphasis is on creating digital effects animation, other important skills such as modeling, rendering, compositing, and lighting, will be presented as you complete the tutorials. It is also the objective of this book that the more you read, the more inspired you will be with many different ideas. You are encouraged to challenge the theory and practice and venture beyond what is covered here.

STRUCTURE OF THIS BOOK

This book is divided into two main parts. The first part consists of Chapters One to Three. Chapter Two covers the fundamental concepts related to digital effects animation. Chapter Three presents complementary concepts such as modeling, rendering, lighting, and camera composition.

When understood and successfully applied, these concepts will help you to become a more well-rounded computer graphics (CG) artist.

The second part of the book divides digital effects into five elements. The first four elements belong to the elements of nature: Fire, Water, Air, and Earth. The fifth element is the elements of Dynamics, both soft-body as well as rigid-body dynamics. These elements are symbolized as five separate Platonic solids. The Platonic solids were first discovered by the Pythagoreans many years ago. They were described by Plato and used by him for his theory of the four elements. The fifth Platonic solid, *dodecahedron*, was described by Plato, in the *Timaeus*, as "... the god used for arranging the constellations on the whole heaven." In other words, it symbolizes heavens or more appropriately, the Universe. The Universe, in essence, is one huge complex mathematical science. Many theories, such as Newton's Law of Universal Gravitation and Kepler's Three Laws of Planetary Motion form part of the Laws of the Universe. Dynamics conform to a subset of these theories. Therefore, it is in this context that I relate these Platonic solids to the digital effects animation covered in this book.

These five elements of digital effects animation are covered from Chapters Four through Twelve. They are presented as tutorials using real-life production requirements as the scenarios. Chapters Four and Five cover the creation of fire, both normal campfire type of fire, and fire that moves with actions and dynamics. It is strongly suggested that you read this section before jumping to other tutorials because most Maya-related concepts are first encountered and presented in this section. In particular, Chapter Four contains very detailed instructions for every step. It is assumed that you may not be sure where all those buttons and menus are in the beginning. However, after Chapter Four, as you gain more experience, the instructions will be straightforward to save space and time.

Chapters Six and Seven cover the creation of the common water effects such as under- and above-water, rain, and splashes. Chapters Eight and Nine cover the creation of different air particle effects. This includes the explosion effects, dusty and sandy effects, and clouds effects. Chapter Ten is dedicated to creating earth, in particular, terrain and grass. An introduction tutorial to creating shader plug-ins is also presented in this chapter. The terrain will be generated using the plug-in created. The last section, dynamics, is covered in Chapters Eleven and Twelve. Chapter Eleven includes the creation of an interesting animation that uses both soft- and rigid-body dynamics. Chapter Twelve presents the challenge of creating a group control system that uses only MEL (Maya Embedded Language).

Finally, an appendix briefly describing the past and future of visual effects animation is presented.

THE APPROACH

Maya is a state-of-the-art software application. Its strength lies in its completeness in providing various tools and options for users to meet the most challenging and demanding production task. However, precisely because of its strength, novice users can easily get confused by its many tool options and wonder where to start, what to try, and why the results did not turn out as they expected.

Michael Porter, the renowned business sage, said that the way to remain competitive is to stay focused. Applying his ideas in problem solving, the approach adopted in this book, is to start simple and stay simple (S^4). That is to say if a tool or method is useful in solving a problem, keep using it. If a problem can be solved in a simpler way, then do it that way. If a new tool does not improve your workflow and productivity, then don't use it. This principle is especially important in today's hectic environment where product cycles are much shorter, and new tools, new hardware, and new methods, keep popping out on the market shelves every quarter. Organizations that do not remain focused end up chasing one product after another and spending more resources for endless retraining and product upgrades instead of generating higher productivity and revenues.

On the other hand, it is important to keep a balanced view and remain open to the needs of research and development for new tools and solutions. A simple way to decide your needs is to ask yourself if the current tools provide sufficient flexibility to direct your scene. For example, if you need to change the lighting on the character, or to expand the explosion a little to cover the windows, do you require a great deal of re-modeling, re-lighting, re-rendering, and re-compositing? Can you simply recycle your current work with little modification and yet achieve your desired results? If your answer is no, then it may be time for you to review your workflow and problem-solving tools.

PREREQUISITES FOR USING THIS BOOK

To successfully complete this book, you should have a basic understanding of 3D animation. For example, you should at least be familiar with using 3D software to view objects in orthographic (top, side, front) and perspective views. In addition, though it is not necessary that you have experience in using Maya, it will certainly enhance your progress if you have explored the basics of Maya so that you know where to look for the various menus and buttons. You should also understand mathematical concepts such as the common trigonometry functions (sine and cosine functions) and three-dimensional vectors. You may have learned these mathematical concepts in your early school days so it is advisable to review them before you begin this book.

The tutorials presented here are independent of one another. However, as you progress from one chapter to another, it is assumed that you have already built up your skills and experience from the earlier chapters. Thus whenever you encounter unfamiliar concepts, they are most likely explained in the earlier chapters. If all else fails, look in the Maya manuals.

WHAT YOU WILL NEED

The tutorials were first developed using Maya 1.0 on NT. Subsequently, I became a Maya 2.0 NT beta tester, so I have updated all the tutorials to Maya 2.0. Therefore, even if you are still using earlier versions of Maya, you should be able to follow the instructions with few modifications.

Software

The tutorials in this book make full use of Maya F/X. This module is part of the standard Maya package. Whether you bought Maya Complete or Maya Unlimited, you should have this module installed in your system.

In addition, you should have access to a composition software of your choice. There are several composition software applications available in the market, such as Adobe Premiere (on PC), Alias Wavefront Composer (on Irix), and Maya Fusion (on NT). When you bought Maya, a Lite version of Composer (on Irix) or Fusion (on NT) is available for you to use. They are more than sufficient for you to complete the tutorials here. A brief discussion of composition is also presented in Chapter Two.

In Chapter Ten, the theory and practice of writing a Maya plug-in is presented. If you would like to try compiling your own tutorial codes into a plug-in, you will need to have the following:

- Microsoft Visual C++ v5.0 or v 6.0 if you are working on NT or
- MIPS Pro 7.2 Compiler if you are working on SGI

In Chapter Eleven, you will also need to have the Maya Cloth module installed, which comes with the Maya Unlimited package, to test the cloth animation tutorial.

Hardware

You are strongly advised to consult your hardware suppliers as well as Alias | Wavefront on the recommended hardware configurations if you are still unsure of what is required to run Maya. However, to give you an idea of what hardware was used for the development of the tutorials and animation in this book, I have included my NT hardware configuration.

In the beginning, the hardware configuration included:

- Single PII processor at 450 MHz
- 384MB RAM
- A medium-range graphics hardware card

At the later stage, in order to speed up the development, the hardware configuration was given a boost to:

- Dual PII processors at 450 MHz
- 512MB RAM
- The same medium-range graphics hardware card
- More hard disk space

ABOUT THE CD

The CD contains the final movie files that I have created for the tutorials. These movie files are the results that you should attain at the end of each chapter. You will be asked to reference the movie files when you complete the tutorial in order to compare them with your results.

The CD also contains various models for you to use during the course of the tutorials. The models provided are courtesy of 3D Café.

The movie files are all without audio. They are in the common Apple QuickTime format.

WEBSITE SUPPORT

A website has been set up as an additional support for this book. You are encouraged to visit the website for the latest updates. This website is my personal effort to help you better understand and complete the tutorials in this book. You may post any problems that you encounter while doing the tutorials to the website and I'll attempt to answer them as much as possible.

The address of the website is: http://www.4deffects.com.

ASSUMPTIONS AND DEFINITIONS

The following assumptions and definitions are made in this book:

Frame Rate

Depending on your medium of output and the region your country belongs to, you may be using a frame rate of 24, or 25, or 30, etc. To standardize, the book will adopt a frame rate of 30 frames per second.

TD versus Effects Animator

Depending on how one defines the title *effects technical director (TD)* and *effects animator*, the job scope is likely to be different. However, as far as the book is concerned, it is assumed that the main task of effects animator and TD involves problem solving and creating digital effects. Thus the term effects TD and effects animator are used interchangeably in the book.

Special Effects, Digital Effects, and Visual Effects

For the purpose of communication in this book, the following assumptions are made:

- Special F/X refers to effects created using physical pyrotechnics and explosives devices.
- Digital F/X refers to effects created purely through computer means.
- Visual F/X refers to effects created using either the digital or special F/X, or a combination of both.

Production Process

As mentioned above, a key feature of this book is the simulated production environment tutorials. However, a true production process is complex and dynamic. Therefore, the book has assumed a very simple and scaled-down version of the process. In the beginning, during the process of understanding a given task and scenario, it is assumed to be the pre-production stage. When the actual instructions and steps are taken to carry out the task, it is assumed to be the production and testing stage. Finally, when all the different pieces of work are output and composited together, the stage will be called post-production.

Production Terms

The terms shot, cut, scene, sequence, and act, are loosely used to mean an animation created with a series of images. The content of these imageries are not related to the actual meaning of these production terms. Therefore, whenever you read any of these terms, you can safely regard them as just a series of animation images that you have or will do.

2

FUNDAMENTALS OF DIGITAL EFFECTS

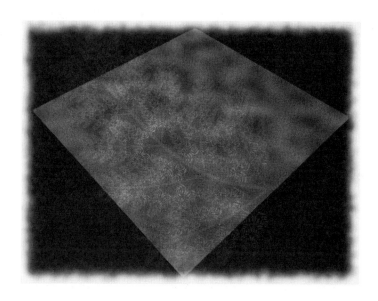

INTRODUCTION

As far as I know, there are no rules that govern the creation of effects animation. It takes time, patience, good observation, and a well-balanced sense of aesthetic judgement. Whatever you may lack from this list, you can try to make up by building a solid foundation of the fundamentals. For a character animator, the fundamentals lie mostly in traditional fine arts training. As a digital effects animator, the fundamentals lie mostly in your technical experience and knowledge of mathematics, in particular, computer graphics mathematics. Whether you have a strong liking for mathematics or a weak heart for even basic calculations, you cannot escape the fact that our universe is made up of a lot of 1s and 0s. Therefore, knowing essential mathematics is a necessary skill that will pay off in the long run.

This chapter covers very briefly the fundamental theory and practice of several technical and graphics-related mathematical concepts. They will be useful in your work as an effects artist. As you read this chapter, whenever you need to get a more in-depth understanding of the concepts discussed, you should consult another graphics textbook or technical papers. Although you will not turn into an instant effects expert by the end of the chapter, hopefully you will have gained enough confidence to move on to the tutorials in the subsequent chapters.

PARTICLE BASICS

Particle system was first introduced by W.T. Reeves in 1983 to model fuzzy objects such as fire and clouds. In a typical particle system, an object is represented by a set of particles. Each particle is born, evolves in space, and eventually dies at different times according to its individual animation. Particles may also generate new particles during their lifetime, gain new attributes depending on their age, and move according to either deterministic or stochastic laws of motion. Thus, by controlling the color, transparency, size, and dynamic behavior using mathematical functions, you can get different overall visual effects of the object.

In a typical particle system, the following parameters are common across all software:

- position
- velocity
- size
- color
- transparency
- shape
- lifetime

As you complete the Maya tutorials, you will see that Maya provides control over all of these parameters and many more.

In addition, Maya supplies a number of preset effects such as Fire, Flow, and Smoke. While these effects are quick and easy to use, it is still important for you to understand the fundamentals of effects creation. Once you have the fundamentals, you will realize that it is not difficult to create your own one-click effects using expressions and MEL.

ADVANTAGES AND DISADVANTAGES

There are several advantages and disadvantages of using particle systems for modeling and animation compared to using the traditional geometrical method. The following table gives a brief comparison.

	ADVANTAGES	DISADVANTAGES
Particle Approach	Procedural control	Computationally expensive
	Modeling of large dataset	Limited visual feedback because rendering is required to see the actual results
	Easily replaceable particle with geometrical objects for group animation, for example, a flock of birds	
Geometric Approach	Direct manipulation of geometry	Impossible to handle large dataset such as creating hundreds of hairs or grass
	High level of user control	Difficult to generate fuzzy objects, such as fire and smoke

Besides the traditional particle system, Maya also implemented its soft- and rigid-body dynamics using particle systems control. Chapter Eleven will provide a tutorial on their usage.

As a general rule of thumb, when an object cannot be described by any form of geometry (such as clouds and fire), it is more effective to use particle systems to generate the object. However, if you are limited by the computational power of your machines or functionality of your software, there is always a simple workaround. You may, for example, scan in a cloud texture and map it easily onto a simple geometry. With an appropriate alpha channel created, you would still be able to get decent clouds moving across your digital environment. Incidentally, such a workaround is often found in real-time animation applications, such as a virtual walkthrough of a city.

PROCEDURAL BASICS

When modeling, it is more manageable to create only a few objects, say, one or two creatures. However, if you are required to model a hundred or a thousand similar creatures, it would be impossible. However, this would not be the case when you procedurally model your object. *Procedural modeling*, also known as *functionally based modeling*, allows you to generate a large class of objects by a single model with easily adjusted and intuitive parameters. Hence, all that you need to keep track of is a list of parameters. For example, for a model that generates different types of leaves, you may have parameters that control things such as the veins, size, and color of the leaves. From that point, when you are required to model hundreds of different types of leaves, all you need to do is to input different parameters to your model and you will be able to create different leaves.

Procedural modeling is applied when creating complex phenomena such as mountains, trees, leaves, clouds, and fire. These models are generally tedious to model by hand. Imagine if you were to adjust individually the vertices of a mountain model! It would be impossible to create.

This technique of procedurally creating and controlling your object is applicable in many contexts of computer graphics. You can also procedurally animate your scene. For example, if you have a scene with a mob of a thousand characters, each with its own action, you're likely to create a control model with necessary parameters that procedurally control the overall characters as a whole. It would be unmanageable to animate each of the characters individually.

When applying a procedural method to texturing your object, you have total control over every single detail of your texture. A typical example is the ramp texture in Maya where you can add or remove ramp entries at will. Procedural texturing is often compared to ad hoc texturing. Ad hoc texturing generally refers to using a fixed image. The image could be from a scanned photo or a PhotoShop-generated image, or a digitally captured picture.

Ad hoc textures provide several advantages. They are detailed, easily created, and simple to texture-map. However, there are several disadvantages. For example, textures taken from photos and magazines often include the environment lighting. Therefore, you may have to retouch the textures before they are usable. In addition, these textures are generally limited in size and are not seamless. Hence, they are a bad source for use in tiling and close-up rendering.

Though procedural means of modeling, animating, and texturing provide great flexibility and control, they are only as good as the functions that define them. Hence, most of the time, use the procedural or non-procedural method, whichever suits you. In Chapter Nine, you will go through a tutorial on creating a procedural cloud. In Chapter Ten, you will write a procedural terrain generator as a form of plug-in. In Chapter Twelve, you will find a tutorial on creating a control system that allows you to procedurally control and animate a group of objects.

CHAOTIC FUNCTION BASICS

In reality, nothing is perfect—neither human beings, nature, nor the trivial objects that surround us. In fact, being imperfect has become a desired feature. Take nature, for example—rocks are beautiful in the way that they have been weathered. You don't see a rock and marvel at how smooth it is; you are more likely to marvel at its unique shape and form caused by the way it has been weathered by nature. Look at a trivial object around you, such as the watch that you are wearing on your wrist. Do you not see some scratches or dirt marks on it? Even for a completely new watch, there are tiny marks on it that may not be visible to the naked eye.

Therefore, to fully and correctly model and mimic reality, it is important to understand that chaos exists everywhere. Organic nature and man-made materials all share a common feature: *chaos*. Mirrors are not perfectly smooth; trees are never perfectly straight; even human faces are not perfectly symmetrical.

Things that are perfect exist only in the world of computer graphics. In the world of CG, you are the creator. You can make perfectly straight coconut trees; you can create a perfectly smooth wineglass; you can even create perfectly flawless human faces. However, the "perfect" nature of CG is also one of the most daunting challenges facing animators. To create a believable world, a believable animation, animators have to *selectively* add in the chaos. Why selectively, you may ask, since chaos already exists everywhere? You have to be selective because in the cinematic world, just as in the photographic world, what interests the audience is not merely a snapshot of the object the way it is. Rather what is important is for you to create imageries that are able to bring out the characteristics of the subject of interest and yet seamlessly mimic the world in which it resides.

For example, if you compare your photographs to the work of great photographers, say a picture of a sunset, have you ever wondered why theirs received awards but yours didn't? The reason is that their pictures are more likely able to bring out the characteristics of the sunset than yours. Not that your pictures are fake. Nor that your picture depicts a lousy sunset. You may be in fact picturing the same sunset. But to carefully photograph it so that the mood, the ideas, and the emotions that come with sunsets are appropriately presented to the audience is a skill. Therefore, to selectively choose the right camera angle, right filter, and right view is analogous to what I mean by selectively adding in the chaos in the CG world.

An important characteristic of chaos is its random nature. There are several ways that you can create the random nature. You can, for example, painstakingly model, paint, or texture the randomness. However, a much easier way is through the use of random functions.

In Maya, there are a number of pre-defined random functions. They include the *gauss, noise, rand,* and *sphrand* functions. The manual provides very good examples of how to use them and their general distribution. You should refer to the manual for more details.

What is of greater interest to discuss in this section is the award winning function: *noise.* As you read more and develop your skill further, you will come to realize that, the random functions such as rand( ), gauss( ), etc. are good, but noise( ) is even better. The main advantage of the noise is its smooth and steady transition of one random value to another. There are several implementations of noise function. Figure 2-1 shows a typical one-dimensional noise function.

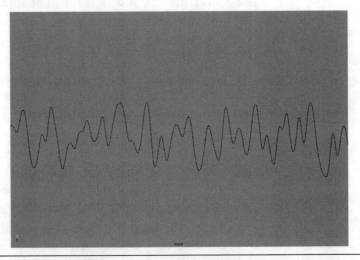

FIGURE 2-1   *A typical noise function curve*

For reasons that some may consider magic, the noise function is able to very closely depict the chaotic nature of much real-life imagery. Among the many common examples is the use of noise to generate realistic marble texture, wood texture, and fire effects.

In Maya, almost all textures, in one way or another, include the use of the noise function. The examples include the ramp texture that allows you to set noise with its HSV values, the 2D placement node that allows you to add noise to its UV values, and the 3D Brownian texture that is embedded with the noise function. As an animator, though you may not be writing your own noise function, you may one day need to write a function that uses noise as your fundamental building block. In fact, in Chapter Ten of this book, you will find a tutorial on building your own terrain generator with the help of a noise function. Thus, it is essential that you understand the basic implementation of noise.

From a simple layperson's perspective, a noise function consists of two parts:

1.   The random part
2.   The interpolation part

The *random part* involves generating randomly positioned points. The *interpolation part* is about how to interpolate between points. Figure 2-2 shows the same noise as Figure 2-1 but with all the random points indicated with a cross.

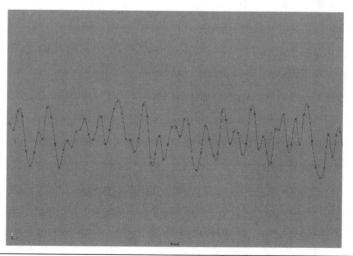

FIGURE 2-2   *A noise curve*

There are of course many different ways to generate the random points and many different ways to interpolate between them. Each method has its own merits. However, among all of them, the most commonly seen implementation of noise is that created by Ken Perlin. Perlin's noise function is implemented using a lattice method. Maya's noise function implementation is based on Perlin's noise function. While it is beyond the scope of this book to indulge in a discussion of the detailed implementation of the Perlin noise function, for those technically inclined individuals, the original Perlin noise code is included, with permission, below. In Chapter Ten, you will need to implement a fractal terrain with the help of a noise function such as Perlin noise.

```
/* coherent noise function over 1, 2 or 3 dimensions */
/* (copyright Ken Perlin) */
        #include <stdlib.h>
        #include <stdio.h>
        #include <math.h>
        #define B 0x100
        #define BM 0xff
        #define N 0x1000
        #define NP 12    /* 2^N */
        #define NM 0xfff
        static p[B + B + 2];
        static float g3[B + B + 2][3];
        static float g2[B + B + 2][2];
        static float g1[B + B + 2];
        static start = 1;
        static void init(void);
        #define s_curve(t) ( t * t * (3. - 2. * t) )
        #define lerp(t, a, b) ( a + t * (b - a) )
        #define setup(i,b0,b1,r0,r1)\
                t = vec[i] + N;\
                b0 = ((int)t) & BM;\
                b1 = (b0+1) & BM;\
                r0 = t - (int)t;\
                r1 = r0 - 1.;
        double noise1(double arg)
        {
                int bx0, bx1;
                float rx0, rx1, sx, t, u, v, vec[1];
                vec[0] = arg;
                if (start) {
                        start = 0;
                        init();
                }
```

```
        setup(0, bx0,bx1, rx0,rx1);
        sx = s_curve(rx0);
        u = rx0 * g1[ p[ bx0 ] ];
        v = rx1 * g1[ p[ bx1 ] ];
        return lerp(sx, u, v);
}
float noise2(float vec[2])
{
        int bx0, bx1, by0, by1, b00, b10, b01, b11;
        float rx0, rx1, ry0, ry1, *q, sx, sy, a, b, t, u, v;
        register i, j;
        if (start) {
                start = 0;
                init();
        }
        setup(0, bx0,bx1, rx0,rx1);
        setup(1, by0,by1, ry0,ry1);
        i = p[ bx0 ];
        j = p[ bx1 ];
        b00 = p[ i + by0 ];
        b10 = p[ j + by0 ];
        b01 = p[ i + by1 ];
        b11 = p[ j + by1 ];
        sx = s_curve(rx0);
        sy = s_curve(ry0);
#define at2(rx,ry) ( rx * q[0] + ry * q[1] )
        q = g2[ b00 ] ; u = at2(rx0,ry0);
        q = g2[ b10 ] ; v = at2(rx1,ry0);
        a = lerp(sx, u, v);
        q = g2[ b01 ] ; u = at2(rx0,ry1);
        q = g2[ b11 ] ; v = at2(rx1,ry1);
        b = lerp(sx, u, v);
        return lerp(sy, a, b);
}
float noise3(float vec[3])
{
        int bx0, bx1, by0, by1, bz0, bz1, b00, b10, b01, b11;
        float rx0, rx1, ry0, ry1, rz0, rz1, *q, sy, sz, a, b, c, d, t, u, v;
        register i, j;
        if (start) {
                start = 0;
                init();
        }
        setup(0, bx0,bx1, rx0,rx1);
        setup(1, by0,by1, ry0,ry1);
        setup(2, bz0,bz1, rz0,rz1);
        i = p[ bx0 ];
        j = p[ bx1 ];
        b00 = p[ i + by0 ];
        b10 = p[ j + by0 ];
        b01 = p[ i + by1 ];
        b11 = p[ j + by1 ];
```

```
        t  = s_curve(rx0);
        sy = s_curve(ry0);
        sz = s_curve(rz0);
#define at3(rx,ry,rz) ( rx * q[0] + ry * q[1] + rz * q[2] )
        q = g3[ b00 + bz0 ] ; u = at3(rx0,ry0,rz0);
        q = g3[ b10 + bz0 ] ; v = at3(rx1,ry0,rz0);
        a = lerp(t, u, v);
        q = g3[ b01 + bz0 ] ; u = at3(rx0,ry1,rz0);
        q = g3[ b11 + bz0 ] ; v = at3(rx1,ry1,rz0);
        b = lerp(t, u, v);
        c = lerp(sy, a, b);
        q = g3[ b00 + bz1 ] ; u = at3(rx0,ry0,rz1);
        q = g3[ b10 + bz1 ] ; v = at3(rx1,ry0,rz1);
        a = lerp(t, u, v);
        q = g3[ b01 + bz1 ] ; u = at3(rx0,ry1,rz1);
        q = g3[ b11 + bz1 ] ; v = at3(rx1,ry1,rz1);
        b = lerp(t, u, v);
        d = lerp(sy, a, b);
        return lerp(sz, c, d);
}
static void normalize2(float v[2])
{
        float s;
        s = sqrt(v[0] * v[0] + v[1] * v[1]);
        v[0] = v[0] / s;
        v[1] = v[1] / s;
}
static void normalize3(float v[3])
{
        float s;
        s = sqrt(v[0] * v[0] + v[1] * v[1] + v[2] * v[2]);
        v[0] = v[0] / s;
        v[1] = v[1] / s;
        v[2] = v[2] / s;
}
static void init(void)
{
        int i, j, k;
        for (i = 0 ; i < B ; i++) {
                p[i] = i;
                g1[i] = (float)((random() % (B + B)) - B) / B;
                for (j = 0 ; j < 2 ; j++)
                        g2[i][j] = (float)((random() % (B + B)) - B) / B;
                normalize2(g2[i]);
                for (j = 0 ; j < 3 ; j++)
                        g3[i][j] = (float)((random() % (B + B)) - B) / B;
                normalize3(g3[i]);
        }
        while (--i) {
                k = p[i];
                p[i] = p[j = random() % B];
                p[j] = k;
```

```
        }
for (i = 0 ; i < B + 2 ; i++) {
        p[B + i] = p[i];
        g1[B + i] = g1[i];
        for (j = 0 ; j < 2 ; j++)
                g2[B + i][j] = g2[i][j];
        for (j = 0 ; j < 3 ; j++)
                g3[B + i][j] = g3[i][j];
        }
    }
```

FUNCTION CURVE BASICS

In animation, there are several function curves that are important to remember. These function curves allow you to control your animation easily without key-framing. For example, when writing expressions to control a bouncing ball, you can easily create the movement with a sine function. And with some simple tweaking on the various parameters, you will be able to create a very realistic bouncing ball animation. And if you need to make changes subsequently, say, to control the bouncing ball based on the movement of a character's hand, you can achieve it by editing some parameters of the sine function.

In Maya, there is already a good set of library functions pre-defined. They are all presented in the *Expressions* manual of Maya. You should refer to this *Expressions* manual for the various explanations. In addition to those presented in the manual, the following functions are also particularly useful in controlling your animation.

Sine Waves

In computer graphics, there are no functions more important than the sine and cosine functions. They are the very first trigonometry functions that you learned in your early school days. Therefore, to re-emphasize their importance as applied in CG, I shall very briefly summarize their common usage:

$$Y = sin\ (time * frequency)*amplitude + offset;$$

Figure 2-3 shows the curves with varying values.

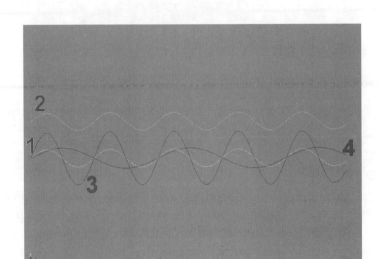

FIGURE 2-3   *Sine waves with varying frequency*

The curves were created using the MEL script shown below:

```
int $i;
float $x=0.0,$y=0.0,$z = 0.0;
int $num_CV = 30;
float $increment = 1.0;
float $amplitude = 1.0, $frequency = 1.0, $offset = 0.0;
curve -d 3 -p $x ($y+$offset) $z -k 0 -k 0 -k 0;
string $curve_name[] = 'ls -sl';
for ( $i = 0; $i <= $num_CV; $i++)
{
$x += $increment;
$y = $amplitude*sin($frequency*$x) + $offset;
curve -os -a -p $x $y $z $curve_name;
};
```

Curve 1 was created using amplitude as 1.0, frequency as 1.0, and offset as 0.0.

Curve 2 was created using amplitude as 1.0, frequency as 1.0, and offset as 3.5.

Curve 3 was created using amplitude as 3.0, frequency as 1.0, and offset as 0.0.

Curve 4 was created using amplitude as 1.0, frequency as 0.5, and offset as 0.0.

To run the above script, go to Window ➤ General Editors ➤ Script Editor… and enter the scripts.

Varying Power

Another very useful function is the power function. When combined with other functions, such as the sine function, it can produce varying results.

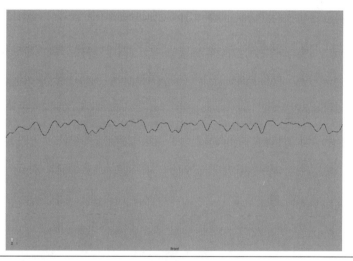

FIGURE 2-4   *Curves created by varying power function*

Figure 2-4 was created using the script shown next. The combined function is particularly useful for creating varying values within a range.

```
int $i;
float $x=0.0,$y = 0.0,$z = 0.0;
int $num_CV = 100;
float $increment = 0.2;
curve -d 3 -p 0 0 0 -k 0 -k 0 -k 0;
string $curve_name[] = 'ls -sl';
for ( $i = 0; $i <= $num_CV; $i++)
{
$x += $increment;
$y = abs(sin (pow($x,1.5)*100.0));
curve -os -a -p $x $y $z $curve_name;
};
```

3D Spiral

3D spiral is another commonly used function. Figure 2-5 shows how it is generated using the MEL script as shown. The height of the spiral and the spiral size can be controlled by varying the $z value.

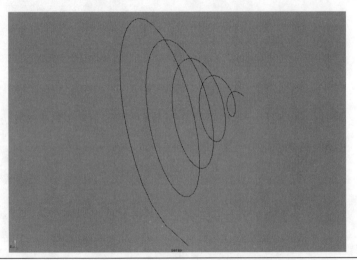

FIGURE 2-5   *A 3D spiral curve generated using sine and cosine functions*

```
int $i;
float $x=0.0,$y = 0.0,$z=0.0;
int $num_CV = 30;
float $increment = 0.1;
curve -d 3 -p 0 0 0 -k 0 -k 0 -k 0;
string $curve_name[] = 'ls -sl';
for ( $i = 0; $i <= $num_CV; $i++)
{
$z += $increment;
$x = cos ($z*10) * $z;
$y = sin ($z*10) * $z;
curve -os -a -p $x $y $z $curve_name;
}
```

Sawtooth Wave

Sawtooth wave is another indispensable function in CG. Figure 2-6 shows how it is generated.

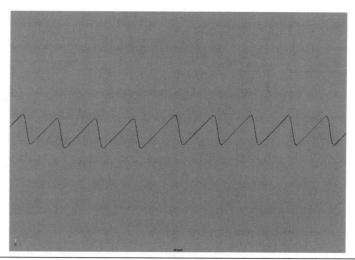

FIGURE 2-6   *A sawtooth wave created using modulus function*

```
int $i;
float $x=0.0,$y = 0.0,$z = 0.0;
int $num_CV = 100;
float $increment = 0.1;
curve -d 3 -p 0 0 0 -k 0 -k 0 -k 0;
string $curve_name[] = 'ls -sl';
for ( $i = 0; $i <= $num_CV; $i++)
{
$x += $increment;
$y = fmod ($x, 1.0);
curve -os -a -p $x $y $z $curve_name;
}
```

Square Waves

Square wave is easily achieved with the help of the floor( ) function (see Figure 2-7).

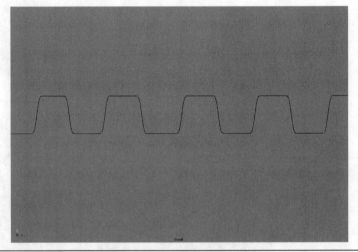

FIGURE 2-7   *A square curve generated with the help of floor () function*

```
int $i;
float $x=0.0,$y = 0.0,$z = 0.0;
int $num_CV = 100;
float $increment = 0.1;
curve -d 3 -p 0 0 0 -k 0 -k 0 -k 0;
string $curve_name[] = 'ls -sl';
for ( $i = 0; $i <= $num_CV; $i++)
```

```
{
$x += $increment;
$y = floor(fmod ($x, 2.0));
curve -os -a -p $x $y $z $curve_name;
}
```

Fadeout Waves

A very simple fadeout function (see Figure 2-8) is achieved by diminishing the amplitude of a sine function.

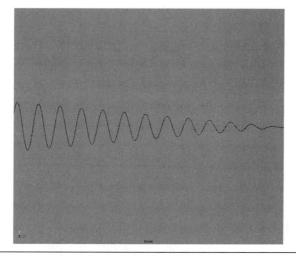

FIGURE 2-8   *A fading-out curve generated using linstep( ) function*

```
int $i;
float $x=0.0,$y = 0.0,$z = 0.0;
int $num_CV = 100;
float $increment = 0.1;
curve -d 3 -p 0 0 0 -k 0 -k 0 -k 0;
string $curve_name[] = 'ls -sl';
for ( $i = 0; $i <= $num_CV; $i++)
{
$x += $increment;
$y = sin(8*$x)*(1-linstep(0.0,10.0,$x));
curve -os -a -p $x $y $z $curve_name;
};
```

In the real world, you seldom see objects move in a linear, unturbulated manner. Therefore, it is very important to be able to create your own desired procedural function curves to describe a motion. They will be extremely useful when you need to use them in expressions to control the motions of your objects. The example functions we've just seen illustrate the power of combining different functions. You should try to experiment with different combinations and parameters.

In the MEL scripts above, all the curves are created using the CVs method. Thus you should not take the curve as absolute representation of the functional values. Instead the representation of the shapes is more important.

COMPOSITION BASICS

Composition is a basic skill for anyone working in a production environment. It is incomprehensible for any animator not to know the basics of composition. There are several composition software packages available on the market. Each has its own strength. However, they all serve the same fundamental goal: to allow different layers of images to be integrated as a whole. The layers of images could be such things as live action footages, background paintings, digitally created 3D shots, or cell-painted animations.

Breaking up images into different layers and composing them at a later stage presents a number of advantages as well as challenges. The advantages include the ability to break up a huge scene that otherwise would use too much RAM to render, the ability to first render confirmed layers thereby saving production time, and the ability to make changes separately based on individual layers. However, the flexibility of modifying individual layers also implies that the integrity of the images may not be maintained. For example, if you have changed the lighting of the background, it may easily end up that the overall lighting for both the foreground and background images do not match. Hence, compositing and editing images is an art to master as much as animating and creating effects imagery.

The fundamental idea behind compositing an image is the use of additional channel information such as the alpha and depth channels. The most commonly used *alpha channel* is sometimes also known as the *mask* of an image. When rendering, you have the option to specify to render with or without the alpha channel. Normally, an image is created with at least three channels: R(ed), G(reen), and B(lue). The alpha channel is the fourth channel of an image. It is always advisable to render an image with alpha channel because you never know when you may need the alpha information to overlay your image. Though it is always possible to generate an alpha channel with the help of composition software, you are likely to face a number of problems such as the common aliasing problem.

A composition software application usually provides many functions for you to composite your images. However, there are a few common operations that you are more likely to use in most of your production work. They are:

Inside. This operation allows image A to be placed inside the alpha channel of image B.

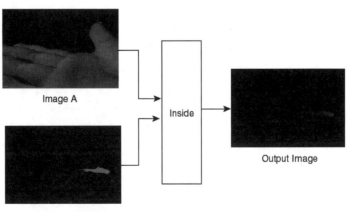

Image A

Alpha of Image B

Inside

Output Image

Multiply.   This operation multiplies the values of image A with the values of image B.

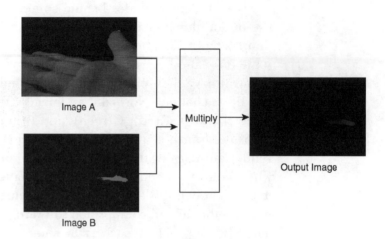

Contrast.   This operation allows you to adjust the RGB and Alpha channels of the image.

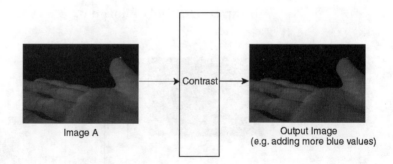

Overlay. This operation allows you to place image A on top of image B using image A's Alpha channel.

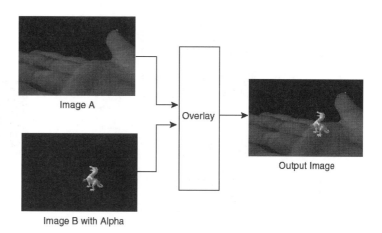

Transform. This operation allows you to perform basic transformations such as translate, rotate, and scale of an image.

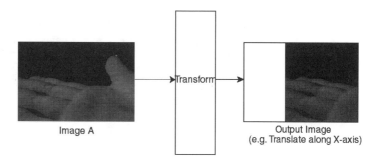

Outside.   This operation allows you to place image A outside the Alpha channel of image B

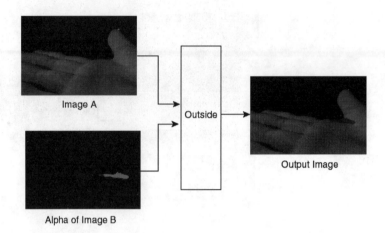

AN EXAMPLE

Apart from the additional channel information, Maya also provides a very useful Use Background shader. Combining this Use Background shader and the alpha information, you can easily create a great many different image layers for use in your favorite composition software. The example below illustrates the few common basic cases that you are most likely to encounter.

Consider the image shown in Figure 2-9.

FIGURE 2-9 *The final image*

To have complete control, the image is divided into five layers.

The Background (BG)

Since this is the BG, it is at the bottom of the layer. Therefore, you can simply render an image without the mask (see Figure 2-10).

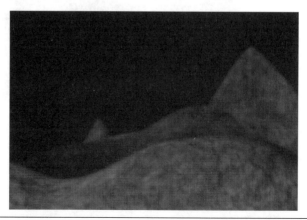

FIGURE 2-10 *The background image*

The Hand

The hand will be overlaid between different layers. Therefore, you should render with the mask on (see Figures 2-11, 2-12, and 2-13).

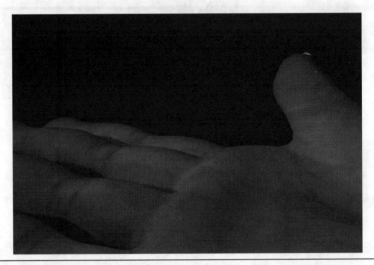

FIGURE 2-11   *The hand layer*

FIGURE 2-12   *The hand image mask*

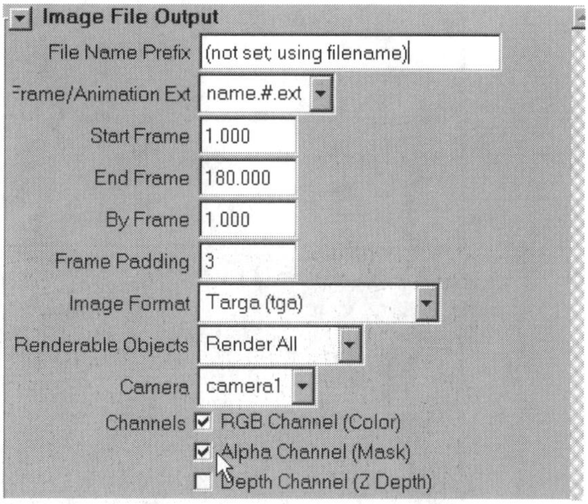

FIGURE 2-13 *Generate an image with Alpha channel (mask) switched on*

The Dragon

The dragon will also be overlaid between different layers. Therefore, similarly, you should render with the mask on (see Figures 2-14 and 2-15).

FIGURE 2-14 *The dragon layer*

FIGURE 2-15 *The dragon image mask*

The Fire

You will need to render the fire with the mask information. However, in addition to that, you will need the shape of the dragon in order to correctly overlay the fire. To include the shape of the dragon without it being rendered out, you will change the shading node of the dragon to Use Background (see Figures 2-16, 2-17, and 2-18).

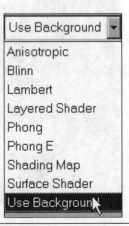

FIGURE 2-16 *Render using the Use Background shader*

FIGURE 2-17 *The dragon fire image*

FIGURE 2-18 *The dragon fire mask*

The Dragon Shadow

A common way of generating shadows is to render in black and white. However, a much better way that provides greater flexibility is to render the shadow as a mask itself. That is to say, the image is black but the mask is shaded with the shadow information. In this way, you can easily create not only shadows that are black and white, but also shadows that contain the texture information of the object.

In this example, instead of simply just black and white shadow, you generate a shadow mask that allows you to include even the texture information of the palm. This should be the case since most shadows are not simply black and white.

To do so, the Hand Shader is changed to the Use Background shader. And the dragon geometry is made invisible but yet able to cast a shadow. This is done through setting the Primary Visibility flag of the dragon geometry off but leaving the main visibility flag on. The flags are available from Window ➤ Rendering Editors ➤ Rendering Flags (see Figures 2-19, 2-20, and 2-21).

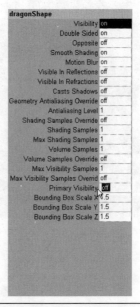

FIGURE 2-19   *Turn off the Primary visibility to hide the geometry*

FIGURE 2-20 *The geometry is not rendered...*

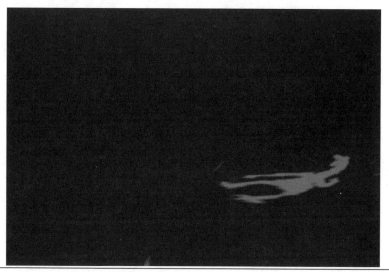

FIGURE 2-21 *but the shadow is still casted*

The Fire Shadow

The way to generate the dragon shadow is also applicable to generating the fire shadow. However, because this time you will also need the dragon shape for the shadow, in addition to setting the dragon with the Use Background shader, you will set it with the Casts Shadows off (see Figure 2-22).

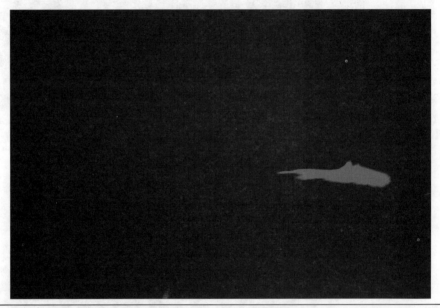

FIGURE 2-22   *The particle fire's shadow*

Creating animation with the help of composition is not necessarily easy. Taking the above example, if you have four layers, and your animation is 6 seconds, then you are likely to end up with 720 frames of images to store instead of only 180 frames to store. Thus, when deciding to layer or not to layer, you must balance flexibility, time, and resources.

3

FUNDAMENTALS OF MODELING, RENDERING, LIGHTING, AND CAMERA COMPOSITION

INTRODUCTION

Creating animation is like conducting a concert. Each instrument is important by itself. You may not be able to play every instrument, but knowing the characteristics of every instrument is vital for you in order to coordinate them all. As an effects TD or animator, knowing other stages of production is similarly essential for you to coordinate and create the desired digital effects. Every motion picture is the result of the work of many artists. Furthermore, in many production environments, it is not always possible to segregate different roles and stages. As an effects animator, you may at times be required to take on the roles of the lighting artist or a modeler. Hence, it is important for you to know about other basic production skills. In this chapter, the theory and practice of the following topics will be introduced:

1.   Modeling
2.   Rendering
3.   Lighting
4.   Camera usage

MODELING ESSENTIALS

For many 3D digital artists, modeling is the very first skill they learn. In fact it is hard to imagine how to learn other practical aspects of 3D concepts such as rendering and lighting without first creating models.

Modeling is a rewarding task because the amount of effort you put into it, is almost equal to how much you will get in return. Unlike writing a shader or lighting a scene, the reward of modeling is immediate and visible. How you push and pull, will be exactly what you get in return in the physical model—no special surprises and no special tricks.

However, as you explore modeling in depth, it turns out that there are indeed many different ways of modeling and different issues that you have to be aware of as a modeler. While there are no hard and fast rules of modeling, there are a few essential theories and practices that will help you make better models.

TYPES OF MODELING

Basically, modeling can be divided into the following three types:

1. Modeling for design
2. Modeling for real-time visualization
3. Modeling for animation

Each of these types of modeling require different considerations.

Modeling for Design. When modeling for design, it is of paramount importance that your model conform to the exact design up to the smallest unit required. In the end, the model may be fed into the process of rapid prototyping and eventually cut into a prototype. Thus, the main characteristic for design modeling is accuracy.

Modeling for Real-Time Visualization.   Real-time visualization includes games, architectural walkthroughs, and virtual reality applied in scientific or medical visualization. For example, when modeling for games, you will be concerned with the number of polygons available for you to model. This is especially important when you are doing real-time 3D games where interactivity is the most important thing. Imagine that you're given a polygon budget of five thousand for the character but the model that you have created ended up with six thousand polygons. It is likely that your console or graphics processor will end up overloaded with processing the additional polygons and the entire game will eventually suffer from the real-time interactivity issue.

Modeling for Animation.   When you model for animation, even though you don't have the precision and real-time issues to worry about, the job does not get simpler. You must pay particular attention to how your model will eventually be modified, textured, rendered, and animated. If your model is sloppy, with lots of folds, seams, and unnecessary details, you will find it hard to modify, texture, and add in the skeleton for animation.

There are generally two approaches to modeling for animation: the polygonal approach or the spline-based approach. In Maya, you can model your characters from a direct polygonal approach or you can model using the well-defined NURBS tools.

There are advantages and disadvantages to both approaches. One of the biggest advantages of using NURBS modeling is that, being spline in nature, the NURBS models that you create are invariantly smooth, no matter how you scale them. This is best illustrated using an example (see Figure 3-1). To simplify, take the NURBS curve instead of a surface as an example.

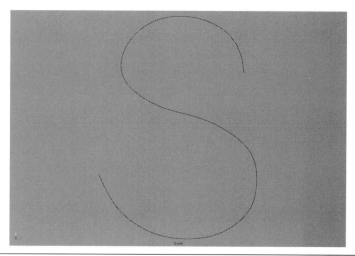

FIGURE 3-1   *A NURBS letter S*

Figure 3-1 shows a NURBS curve that forms the letter S. So, using polygon lines, the letter S will be closely approximated as shown in Figures 3-2 through 3-5.

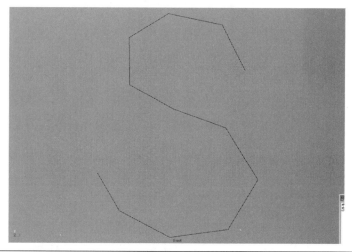

FIGURE 3-2   *A medium polygonal approximation to the letter S*

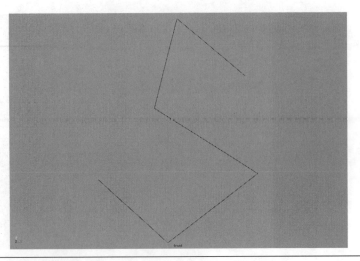

FIGURE 3-3   *A low polygonal approximation to the letter S*

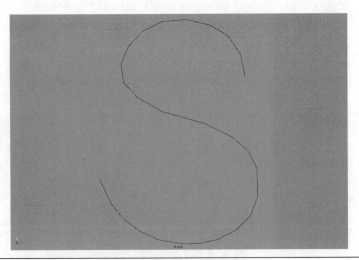

FIGURE 3-4   *A higher polygonal approximation to the letter S*

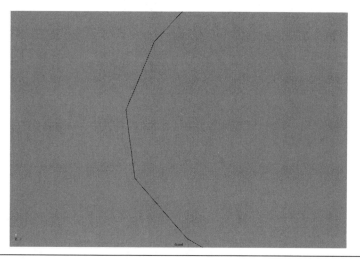

FIGURE 3-5   *A closeup view of a part of the high polygonal approximation*

From Figures 3-2 through 3-5, it is evident that even if you use a high-resolution model (the Figure 3-4), when you scale the character for a close-up view (Figure 3-5), the initially unnoticeable edges become obvious, which is undesirable. Where as using the NURBS model, how smooth the surface turns out depends on how much you tessellate the model. And this process of tessellation is often easily controlled from within the software. Therefore, modeling with NURBS is a very favorable choice.

To understand tessellation, imagine that it is a way of breaking up a NURBS surface into smaller pieces of polygons (three-sided or four-sided polygons), so that the surfaces can be rendered into images. For some, this appears to be the same as polygonal modeling. However, the main difference is that tessellation occurs as a stage in the rendering pipeline. Therefore you can always fine-tune and adjust the tessellation parameters based on your rendered output. In polygonal modeling, you don't have this control. You have to decide how many polygons you would like to use and you are unlikely to be able to, say, change a one-thousand polygonal model, into a more detailed, two-thousand polygonal model. This is why in most NURBS/spline-based modeling applications you can easily turn the NURBS/spline models into polygon models, but not the other way around.

So why use polygonal modeling when NURBS modeling appears to be the preferred approach? The answer is that polygons are basically stored as lines and vertices where as NURBS are most often described with cubic functions. This makes the computation of the polygon information much faster, which is also why game models are polygonal and not NURBS based. Besides being easier and faster to compute, the flexibility of being able to create and move lines and vertices makes it easier to create models with sharp edges and abrupt angles. While NURBS can also produce sharp corners and edges, its topology makes it less than ideal to do so. In addition, because of its simplicity, editing polygonal models is sometimes much faster and easier.

AN EXAMPLE OF NURBS MODELING AND TEXTURING

One of the many strengths of Maya is its set of powerful NURBS modeling tools. From the simple primitives, to the common NURBS booleans functions, to the various deformations and sculpting tools, Maya allows the artist to create and easily animate virtually any imaginable form of characters.

This section will illustrate briefly a basic method of NURBS modeling and texturing using Maya. The model in this example is a simple hand model.

Create the finger

1. Create a sphere.
2. Rotate the sphere along the Z axis by 90 degrees.
3. Select an isoparm of the sphere and detach a part of the sphere.

Your result should look like Figure 3-6.

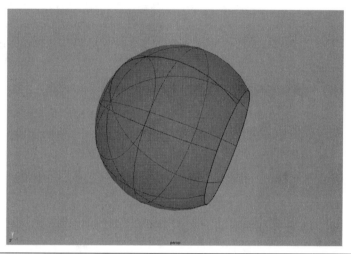

FIGURE 3-6   *A detached sphere*

Fine-tune the finger model

4. Scale the finger along the horizontal axis.
5. Insert several isoparms at various places on the finger.
6. Move and scale the various set of points you have created as you insert the isoparms.

You should get the shape of the finger as shown in Figure 3-7.

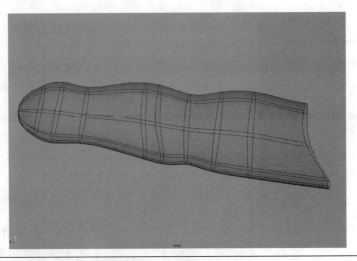

FIGURE 3-7   *A finger shape created by simple transformations*

More fingers

7.   Repeat the steps above to create more fingers.
8.   The creation of the thumb is similar except that the orientation is by the side (see Figure 3-8).

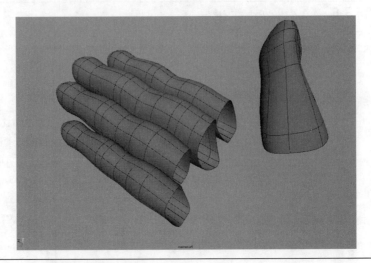

FIGURE 3-8   *Creating the rest of the fingers*

Create the palm

9. Create another sphere.
10. Rotate the sphere along the Z axis by 90 degrees.
11. Select an isoparm of the sphere and detach a part of the sphere.
12. With the help of the Sculpt Surface Tool, edit the surface so that it resembles a simple palm, as illustrated in Figure 3-9.

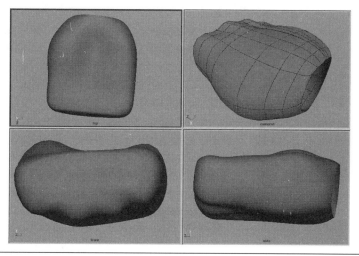

FIGURE 3-9 *A general shape of a palm*

Join the fingers and palm together

13. Position the fingers and the palm together as shown in Figure 3-10.

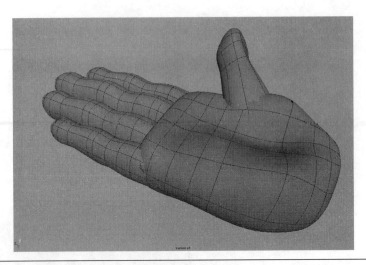

FIGURE 3-10   *Putting the palms and the fingers together*

14. With the help of the Circular Fillet tool, create a fillet between each finger and the palm. Make sure
that you have the Create Curve On Surface checked
On (see Figure 3-11).

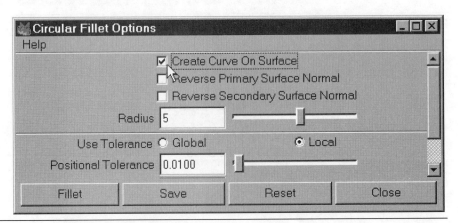

FIGURE 3-11   *Create the curve on the surface*

15. With the help of the Trim tool, trim away the fingers and the palm that are hidden away from the surface. However, this step of trimming is not really necessary since the hidden surfaces are inside the palm and are not seen from the audience. You should now have a seamless hand. Figure 3-12 shows the entire hand, which includes those finger nails *created by simple deformation of spheres.*

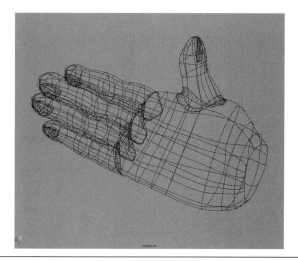

FIGURE 3-12 *Trim the surfaces to get a complete hand*

Texture the hand

16. Texturing the hand is in fact a simple step. Make sure that you have scanned-in a texture of a real person's hand (see Figure 3-13).

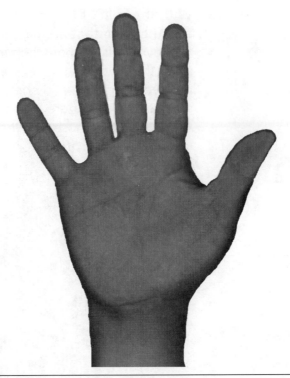

FIGURE 3-13   *The scanned-in hand texture*

17. All you need to do now is map the hand with the help of the 3D Texture Placement node. However, to have more control over every detail of the finger and hand, you should cut the image into individual fingers and palm and texture them separately (see Figures 3-14 through 3-16).

FIGURE 3-14 *A cutout index finger texture*

FIGURE 3-15 *A cutout palm image texture*

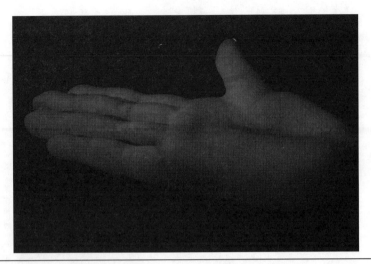

FIGURE 3-16   *The final rendered hand image*

Though texturing appears to be a straightforward process of adding shading and details to an object, it can become rather complex, especially if you have a single complex model. Therefore, when creating a model, you should always be sure to create a clean model with properly created UV spans.

ADVANCED MODELING—USING SUBDIVISION MODELING

Among Maya's advanced modeling tools is the revolutionary Subdivision Modeling tool. Subdivision modeling allows models to be fine-tuned according to the required details. For example, if you need to create a model where certain parts are detailed and other parts are not, all you have to do is convert the model into a subdivision surface. From there, you have the control to subdivide the required part into more detail while leaving the rest untouched. Without subdivision, if you need to add detail at a certain part of the model, you will increase the UV spans of the entire model and thus introduce other unnecessary details.

The example below illustrates a simple use of subdivision modeling. The model to be created is a basic cartoonic spacecraft.

Create the sphere

1. Create a sphere.
2. Select the sphere and convert it into a subdivision surface.

Model the shape

3. Select all the middle points of the sphere.
4. From the Subdivision menu (F3), Crease the points.
5. Scale the points.

Your results should look like Figure 3-17.

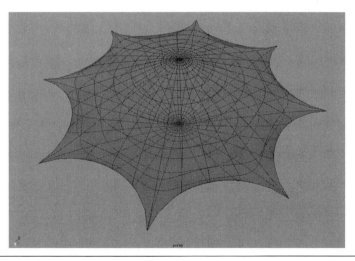

FIGURE 3-17 *Subdivision shape created by creasing*

Model the legs of the spacecraft

6. From the bottom side of the model, select four diagonal CVs as shown in Figure 3-18.

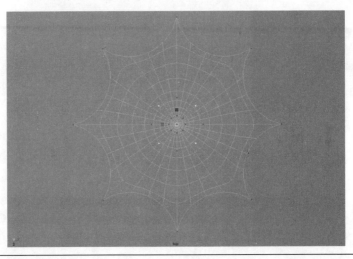

FIGURE 3-18 *Select the CVs as shown*

7. Do a Subdivision ➢ Refine Display Region.
8. The region is refined. Reselect the points and refine the region one more time.
9. Your results should look like Figure 3-19. Notice that only those regions that you selected are subdivided and refined.

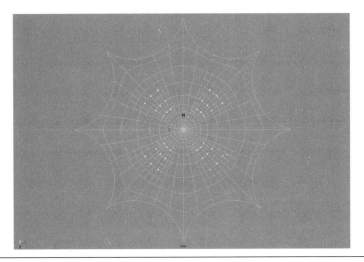

FIGURE 3-19   *Subdivide the region*

10. Repeat refining the region if you want the legs to be thin.
11. With the refined region points selected, move them along the Y-axis.
12. Scale the points.
13. You should get an image similar to the one shown in Figure 3-20. They are the legs of the spacecraft.

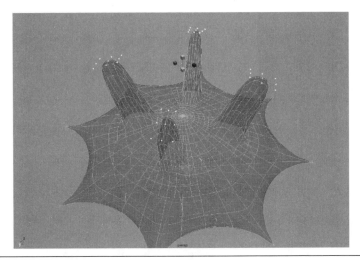

FIGURE 3-20   *Create the legs of the spacecraft*

Model the head of the spacecraft

14. From Subdiv Surfaces ➤ Base Mesh Display, switch the subdivision points back to the original amount of detail.
15. Select the top points as shown in Figure 3-21 and do a Refine Display Region.

FIGURE 3-21   *Select the CVs as shown*

16. Select the ring of outer points and Crease the points.
17. Select the ring of inner points and Refine the region again.
18. To create the head, all that is left is to translate the refined region along the Y-axis, followed by Scaling the points in the way that you want the shape of the head to form.
19. The final model is as shown in Figure 3-22. Notice that the number of CVs on the model is the same as when you first created the sphere. The subdivision surface method allows you to easily fine-tune and create any details you need.

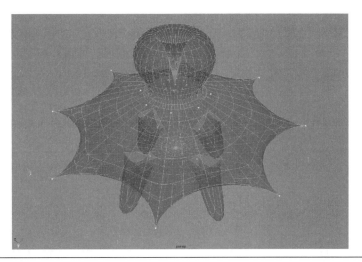

FIGURE 3-22 *The final subdivision model*

20. Finally, because Maya does not allow the subdivision surface to be rendered directly, you will have to go to the Subdiv Surfaces and choose to tessellate the model into a polygonal model.

A Note on Level of Detail (LOD) Modeling. A final note about modeling is that normally in complex production modeling, a given character is likely to have several levels of detailed modeling. Typically, a very fine resolution model is used for close-up shots, and a lesser detailed model of the same character is used for a distance shot. This idea of level of detail is in fact a common practice in real-time visualization. For example, in a walkthrough of a city, it is impossible to keep the processor busy with all the detailed models. Thus, the real-time engine is normally able to switch between different LOD models depending on where the camera is viewing and how far away the models are from the view.

In PhotoRealistic RenderMan, there is already a smart implementation of LOD that allows you to specify various

LOD models. From the specification, the renderer is able to automatically select the correct detail to render. In addition, the transition of the various LOD models are smooth. Currently Maya's native data files (.mb and .ma) do not have LOD routines. Hopefully, in the future, Maya will not only be able to automatically select and render smoothly the LOD models, but be able to automatically generate the various LOD based on the finest model itself.

RENDERING ESSENTIALS

Rendering is one of the final and most important stages in creating digital imageries. Any experienced production animators could tell you how, at one time or another, they were "betrayed" by their renderer: either the renderer took an unexpectedly long time to render or they hit the wrong camera to render. While making a mistake in rendering is a common occurrence, you can also minimize your rendering pain if you have a good understanding of the entire pipeline of rendering.

Many computer graphics textbooks provide a clear explanation of what actually happens when you hit the render button. In my opinion, knowing what happens in a 3D rendering pipeline is essential. Therefore, I recommend that you refer to those computer graphics books for a detailed explanation. In addition, particularly related to Maya's rendering pipeline, there is a document available from the Alias | Wavefront website: *Maya Software Rendering—A Technical Overview.* It is worth the effort to read it if you hope to use Maya's renderer to its fullest capability.

ILLUMINATION MODELS

In the world of CG, it is almost impossible to discuss rendering without mentioning the term illumination model. Surprisingly, many digital artists are not familiar with this concept. They perceive the jargon as something that only the technically-minded artist needs to understand. While knowing the concept of illumination models may not turn you into an instant expert artist, it will help you to be more aware of the limitations of your rendering and lighting software and enable you to create your animations more efficiently.

Illumination models describe how light is reflected and refracted from surfaces. In modeling, you create a geometrical model to represent your character. In CG lighting, you don't physically create an illumination model to describe how light is reflected and refracted. Instead, illumination models exist as an integrated mathematical function within your CG software application. So, you don't have to tell your system how to model the way light is reflected or refracted from, say, the mirror to the surface, each time you create a scene. Instead, you just hit the render button and everything within the camera view, from the geometrical model to lighting of the scene, will be calculated and rendered into a final imagery for you.

There are generally two types of illumination models: *local* and *global*. A local illumination model describes only the light that goes directly from the light source and gets reflected from the surface into the camera. However, you know that the light that hits and reflects in the surface does not come from the light sources alone. There are also other lights that fall on the surface from other sources such as light that gets bounced from the wall and reflected from the glass. Global illumination refers to light that is reflected from other surfaces to the current surface.

So, what do these illumination models have to do with the way you render your scene in CG? Very much indeed. In most applications, the local illumination model, which is also known as the reflection model, is incorporated as part of the shading material. A widely used example is the Phong model. And the global illumination model is commonly available as raytracing or radiosity. Each of these different types of illumination models, even if given the same scene, will create different rendered imagery.

For example, when you render an image using ray tracing, you will probably get dark and sharp-edged shadows. Ray tracing works by tracing the rays of light from the eye back through the image plane into the scene. It then makes a decision on how to color a pixel based on what it hits. It is essentially a point-sampling algorithm. Therefore using ray tracing, you may easily end up with several aliasing problems. Compared to rendering with radiosity, you will be able to get more diffused, realistic images. In addition, radiosity rendering is view-independent. Once rendered, you can, for example, easily do a walkthrough of the scene without having to re-render.

Maya's rendering implementation allows you to selectively raytrace the scene. That is to say, instead of a global ray trace button, you are able to save substantial time and apply ray tracing only to objects that require the characteristic of ray trace reflection or refraction. However, Maya's rendering does not cater to radiosity rendering. Figure 3-23 illustrates a very simple test example of Maya's rendering, and the popular, RenderMan compliant shareware, Blue Moon Rendering Tools (BMRT) of Larry I. Grits.

FIGURE 3-23a *Image created using BMRT's radiosity and ray tracing method*

FIGURE 3-23b *Image created using BMRT's ray tracing only method*

FIGURE 3-23c *The same image created in Maya's default render setting*

The test scene for all the images is the same. It consists of a simple point light source with shadow. The intensity of the point light is normalized so that it is about the same value in both the Maya and BMRT. You will notice the presence of substantial diffuse information for the image that was done with ray tracing and radiosity using BMRT (Figure 3-23a).

What is important here is not for you to comprehend the technical accuracy of these different illumination models. Rather, it is that you should overcome the limitations of the different rendering methods. For example, if you were to ray trace an image in Maya, given your knowledge of raytracing and radiosity, you could pay more attention to, for example, the hard edges of ray traced shadows. This will help you be more innovative and find solutions to create better imagery.

MAYA RENDERING

Maya's rendering manual provides a very clear explanation of various rendering concepts and methods. Therefore, this section will not repeat the contents of the manual. Instead, we will highlight several important concepts.

Optimization.   Speeding up rendering time is always an important task. The list below provides brief instructions to improve your rendering time. For more detail, you should refer to the manual.

- Hide objects that are not visible from the camera. For example, given a 6-sided cube, if you won't see the bottom side of the cube, hide it from view.
- Don't use an anti-aliasing level that is too high and yet does not improve your imagery output. Always start with a low anti-aliasing level.
- When motion-blurring objects, use low anti-aliasing since you won't see details anyway.
- Use a low resolution model, if possible.

- Render scenes in layers, if possible.
- Bake your IK, softbodies, and dynamic objects once you are happy with your animation.
- Avoid creating too small a geometry in your scene. Small geometries always end up with serious aliasing problems and you will have to use a high level of anti-aliasing in order to solve the problem.
- Always run the renderChecker MEL script before you commit to a large rendering job. The renderChecker script examines your scene and checks for various details and warns you of any possible rendering problems.
- Use textures that are a power of 2, for example, 64, 128, 256, or 512.
- Always use texture formats of iff or SGI. They are the native textures to Maya and do not require intermediate conversion.
- Turn the cast shadow rendering flag off for objects that you don't want to cast shadows, such as a big piece of floor. While it cannot cast shadow, it can still receive shadow.
- Create Instances of geometry instead of duplicates. Instances do not require you to store and compute again the geometry information and thus save rendering time.

Interactive PhotoRealistic Rendering. Maya provides an innovative fine-tuning rendering method called Interactive Photo-Realistic Rendering (IPR). Traditionally, images will have to be re-rendered whenever you make even a simple change, such as the color of the objects. When rendered with IPR, an image is stored as a huge file that contains information such as the shader, light, and glows. From there, you can interactively adjust the parameters. For example, when you change the color of the object or map a bump map to the object, this information will be updated interactively. This saves you tons of precious time especially if you have a huge scene and all you want to do is fine-tune the color to one that is artistically acceptable.

However, with IPR, if you were to change the view, and adjust the object by deforming it, you have to re-IPR-render the scene because this information must be updated in the IPR file. In addition, interactively fine-tuning the particle effects is currently not possible.

Building Your Shader with Hypershade.   In addition to IPR, Maya also allows you to easily build your shader. In the earlier version of Maya, building a shader was fast but only if you had an idea of what you wanted and were able to picture it in your mind. However, with Maya's hypershade, you can easily build your shader by simply clicking and connecting visually the various nodes. This is especially time-saving when you have complex shaders that you would like to build. (Refer to the Maya manuals for the details of using hypershades.)

LIGHTING ESSENTIALS

Lighting is an essential component to create visually rich cinematographic images. Whether in actual filming sets or in the digital CG world, lighting is one of the toughest challenges. Simply because human eyes are so accustomed to seeing things the way they are, any slight abnormal differences in the lighting condition is immediately obvious, either consciously or subconsciously.

Lighting in CG is not all about mimicking reality. It is more than that. It is about bringing out the essential characteristics of the subject seamlessly and in a way that conforms to the believability of the scene. It means bringing out the best in a picture. For example, when you light your scene, you do not think in terms of "I'm creating this as sunlight and this as the street light." Rather, you think in terms of "How do I create and position the light so that I can create an image that tells the audience how sad my character is?" In other words, you put the subject of interest as the center of the reason for the lighting. Trying to mimic the actual lighting in the world is never the right way to start lighting your scene.

Just as traditional film-making is termed painting with light, analogously, in the CG digital world, you should attempt to model with light. In addition to creating a physical model, the task of a modeler may extend into making use of light to bring out the best of the model. Achieving this doesn't require the knowledge of your lighting director. But you must remember and put into practice the simple principle of paying attention to which details should be put in the light and which in the shade.

In addition, it is also important for you to know the theme of your scene. For example, if your scene is part of a comedy sequence, then it is likely that you will be using a generally high-key, well-illuminated lighting for your overall scene. On the other hand, if you want to create a moody scene, you are likely to use a darker light setting.

In Maya there are currently four types of basic light sources: *ambient, spot, directional,* and *point.* While theoretically, with these light sources you are able to light up almost any required scene, in practice these CG lighting models are still not versatile enough for cinematographic-quality lighting. This is the same for most other 3D software on the market. Therefore, you are likely to end up with several light sources in order to light your scene appropriately. This also explains why, for example, in *A Bug's Life,* it was common for a CG scene to have as many as fifty or even more than a hundred lights.

LIGHT SOURCES

There are several basic terms and concepts commonly used in lighting, both in CG as well as in cinematic filming. This section will introduce some of them. And depending on your references, some books may use different terms to describe the same concept. Therefore, what is important here is not to take these concepts as lighting formulas but to always exercise your own creativity in applying the concepts to your scene.

In general, every scene should be lit from four basic light sources:

1. Key light
2. Fill light
3. Back light
4. Set light

Key light is also known as principle light. It is generally the light that casts the primary shadows and creates a sense of directionality to the lighting. There is often the misconception that a key light must be placed somewhat by the side and above the camera. This is not always true. A key light is also the main light that will model the subject of interest. Therefore, whichever position that will provide the best features of the subject will become the key light position. In most situations, placing the light on the side toward the subject does provide a good modeling of the subject.

There are two purposes for the existence of *fill light*. One is to fill up the scene and ensure that no surface in the field of view is underexposed without any light. Another is to fill in the shadows produced by the key light so that the shadows do not appear to be completely opaque and harsh. Fill light often exists as shadowless soft light in the CG scene.

As its name suggests, *back light* is normally placed directly at the back and above the subject. Its purpose is to create a silhouette outline of the subject so that it is fairly clear that the subject is separated from the background. Back light is usually specular enough to produce highlights on the subject. Another term, *kicker,* is often confused with backlight. Kicker is similar to back light except that it is placed about the same level, to the side, and at the back of the subject. If you imagine that the subject is a human, then back light will serve to bring out the outline of the human with highlights on the hair, whereas kicker light will illuminate the person's shoulder.

Set light is also known as background light. It is used to illuminate the background since the background is usually partly lit by the key and fill lights.

CG LIGHTING VERSUS REAL LIGHTING

Light itself is a complex and beautiful phenomenon. From the rainbow that you see after a summer rain, to the colorful imagery that focuses at your iris, they are all a result of the millions and billions of constantly moving photons.

Therefore, it is no wonder that CG light finds it hard to mimic this wonderful natural creation.

Contrast.   In the world of CG, light exists in a different form. In the case of a common CRT (Cathode Ray Tube) monitor, it is the result of the electrons hitting the sulphide-coated screen. However, whatever the medium, the truth is that CG light is bounded by the physical ability of the display medium, whereas in real life, light is never bounded by any limits. Therefore, it is not enough to position and know how much to shade and light. You have to also understand the importance of contrast. Contrast is the difference between the brightest and the darkest. For example, in a fairly flat and uniform frame, the light will appear to be brighter and create a better depth when there is a higher difference in the bright and dark regions. Hence when you create CG light, you must not overlook the importance of the contrast of your scene.

Decay.   In real life, light decays, which means that light that is farther away will appear to be dimmer than light that is closer to you. In CG, you have the option of deciding if your CG light will ever decay or to what extend it will decay, proportional with the distance, or double it? Though depending on the scene, it is almost always a good practice to have your light decay linearly with the distance. A non-decaying CG light, though convenient to use, seldom produces realistic results.

Lighting in Stills Versus Lighting in Animation. Lighting in animation can prove to be a very different experience than lighting in stills. Lighting in stills, such as during a photo-taking session, is straightforward. Lighting in animation, on the other hand, requires you to pay particular attention when a character moves. As mentioned earlier, if lighting is merely mimicking reality, then there would be nothing to worry about. However, this is not the case. A character may appear to be beautifully portrayed in one angle of lighting, but not in another when it moves. For example, what should happen when your character move to the shaded part of the scene? If you simply move the light with the character, it may offset the balance of the light in the scene.

Therefore, as the most general rule of thumb, when lighting, always strive to maintain the balance of the scene. As with everything in life, a good image is an image with well-balanced details and well-balanced lighting. You will be able to achieve this through lots and lots of practice.

CAMERA ESSENTIALS

The camera is the eye of the audience. When it moves closer, the audience moves with it. When it concentrates on a particular item, the audience concentration is devoted to that item alone. Therefore, skillful employment of the camera is critical, even if you have a good story and plots.

This section will present two fundamental skills of using the camera in computer graphics. They are:

1. Camera movement
2. Camera angle

CAMERA MOVEMENT

The use of camera movement is an art. Too much movement is just as bad as none at all. To properly master the movement of the camera requires lots and lots of trial and error. This art becomes even more challenging when you are integrating the movement of the camera in CG with a live-action camera. Maya *Live* is a solution to this problem. Maya Live enables you to integrate live images with the digital images, complete with different camera movements.

This section is not a tutorial of Maya Live. Instead, I will present the fundamental methods of creating camera animation. In the world of digital imagery, the camera is defined with three main components:

1. The eye of the camera, which is analogous to the view finder of the real camera.
2. The look at point, which is analogous to where you are aiming your object.
3. The up-vector, which is analogous to how you rotate your camera, landscape picture, or portrait picture, or in- between.

In Maya, by default, the camera you create is a single node camera. That is to say, all three components are integrated into one. If you would like to create a camera with two or three components, you have the option to set it under the Options window (see Figure 3-24).

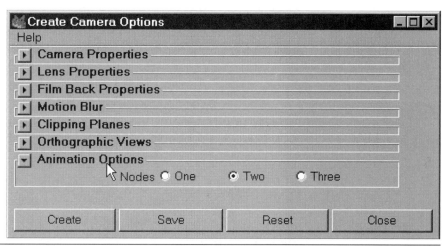

FIGURE 3-24 *Options to create a one, two, or three node camera*

A two-node component camera allows you to have access to the *look at value,* which is called the camera_view, and the *camera eye value,* which is called the camera. They are all grouped together under the camera_group node. A three-node component camera allows you to have access to all three components of the camera. This provides great flexibility. However, unless you need to roll and pitch your camera, it is not a preferred choice. Most of the time, a two-node camera allows you to create almost all the camera animation. With the two-node camera, the camera_up value automatically remains vertically upwards of the camera node. Therefore, creating the camera animation is simply a matter of fixing one, animating the other, or animating both at the same time.

The following table defines how you can create different camera animation by animating the node.

ACTION REQUIRED	STEPS
Animate the camera to move around an object similar to a turn table animation.	• Create a two-node camera. • Keyframe or constraint the camera_view node so that it will keep looking at the object of interest. • Tumble and move the camera node (not the camera_group node) around and set keyframe on the translation values.
Create a roller-coaster animation.	• Create the motion path curve. • Create a two-node camera. • Set the camera_view node to follow the motion path. • Set the camera node (not the camera_group) to follow the same motion path. However, this time, make sure that the start time is say, 30 frames, later. When you play the animation, you should see the camera move as if you were on a roller coaster

Camera Angle. As in photography, the employment of the camera is extremely important. To merely position your camera and snap or animate will seldom get you close to creating good imageries.

There are a few general practices in employing a good camera angle.

Dimensionality. A screen is a one-dimensional flat surface. Therefore, it is important that when you position your camera, the most number of surfaces is visible. Figure 3-25a-d illustrates that even when you have a top, front, and side view, you may not be able to comprehend what is actually the object unless you have a good camera position that shows the most number of faces.

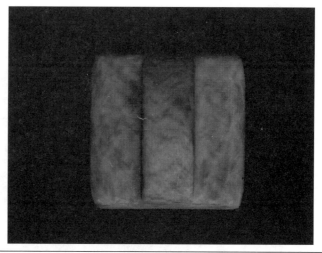

FIGURE 3-25a *The top view*

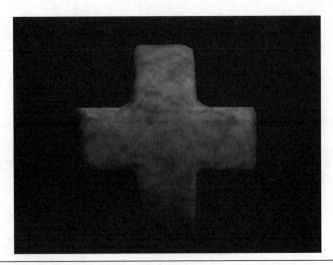

FIGURE 3-25b *The front view*

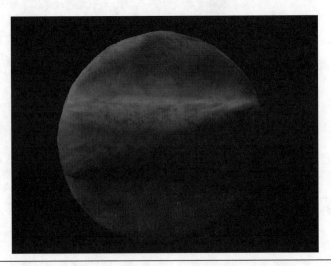

FIGURE 3-25c *The side view*

FIGURE 3-25d *A complete picture is shown from perspective view*

Up or Down View. When positioning the camera, there is a great difference between an up and down view. A camera viewing upwards to a character will create an authoritative and perhaps even menacing view. A camera that shows trunks of legs is likely to imply a child's view.

Camera Depth. To increase the depth of the scene, employ the following methods:

- Render with the depth of field. This is identical to the real camera term, depth of field. The focused object could be the foreground or the background object. The distinction between the clear and focused, and the blur and out-of-focused, is that objects will be able to separate and thus create a good sense of depth.
- Use fog. Employing the use of fog will reduce the visibility distance. This is a common trick to create the illusion of depth. However, the use of fog will often

flatten your final imagery. Thus, you should exercise good lighting skills when including fog effects into your scene.

CONCLUSIONS

This chapter together with the earlier chapters, has covered the basics of creating effects animation. The concepts and ideas discussed are by no means exhaustive. You are encouraged to further explore the various topics covered by referring to other manuals and references.

The rest of the book will take you through the practice of these theories using Maya.

THE BURNING
FIRE

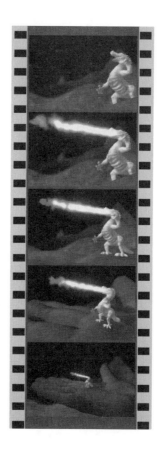

INTRODUCTION

What is fire? A dictionary will give you a range of explanations, depending on where and how you use it. Fire can be explained from a chemical perspective as a phenomenon of combustion that manifests itself in *light, flame,* and *heat.* It has no particular form, but yet can take the shape of any combustible medium. You cannot grab it, but you can hold it. You cannot touch it, but you can feel it. It is one of the most amazing discoveries that our ancestors experienced thousands of years ago and yet remains the same today.

Fire can also mean liveliness, passion, excitement, and enthusiasm. When your drama teacher instructs you to show her the fire in your eyes, you know well that it is the passion and excitement that she wants to see in your performance. But fire can also take the form of attack, ordeal, irritation, and anger. In military terms, if you are "under fire," you must fight and counter attack, hold and dig in, or retreat and flee. In a matter of seconds, fire can give spirit to life or it can cause great destruction. However, among all these varied explanations, I think the moment of being told "You're fired!" gives the strongest impression of fire.

As varied as the explanations given to the meaning of fire, the computer graphics (CG) form of fire that most animators and technical directors are required to create is equally varied. This chapter and Chapter Five: *The Dynamic Fire,* will guide you through the process of creating two different types of commonly seen fire effects. While it is not possible to create a library of fire, the techniques for creating these CG fire effects will help you with the required fire effects in most other situations.

TYPES OF FIRE

I have very broadly categorized fire effects into two arenas. The first type is characterized by its burning effects, one that gives the feeling of spontaneous and smooth burning flames. Examples of such fire effects are torches of flames, burning woods, and candle flames. Some of you may be able to remember the experience of such fire effects when you recall your first campfire night: the cracking sound of the burning woods, and the warm feelings of the fire. The effect of such fire is a result of instantaneous and spontaneous burning under a good and continuous presence of oxygen. The apparent movement of the fire follows the theory of hot air rising and cool air falling. Therefore, you will be able to see the obvious fragments of flames flickering, rising, and disappearing in the air.

The second type of fire effect is characterized by its rapid movement. It presents a stronger threat to the viewers. It is a direct contrast to the first type of fire, which is generally smooth and spontaneous. This second type of fire effect does not have a rolling and burning look. Chapter Five will present a closer look at this type of fire.

PRE-PRODUCTION: UNDERSTANDING THE SCENARIO

TASK

- In this project, you are the sole effects animator on your team. You are called upon to create fire effects that breathe life into a dragon statue. The dragon model will be given to you by your fellow modeler. It is a jade, greenish-looking dragon. A preliminary sketch is available to you as shown in Figure 4-1.

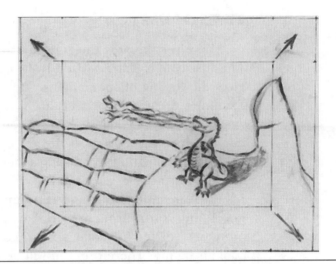

FIGURE 4-1   *Sketch*

After some discussion, you know that you will create a six-second animation. The dragon will not be moving in this shot. Only the camera will be moving. You are required to carry out the animation to the best of your knowledge and make any other decisions based on available resources and your skills.

ANALYZE THE PICTURE

Whenever you receive a sketch for a new project, you should take some time to study it. In a typical production process, there may be more than one sketch of the required shot. If so, you are in luck. You will be able to compare the look of the sketches and decipher what exactly is required. You would be even luckier if, the director is available to tell you precisely what he or she expects from your animation. However, most artists rarely have a specific goal in mind before beginning work. Consequently, the process of visualization is actually the search for a goal rather than the attainment of one. As an effects specialist, most of the time, you are trusted to exercise your own creativity and present the best effects imagery possible.

On the other hand, even when the work is fixed during the early production stage, you should be prepared to make changes any time during or after the completion of your task. Ask any director or animator, and they will tell you that last-minute changes are part and parcel of a production cycle. In fact, the challenge of working and being a good animator often takes into account whether you can meet the last-minute changes and accommodate the art direction required by the director or your clients.

In this project scenario, for example, even though you are told that the animation required is a six-second fire effect, this six-second shot could easily become a seven-second shot. If you dislike making changes, let alone last-minute changes, you may feel particularly frustrated when pursuing your career in a production environment. However, if you understand and accept changes in the spirit of making better and livelier motion pictures, then it will be enjoyable rather than an ordeal for you.

TASK

- Write down a list of ideas that you have in mind on how you think the effects could be done as you analyze the picture. It doesn't matter if you are inexperienced in creating such effects. At this stage it is important to be creative and use your imagination and think about what the fire spitting from the dragon should be like.
- Your list should include questions such as:
  - How fast should the fire be shooting out?
  - When does the fire reach its peak position?
  - What should the timing curve be like? Meaning if you were to sketch a distance-time curve for the movement of the fire, should it be linear? Or should in be fast-in, slow-out?
  - How should the color of the fire evolve as the fire zooms across the screen?

- Make sure that you note all your questions before proceeding to the next section.
- Next, for each question, try providing an answer yourself. For example, take into account the style of your director. This is especially important if you're not doing a realistic shot but more of a stylized animation. In stylized animation, different directors prefer a different look for their work. For example, a director who is influenced by Disney animation and a director whose work depicts Japanese anime style, will ask for entirely different results even for the same shot.
- Once you have an idea of the answers to your questions, sketch them. For example, you may sketch the time-distance curve of how you think the fire should travel.

At the end of this preparation stage, you should have an idea of how and what you are going to achieve. Don't undermine the preparation stage and jump straight in front of your workstation and start modeling or animating. Without good preparation, you may easily end up with the wrong approaches and never achieve your goals with the given timeframe.

APPROACHES

The approach that I adopt to creating digital effects in Maya is a divide-and-conquer approach. The overall requirement is first broken down into various layers. Each layer is in turn focused and solved. For example, in this production scenario, the general movement and look of the fire is first achieved and the fine tuning of the details are followed in the subsequent steps. Figure 4-2 illustrates very generally the process of creating the digital effects in Maya.

The first step is to determine the method of creation for the particles. Each method is suitable for different purposes. The manual provides very straightforward explanations of each type of creation. As you go through the tutorials, you will better understand when to use each of the different types of creation.

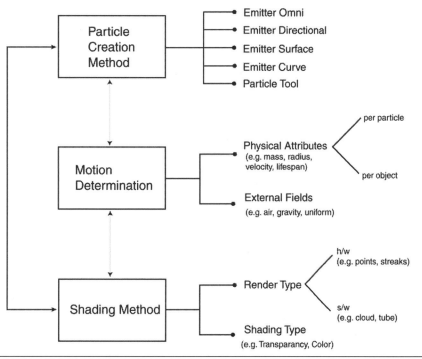

FIGURE 4-2   *Workflow of creating particle effects in Maya*

After the particles are created, the motion required of the particles is usually controlled in two ways: either by setting the physical attributes of the particles or by creating the dynamic fields to control them, or using both ways together. For example, if your animation requires that the particles will move like cigarette smoke, you would likely create the particles with a small radius and reasonably short life span and link a turbulence dynamic field to it. There are other ways to control the particles, such as keyframing the particle movement, and using expressions. You will experience the different methods in the later tutorials.

Once the movement of the particles is achieved, you will move on to render the particles. Depending on the types of particles you created, you can hardware-render or software-render the particles. Each type of particle rendering has its own merits. For example, to create the effects of fireworks, smoke, and sparks, hardware-rendering generally provides convincing and fast results. If you require reflection or refraction of your particles, software-rendering is generally preferred. With each render type, you are able to fine-tune the look of the particles by mapping and controlling the various parameters such as transparency and color.

Creating the desired effects is an interactive process. Therefore, during each stage of the creation, you are likely to loop back to the previous or beginning stage and further fine-tune various parameters until you achieve the desired results.

This workflow model may seem rather logical and simple. However, do not underestimate the process. Once you get used to organizing your work and eventually develop your own processes and procedures, you will realize that organizational skills are especially important when you work on more complex projects.

TASK

- Based on this work flow model, develop your own procedures. There is no single best model. The important point is to develop your own working habits and processes.
- Add more detail and more stages as necessary.

PRODUCTION AND TESTING

To manage your files, you will set a new project for this Fire Dragon tutorial.

Create a new project

1. Go to the File menu and select Project ➤ New… .

A window opens to let you set the name and location of the new project.

2. Enter Fire_Dragon as the name of the new project.
3. Click on the Use Defaults button.
4. Click Accept to set Fire_Dragon as your working project (see Figure 4-3)

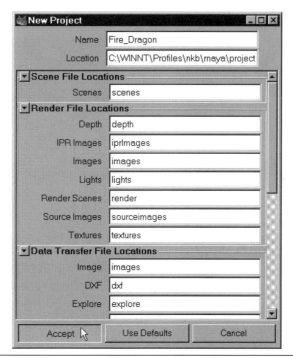

FIGURE 4-3   *Create a new project*

You will next load in the dragon model.

The purpose of loading the model is to help you more precisely locate the fire's starting point and set up the camera position and angle. However, at times, your required model may not be available for you to use or your model may be too complex to be loaded. If this is the case, you may create a simple stand-in model or load a sample image as a simple reference.

Load in the dragon model

5.   Go to File ➤ Import… .

A window opens and lets you choose a file to load.

6.   Select your CD-ROM drive and select the file dragon.ma or dragon.mb. The files are located under the directory of 3Dcafe/Animals.
7.   Click Import to import the dragon model into the scene.

The dragon file is a highly detailed dragon model. Therefore, depending on your machine speed, it may take some time to load.

Maya supports several file formats for both import and export. Some of these formats are integrated as plug-ins. Therefore, you will have to load the plug-in before you are able to import or export the files. To load a plug-in, go to Window ➤ General Editors ➤ Plug-in Manager… . From the Plug-in Manager window, load the appropriate plug-in. It is always faster to save or load a Maya binary file (.mb) than an ascii file (.ma) since binary files are usually more compact. Use only Maya ascii file format when you need to physically edit the file or when ascii file transfer is preferred. One advantage of using Maya ascii file format

is that you can cut and paste the file into an email and send it out as a normal text email. This is especially useful when the receiver's email program is set to always decode with error any binary files.

To better manage your scene, you will next create a layer for the dragon model.

Layer the dragon

8. With the dragon model still selected, go to Window ➢ Layer Editor... .

The Layers window opens.

9. Click on the New Layer button.
10. A new layer is created. Click on the Assign to Current button to assign the current selected dragon to the layer.
11. Double-click on layer1 and rename it layer_Dragon.
12. Click on any of the colors to set the current color for the layer.
13. Tumble around to see the dragon and have an idea of how to position your fire and also have an idea of the size of the fire.

Once done, you will hide the dragon for now.

14. Click on the Invisible button to make the layer_Dragon invisible (see Figure 4-4).

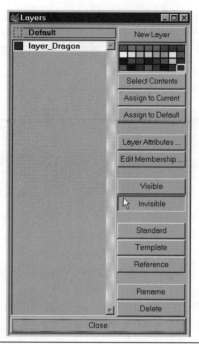

FIGURE 4-4   *Layer your model*

15.   Click Close to close the Layers window.

In Maya 2.0, the Layer Editor has an improved functionality. Therefore, if you open a scene created with layers using an earlier version of Maya, you are likely to experience some problems as some of the old functionalities are no longer supported. Refer to the Maya manual for details. It is always advisable to create multiple layers in your scene for different parts of the models. This allows you to better control and manage your scene especially when developing complex models or animation. Besides, in Maya 2.0, you are able to assign different colors to different layers. For example, you can assign a character head to be blue, and assign the limbs of the character with green. This allows you to easily compare layers and make references.

If a model is complex and huge, for example, the dragon model, using the Layer Editor, you can always display it as bounding boxes and thus speed up your interactivity. To display a layer as bounding boxes, from the Layers window, click on the Layer Attributes button. The Attribute window opens. Click on the Level of Detail listbox and change the level of detail to Bounding Box (see Figure 4-5).

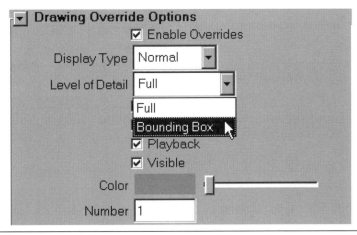

FIGURE 4-5   *Display using bounding box*

CREATE THE DRAGON FIRE

You will first create an emitter that will function as the fire that the dragon shoots out. Since the fire will generally be shooting in a single direction, you will use a directional emitter, which will emit particles in only a single direction.

TASK

- Experiment with the effects of using different emitters. Bookmark this point and come back again later to see if you can achieve your desired results using a different emitter.

Create the fire particles

1. Press F4 to switch to the Dynamics menu set.
2. Select Particles ➤ Create Emitter -❏.

   The Emitter Options window opens.

3. Enter E_DrgFire as the Emitter Name.
4. Set the Emitter Type as Directional.
5. Click on the Emission Direction and set the DirectionZ to 1 and the rest of the X and Y directions to 0.
6. Leave the rest of the parameters as default and click Create.
7. Click Close to close the window.

   The emitter E_DrgFire is created, together with the particle object particle1.

8. Go to Window ➤ Outline… .
9. Double-click on the default name of particle1 and change it to particleFire (see Figure 4-6).

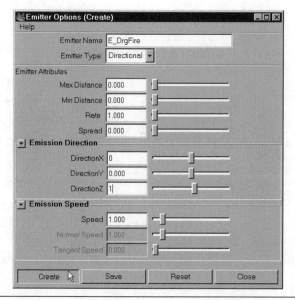

FIGURE 4-6   *Create the fire emitter*

Play back the animation

10. Go to Display ➤ Grid to toggle off the grid display.
11. Dolly in to have a better look at the emitter.
12. Click on the Play forwards button at the bottom of the screen to view the playback of the fire particles.

Depending on the rate of emission, you should see a string of particles from the emitter.

13. Toggle the Grid back on.

You have now achieved the first basic movement of the fire. While it is obviously far from complete, you are a step closer to the final results. With this basic movement, you will now fine-tune the animation to add details.

FINE-TUNE THE FIRE MOVEMENT

Fine-tuning is different than making changes. Fine-tuning should help you get a step closer to your desired goal while making changes may result in a completely different direction or idea. Having an organized working method such as keeping regular and different versions of backups during the different stages of your work, will certainly help you when changes are required.

Adjust the emitting speed

Looking at the particles, you will realize that the movement lacks dynamics. A typical emission often occurs after the substance is compressed under pressure and released. Therefore, you will now introduce the dynamics by increasing the speed of emission.

TASK

- Besides increasing the speed, think of other ways to improve the dynamics of the fire.

1. Go to Window ➢ Outliner… .
2. Click on the node E_DrgFire.

Its keyable channel information is displayed in the Channel Box on the right side of the window.

3. If the channel box is not shown, go to Options ➢ Channel Box.
4. From the Channel Box, set the speed value to 48.
5. Set also the Rate value to 100.

NOTE

There are several ways to select your objects. Selecting through the Outliner window provides a detailed and direct approach. To more quickly select any node, you may simply draw a bounding box around the object. Refer to the Maya manual for more details on selection priorities, different components, and object selection methods. For earlier versions of Maya, the E_DrgFire node is known as E_DrgFireShape node.

Add in the air resistance

As the fire zooms itself forward, like any other object, it should gradually lose its momentum due to the air resistance. To achieve such effects, a Drag field is added.

6. From the Outliner window, select the particleFire node.
7. Go to Fields ➢ Create Drag -❑.

The Drag Options window opens.

8. Enter the Drag Name as F_AirResist and set the Magnitude to 1.5.
9. Also set the Z direction to 1 and the rest of the directions to 0.
10. Click Create to add the field to the scene.

This will add the F_AirResist field to the scene and connect it to the particleFire node.

11. Click Close to close the window (see Figure 4-7).

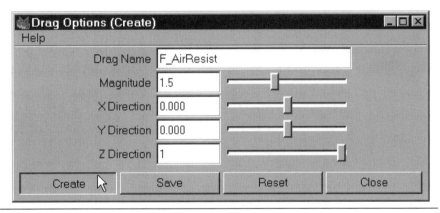

FIGURE 4-7   *Create the air resistance*

In Maya, there are several already defined force fields such as Drag and Gravity. They are convenient ways to introduce forces to control the movement of the models. However, it is also not too difficult for you to introduce your own similar controls with the help of the MEL scripts. You will get to try this in subsequent chapters.

12. Play back the animation. You should see the slowing down of the particles as they move farther away from the emitter source.

Set the preliminary particle rendering type

You will set the rendering to Cloud type rendering.

13. Select the particleFire node.
14. Go to Window ≻ Attribute Editor. Or you may press Ctrl-a to activate the hot key for the Attribute Editor window.

The Attribute Editor opens.

In Maya 2.0, the Attribute Editor usually opens as part of the main window. If you have the channel box shown on the right side of the main window, the Attribute Editor will replace the channel box in the same position. If you prefer to have the Attribute Editor as a separate window, as in the earlier version of Maya, you can, from the menu bar of the Attribute Editor, go to Copy ≻ Tear Off Copy… . A separate window of the current Attribute Editor appears.

15. Under the Render Attributes section, set the Particle Render Type to Cloud (s/w). (see Figure 4-8)

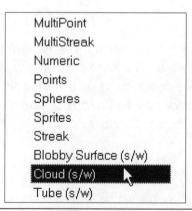

FIGURE 4-8   *Change the particle render type*

16. Play back the animation for a better view of the particles movement.

*Depending on your hardware running Maya, sometimes you may experience that the display rate drops significantly if you switch to Cloud or other rendering types. One way to improve your response time is to display only one window during the playback. To see the speed of your display rate, type the following at the command-Line prompt: **displayStats -fr true.** To turn it off, type in the command: **displayStats -fr false.** In general, a real-time display rate is optimal at 30 Hz and above. But a more likely value of 20 or even 15 Hz is acceptable. With anything less, you may experience jerky images. In Maya, you may choose to play your animation at a different default rate. If you choose to play in real time, most likely your system will not be able to cope if your scene is loaded with several models. To set your playback speed, go to Options ➢ General Preferences... . The General Preferences window opens. Click on the Animation tab and set the Playback Speed to your choice. To ensure that every single frame is played back, set the option to Free (see Figure 4-9).*

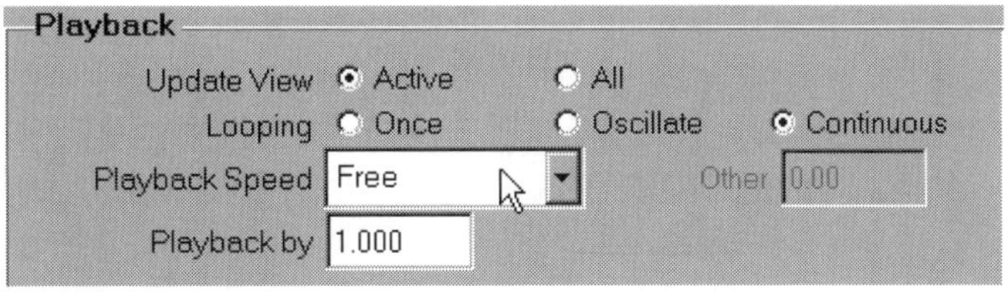

FIGURE 4-9 *Play back at free speed*

Looking at the particles movement, you will realize that it does not look good. The particles are all moving in a nice linear manner. Typical fire exhibits turbulence. Therefore, the next thing to add is more turbulence to your fire.

Adding turbulence to the movement

17. Select particleFire.
18. Go to Fields ➣ Create Turbulence -❑.

The Turbulence Options window opens.

19. Enter F_Turbulence as the Turbulence Name.
20. Enter 50.0 as the Magnitude of the turbulence force.
21. Set the Attenuation to 0 and the rest as default.
22. Click Create to create the turbulence field.
23. Close the window.
24. Play back the animation. You should see more turbulence in the particle movement (see Figure 4-10).

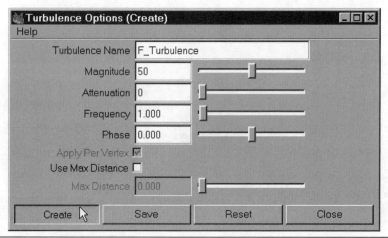

FIGURE 4-10   *Create turbulence field*

TASK

- What are the parameters that control the speed and movement of the particles now? They are—the air drag, turbulence, and the speed of emission. It is a good habit to always record which parameters control which objects in the scene. This is especially useful when you need to make changes to your scene and animation, say, two months later. It will also be useful if you were to implement your own user interface with customized control and sliders using MEL in Maya.

SET THE PHYSICAL ATTRIBUTES OF THE FIRE

Currently, the particles appear to last forever. Knowing the length required of your animation, you will set the life span of the particles to an appropriate value.

In Maya, you have the choice of setting the life span of your particles to base on per object or per individual particle. Whether to set the particle to die at the per particle or per object levels has a lot to do with the randomness that you want to introduce. If you are not sure what would be appropriate, set the life span to be per object first. Once you realize that the movement or the animation appears to be rather dull, you can add more randomness to it by deleting this attribute or simply override it by adding the per particle attribute. The per particle attribute has a higher priority than the per object attribute.

Set the life span of the fire

To introduce more randomness to the fire effects, you will set the life span of the particles to per particle. However, I have also managed to get good random results through the use of per object life span. You are encouraged to experiment with the different settings.

1.   Select particleFire.
2.   Open its attribute editor.
3.   Under the Add Dynamic Attribute section, click on the Lifespan button (see Figure 4-11).

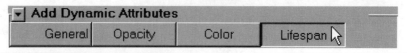

FIGURE 4-11   *Add a lifespan dynamic attribute*

A window opens to let you set the life span to either per particle or per object.

4.   Check on the Add Per Particle Attribute.
5.   Click on Add Attribute.

A new attribute lifespanPP is added to the Per Particle (Array) Attributes section.

6.   Right click on the lifespanPP box and choose Creation Expression… .

The Expression Editor window opens.

7.   Enter the following expression into the Expression Editor window:

```
float $Life = rand (0,2);
particleFireShape.lifespanPP = $Life;
```

8.   Click Create to create the expressions.

The first statement of the expression declares the variable Life as a floating variable and assigns the output of the random function rand( ) to it. The rand( ) function is able to generate a random value each time it is called. In the case above, the rand( ) function returned values that will always lie between 0.0 and 2.0. Therefore, each particle will end up with a different life span when first created. For a detailed explanation of the rand( ) function and its distribution curve, refer to the Maya manual.

The second statement assigns the variable to the particle's life span.

TASK

* You are encouraged to change the values to other numbers such as (1,2) or (0,3) etc. However, take note that the life span of particles is often used later as a reference map for other parameters such as the color or transparency. So, take note of the values you've chosen.

When you do a playback, you should see the particles disappearing towards the end of the particle instead of lasting forever in the scene.

You will now set the physical attributes of the particles. Bear in mind that the physical attributes such as the radius, will affect the final render of the fire effects.

Set the size of the particles

9. From the Add Dynamic Attribute section of the Attribute Editor, click on the General button.

The Add Attribute window opens.

10. From the window, click on the Particle tab.
11. Highlight radiusPP and click OK (see Figure 4-12).

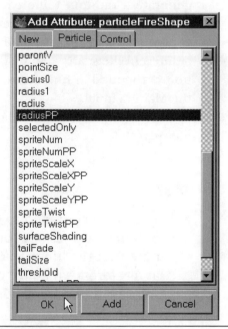

FIGURE 4-12   *Add a radiusPP dynamic attribute*

A new attribute, radiusPP, is added to the Per Particle (Array) Attributes section.

12. Right-click on the radiusPP box and choose Create Ramp.

A default ramp is created that maps the life span of the particle with the radiusPP.

13. Right-click on the radiusPP box.

14. Select ≺ arrayMapper1.outValuePP ≻ Edit Ramp.

The Attribute Editor of the ramp opens.

15. Enter ramp_radiusPP as the name of the ramp
16. Set the ramp values and positions as shown in the following table:

POSITION	RGB VALUES
1.0	1.5, 1.5, 1.5
0.815	1.905, 1.905, 1.905
0.0	2.0, 2.0, 2.0

Mapping various functions and parameters using the Ramp texture is a common technique in Maya. As you go through the tutorials in the book, you will realize that the Ramp function is a versatile texture that provides great flexibility and ease of use.

In the above example, the alpha values of the ramp are mapped to the size (radius) of the particles based on their life span. At the beginning of the life span, the particle radius is 2.0. As individual particles age, the radius will reduce according to the interpolation of the values. For example, if a particle is born with a life span of 2.0, it will reach a radius value of 1.5 towards the end of its two-second life span. And at $0.815*2.0 = 1.63$ seconds of its life span, it will have a radius of 1.905.

The purpose of the ramp is to reduce the size of the particle as they age. It follows the logic of dispersion of fire as the distance the particles travel increases. You are very likely to have to keep tweaking the values of the ramp in order to get the desired effects.

It is a common method to reduce the radius of particles as they age. However, at times, you may want to instead increase the size as they age. This circumstance arises when you would like to create the effect of diffusion of gas particles. You can achieve gas diffusion by generally reducing the transparency and increasing the radius of the gas particles. Make this an exercise to explore yourself.

TASK

- Test some extreme values of the ramp to compare the effects.

CREATE THE FIERY LOOK

Create the fire shader

1. Go to Window ➢ Rendering Editors ➢ Multilister…. . The Multilister window opens.

2. From within the Multilister window, right-click to go to Edit ➢ Create…. .

    The Create Render Node window opens.

3. From the window, click on the Particle Cloud button under the Volumetric Materials section (Figure 4-13).

    A new particleCloud2SG shader is created as shown in the Multilister window.

FIGURE 4-13   *Create a new particle volume shader*

4.   Change the name of particleCloud2SG to
     particleFireSG and its volume material from
     particleCloud2 to particleFireM.

Assign the particle shader to the fire

5.   Select the particleFire node from the Outliner.
6.   Select the particleFireSG node from the Multilister
     window and right-click to go to Edit ➢ Assign.
7.   The particleFire is assigned with the new
     particleFireSG volumetric shading group.

Test-render the Fire

Before you test-render the scene, add a simple light
source. For test-rendering purposes, you will add in a spotlight.

NOTE

*For quick testing of scenes, I prefer to use spot light because it is
directional and you are able to easily control and focus the spotlight at any desired objects. In Alias PowerAnimator, another
excellent product of Alias Wavefront, the default light source is
an ambient light plus a directional light. You may also try using
this setup to test your scene.*

8. Press F5 to go to the Rendering menu.
9. Go to Lights > Create Spot Light.

A default spotLight1 is created and positioned at the origin.

10. From the Outliner Window, using your middle mouse button, click, drag, and drop spotLight1 into the perspective window.
11. Tumble and Track the view until you get to a view similar to the one shown in Figure 4-14.

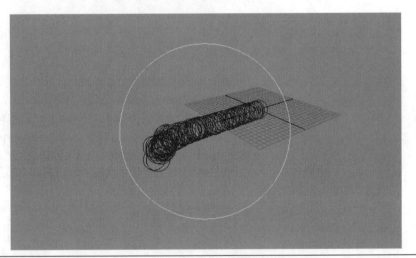

FIGURE 4-14   *Setting the spotlight view*

12. Click, drag, and drop the persp camera from the Outliner Window to get back your perspective camera view.
13. Play back the animation to an arbitrary frame number, for example, 45.

14. Go to Render ➤ Render into New Window... .

You should get a rendered image similar to the one shown in Figure 4-15.

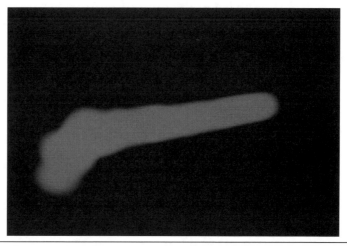

FIGURE 4-15 *A rendered image of the fire*

The image now lacks color, surface depth, and various details, which you will add in the following sections.

For now, if you are happy with the motion and are only testing the look of the fire, you will cache the particle. In Maya 2.0, you are able to selectively cache your particles.

Cache the fire particles

15. Select particleFire.
16. Go to Solvers ➤ Scene Caching ➤ Enable.
17. Play back the animation to allow the system to start calculating the various parameters and cache them.
18. Scrub the animation and you should be able to see that the particles are correctly displayed all the time.

19. At any time if you want to disable or delete the cache, select the object and go to Solvers ➤ Scene Caching ➤ Delete or Disable.

If you have a large amount of information and can't afford the memory to cache the animation, you can always go to Solvers ➤ Run-up Caching ➤ Run-up and Cache. This will run up the particles to your current frame position. However, you won't be able to scrub the animation. There are several more options for you to efficiently play back your particle animation. Refer to the Maya manual for more details.

Another point to remember about playing back animations is that if you drag using your middle mouse button, the scene will not be updated. This applies to all objects. This is useful for setting keyframes without updating the scene.

Bookmark the Camera View

20. Go to View ➤ Bookmarks ➤ Edit Bookmarks… .

The Bookmark Editor (persp) opens.

21. Enter cameraView_f45 as the name. Choose any frame value that you will want to consistently test and see the results.

It is always better to bookmark a camera view to compare different images. With the same camera setting, you will be able to tell if the adjusted parameter has any significant influence on your image.

Add Color

In Maya, there are two common methods for adding color, transparency, and incandescence:

- Adding through standard mapping
- Adding through the life span.

Adding through the standard mapping swatch will cause individual particles to exhibit the same color texture throughout their entire existence. Imagine the particles as individual spheres. If you map a standard ramp as its color, the ramp color will exist and remain the same throughout the life span of the spheres. The color will not change (see Color Plate).

Compare mapping the color to the life span of the particles: the particle will appear to be Red in the beginning and Blue towards the end of its life span (see Color Plate).

Adding through life span will result in a change of color as the particles age.

TASK

- Think about how to map the particles so that the color changes according to their age and at the same time exhibits the same pattern of colors throughout their life span. In other words, how do you achieve a combination of both life span and standard color mapping?

You will map the Life Color with a standard Ramp texture.

22. Select the particleFireM from the Multilister window.
23. Open its Attribute Editor.
24. Click on the Map button beside the Life Color.

The Create Render Node window opens

The Map button in Maya 2.0 is represented as a simple checker pattern button. To perform operations such as delete, ignore, and create expression on the map button, you have to right-click on the function name itself. For example, to create the expression for the color map, right-click on the word Color and select Create New Expression. Notice the difference from the older version of Maya, where it required a right-click on the Map button itself.

25. Click on the Ramp button.

　　The Attribute Editor for particleAgeMapper1 opens.

26. Check on the Relative Age box (see Figure 4-16).

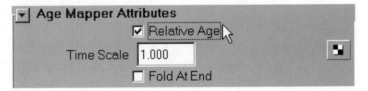

FIGURE 4-16　*Set the relative age of the particle*

As a general rule of thumb, I always have the Relative Age box checked on whenever I map using the Particle Age. It is also written in the manual that if you do not get your expected results, you should turn this box on.

27. Click on the Go To Output Connection button and navigate to the default ramp1 texture that has been created (see Figure 4-17).

FIGURE 4-17 *Input and Output connection*

28. Enter ramp_LifeColor as the name of the ramp.
29. Set the entries of the ramp as shown in Figure 4-18.

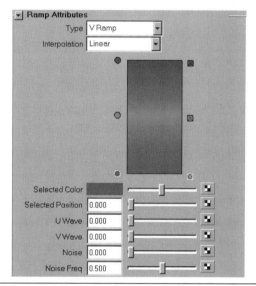

FIGURE 4-18 *Create the ramp texture for the Life Color*

The ramp values are as shown below:

POSITION	RGB VALUES
1.0	0.710, 0.0, 0.0
0.515	1.0, 0.458, 0.0069
0.0	0.489, 0.440, 0.2

TASK

- For a particle with a life span of 2.0 seconds, what would the color at the beginning of the life span be and what would it be at, for example, 1.5 seconds?

In the world of colors there are several models: the HSV (Hue, Saturation, Value), CMY (Cyan, Magenta, Yellow), and RGB (Red, Green, Blue) models. In Maya, both the HSV and RGB models are available. Each model is suitable for different circumstances. For example, if you would like to have a colorful but soothing image, it is generally advisable to use the HSV model. You can adjust the H values to obtain different color but maintain the same S and V values throughout to keep the integrity of the colors.

Add Transparency

From the wireframe playback, you will notice the popping problem. That is, instead of seeing the particles disappear gradually, you will notice that the particles pop out of the scene suddenly when their life span reaches the peak values.

One solution to this problem is to add a transparency to the life span of the particles. In this way, towards the end of the life span, the particles will become more transparent and eventually completely transparent before they die.

You will create the transparency using ramp and set the particles to be near-transparent throughout and completely transparent at the end.

1. Map the Life Transparency of particleFireM using the same method as described above for the Life Color.
2. Rename the ramp ramp_LifeTrans.
3. Set the entries of the ramp as shown in Figure 4-19.

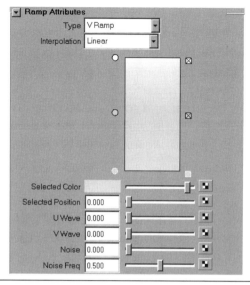

FIGURE 4-19 *Create the ramp texture for the Life Transparency*

POSITION	RGB VALUES
1.0	1.2,1.2,1.2
0.515	0.9, 0.9, 0.9
0.0	0.935, 0.935, 0.935

When setting the values, note that it is not necessary to have them fall within a standard value of 0.0 (opaque) to 1.0 (transparent). As in the above ramp, the values corresponding to the last entry on the ramp have a value of 1.2. This in fact will cause the particles to be transparent even before they die. You should try different values and experiment with how the final particles are rendered.

In general, I would suggest that the ramp values be slightly higher than 1.0 towards the end to be sure that the particles disappear particles before they die. Another method is to give the transparent values of 1.0 at an earlier position. For example, you can set the values to be 1.0 at a position of 0.995. This will ensure

NOTE

that the particles will reach complete transparency just before they die. However, if you have a life span of say 20 seconds, setting a value of 1.0 at 0.99 will result in the particles starting to disappear at 0.99*20*30 = 594 frames, which is 6 frames before the end.

Whenever you are dealing with long animation time, always use a simple proportional formula to compute your ramp values so that you know when the particles appear and disappear.

TASK

- Given a particle life span of 1.5 seconds and assuming a 30 fps setting, what should the ramp position be if you want the particles to disappear at say the 43rd frame?

4. Go to the bookmark cameraView_f45.
5. Test-render the image.

You should get an image similar to the one shown in Figure 4-20.

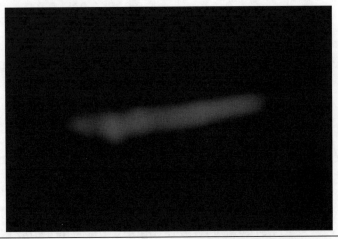

FIGURE 4-20 *A rendered image of the fire*

FINE-TUNE THE LOOK

Add the Incandescence

Adding incandescence allows you to create the self-illuminating effects. This function is particularly useful when you need to have that extra high fluorescent look. In effects such as fire, hot liquid, and lava, you will almost always need to add this incandescent effect.

1. Map the Life Incandescence of the particleFireM using the same method as described above for the Life Color.
2. Rename the ramp as to ramp_LifeIncand.
3. Set the entries of the ramp as shown in Figure 4-21.

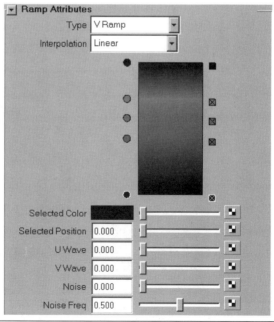

FIGURE 4-21 *Create the ramp textures for the Life Incandansance*

POSITION	RGB VALUES
1.0	0.0, 0.0, 0.0
0.725	0.722, 0.527, 0.035
0.58	0.827, 0.307, 0
0.425	0.796, 0.173, 0.110
0.0	0.0, 0.0, 0.0

TASK

- Can you achieve the incandescent effect, without using incandescence, by just creating very high values, greater than 1.0 for the RGB values of the color map?

4. Do a test-render and your results should look like Figure 4-22.

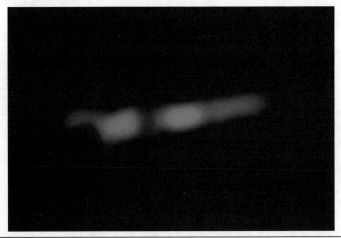

FIGURE 4-22   *A rendered image of the fire*

TASK

- Comment on the look of the render. What do you think is lacking in this image?

Add the blob map

A problem with the look of the image is that it doesn't have any random color that you expect to see in a fire effect. So, you must add random details to the fire.

There are several ways to add detail to a particle effects. For example, instead of using a simple ramp for the color above, you can overlay the color with a noise function texture such as Solid Fractal. However, in this section, you will add the noise detail using the Blob Map function available in the shader.

The Blob Map function is directly related to Transparency function of the Particle Shader. According to the explanation in the Maya manual, it is a scaling factor for the particle clouds' Out Transparency attribute. You will map this function with a noise/fractal type shader.

5. Select particleFireM and opens its Attribute Editor.
6. Click on the Map button of the Blob Map.

The Create Render Node window opens.

7. From the 3D texture section, click on the Crater button to create a 3D crater texture node (see Figure 4-23).

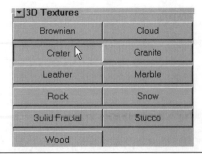

FIGURE 4-23   *Create the 3D crater texture*

8. Enter the name of the 3D crater texture as crater_BlobMap.
9. Edit the crater to the values as shown (see Figure 4–24).

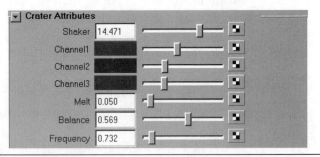

FIGURE 4-24   *Set the crater node attributes*

	RGB VALUES
Channel 1	0.416,0.149,0.075
Channel 2	0.251,0.114,0.043
Channel 3	0.235,0.208,0.122
Shaker	14.47120
Melt	0.05
Balance	0.56910
Frequency	0.732

TASK

- Will Blob Map work if your transparency is black? That is, if you were to have opaque particles (no transparency), will the Blob Map have any effect? When you have tested and found out the answer, remember this point because it will save you some time when trying out various mapping functions.

For a detailed explanation of the Crater function parameters, refer to the Maya manual.

One problem with using 3D Texture node is that the patterns are random, but because of the nature of its 3D node, it exhibits a fixed pattern of randomness. This fixed pattern of randomness is obvious and undesirable in animation. To break such a sequence of dull predictability, you may choose to change the various parameters of the texture. For example, you may animate the shaker or frequency values over time. However, a simple, and quick alternative is to transform the 3D Placement node. In this case, you will animate the translation value of the node.

The question now is which translation value should you use? A common rule of thumb is to translate the node that is in the direction opposite to the movement of the particles. In this case, since the particles move in on the Z-axis, you will animate the movement in the opposite Z-axis.

TASK

- Instead of translation, experiment with scaling and rotation values of the node.

To achieve the translation of the node, a common method is to keyframe the movement. However, the practice I adopt is, whenever possible, try to do a procedural animation rather than keyframe animation. Procedural allows you to have a more direct and faster control than keyframing. Therefore, for this case, you will use an expression to control the animation of the node.

10. Select the 3D Placement node of crater_BlobMap.
11. Open its Attribute Editor.
12. Right-click on the translation values and select Create New Expression... (see Figure 4-25).

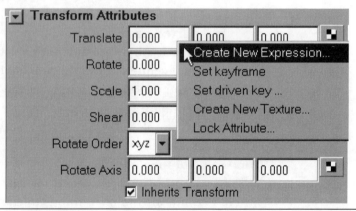

FIGURE 4-25   *Create a new expression for the translation values*

The Expression Editor opens .

13. Enter the following expression:

$t = 10*time;
place3dTexture1.translateZ = -$t;

14. Enter the name of the expression as FireRandom (see Figure 4-26).

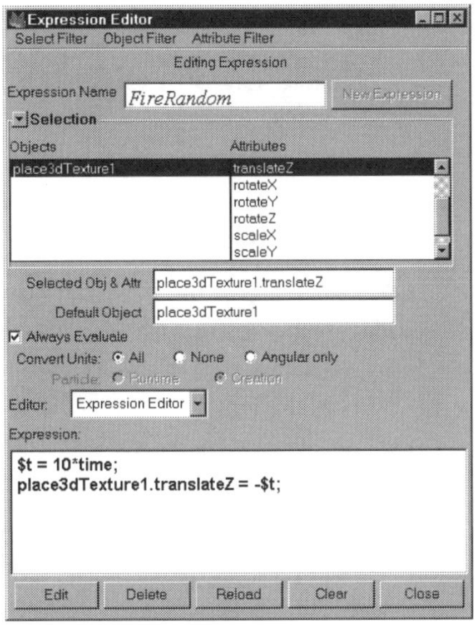

FIGURE 4-26 *The expression window*

15. Render the view. You should get an image similar to the one shown in Figure 4-27.

FIGURE 4-27 *A rendered image of the fire*

Highlighting the Fire

In the introductory chapters, you have learned that light plays a significant role in modeling your scene. So far, in this example, your scene is lit by a single spot light. You will now put into practice how to model a scene using this spot light.

Currently, from the rendered scene, the fire does not appear to resemble a luminous fire. So, you will attempt to model this effect by increasing the intensity of the spot light source.

16. Select spotLight1.
17 Go to its Attribute Editor.
18. Change the intensity of the spot light to 10.0 (see Figure 4-28).

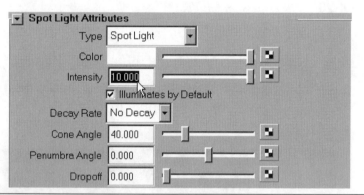

FIGURE 4-28 *Set the intensity spotlight*

19. Test-render the scene. You should now get an image similar to the one shown in Figure 4-29.

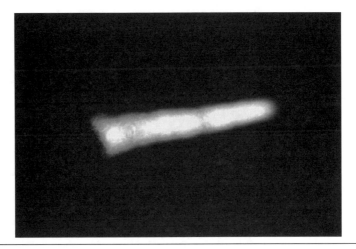

FIGURE 4-29   *A rendered image of the fire*

To create a more realistic effect, you will add more glow to the fire particles.

20. Select the particleFireM.
21. Set the Glow Intensity to 0.1 (see Figure 4-30).

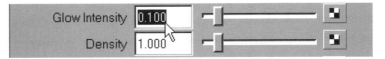

FIGURE 4-30   *Setting the glow intensity*

22. Test-render and you should get an image similar to the one as shown in Figure 4-31.

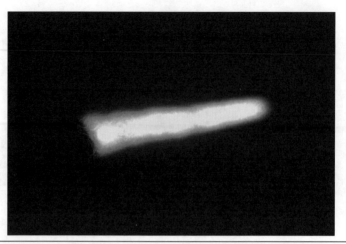

FIGURE 4-31   *A rendered image of the fire*

FURTHER FINE-TUNE THE MOVEMENT

You will now fine-tune the movement of the fire by adding more randomness to it.

Recall the three factors that affect the movement. To increase the randomness, a straightforward approach is to increase the magnitude of the turbulence field. When increasing the turbulence, take note that you do not want the entire fire to be turbulated. Rather, you will set the fire to be stable at the beginning and slowly lose momentum and become more turbulent towards the end.

Create stronger turbulation

1. Select F_turbulence.
2. Set the turbulence fields to the following values:

Magnitude	200
Attenuate	1.0
Frequency	100

TASK

- Try out different values.
- Try introducing the different phase values of the turbulence and observe the difference in your animation.

More Emission

There may be some intermittent break of your fire. One way to remove it is to control the transparency of the particle. Another way is to control the turbulence of the fire, or have more particles emitted per second. You should be able to fine-tune based on your understanding of what controls the look and movement of the fire. A better result is obtained by setting the emission to a higher value.

3. Select the E_DrgFire.
4. Open its Attribute Editor and set the emission rate from the original 100 to 250.

After you have made changes such as increasing the rate, if you don't see any difference in the generation of the particles, first make sure that you have deleted your particle cache and regenerate a new one, and second check that you have the Cache Data turned off (see Figure 4-32).

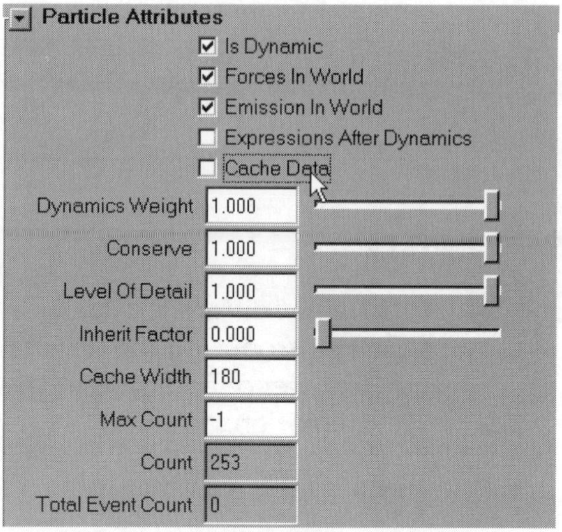

FIGURE 4-32 *Toggle off the particle cache data check box*

FURTHER FINE-TUNE THE ANIMATION

At this stage of your work, you should have achieved a fundamentally good-looking fire. Depending on the requirements and your personal aesthetic feeling, you may repeat the process of adjusting the movement and texture values to achieve your final imagery. You should experiment with different adjustments to see what you can achieve.

I have been able to get a better looking fire by making the following adjustments.

Final tunings

1. Select the Crater 3D placement.
2. Edit the Scale X,Y,Z values to 1.883,2.258,1.885.
3. Select particleFireM.
4. Change the Noise to 0.236 and the Noise Aspect to –0.675.

These four steps will create a more noisy fire effect. You should try scaling the 3D Placement node, and add in more noise to the shading node.

5. Select E_DrgFire, and change the Direction Y value to 0.2.

This will set the fire to move upwards as it travels horizontally. Remember that nothing in real life moves linearly. In addition, you may try introducing more variation the movement by adding more dynamic fields such as gravity.

6. Select spotLight1.
7. Open its Attribute Editor.
8. Go to the Shadows section.
9. Check the Use Depth Map Shadows.

This will create depth map shadows for spotLight1 (see Figure 4-33).

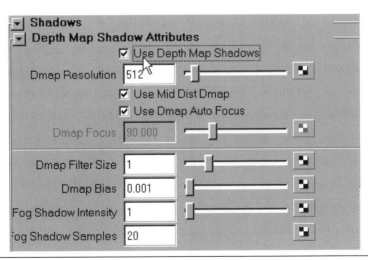

FIGURE 4-33 *Turning on the shadow option of the light source*

10. Add any additional light source that you deem necessary to help model the fire.

PUTTING EVERYTHING TOGETHER

You are now ready to bring back the dragon, and add in other details.

1. Open the Layer Editor.
2. Set the layer_Dragon Visible.
3. Adjust the position of the dragon so that it appears to be emitting fire from its mouth.

You may need to further adjust the Direction Y of the E_DrgFire so that the mouth position and the fire emitting will blend nicely.

It is always easier and more predictable to position geometries than particles. This is especially the case when you have complex dynamics linked to the particle movement.

4. If you have done the hand model in the earlier chapter, load it in and adjust the position according to the sketch given in Figure 4.1.

Camera Movement

So far you have been using the default camera to tumble around and check your animation. Now, you will add in your own camera to the scene.

1. Go to Create ➤ Camera -❑.

The Create Camera Options window opens.

2. Under the Animation Options section, click on Two to create a two-node camera.
3. Click Create and Close the window.

A new camera is created.

4. From the Outliner Window, Drag and Drop the camera1_group into the perspective window.

This will set it as the current camera.

5. Go to View ➢ Camera Settings ➢ Resolution Gate.
6. A default resolution gate is shown in the perspective window.
7. Adjust the camera view until you get a setting similar to the given sketch in Figure 4.1.

NOTE

The resolution gate is especially useful for you to check if the entire scene fits according to your given sketch. For example, if you were to render out at 640 by 350 resolution, from just the normal perspective view window, you will not be able to tell if the corner object in the scene is visible in the final rendering. In addition, you are able to view the safe region to ensure that your output will be fully visible. To view the safe region, go to View ➢ Camera Settings ➢ Safe Action or Safe Title or Field Chart.

8. Select camera1_view
9. Set the translation values to 0.0, 0.0, 0.0.
10. Press F2 to go to the Animation menu.
11. Go to frame 1.
12. Highlight the translation X, Y, Z box (see Figure 4-34).

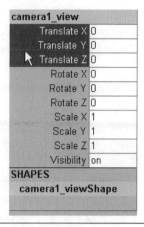

FIGURE 4-34   *Highlight the translation channels from camera1_view*

13.   Go to Animate ➤ Set Key -❑.

The options window opens.

14.   Make sure that the options are set according to Figure 4-35.

FIGURE 4-35   *Making sure that only the selected channels from the channel box will be keyframed*

15. Click on Set Key and Close the window.

The view of the camera is now fixed at the origin.

16. Select the camera1 node.
17. Set various keyframes and animate the movement of the camera according to how you want it to move.

POST-PRODUCTION

Before you render your scene, make sure you have an idea of how you would like to layer and composite your animation.

In order to have good control over every single detail of your scene, you may want to render the scene into the following layers and composite them. You should also refer to Chapter Two on the introduction to composition:

- Fire effects
- Shadows of the fire
- Dragon image
- Dragon shadows
- Textured hand image
- Static background (BG) image

The following instructions will take you through the creation of the fire effects rendering.

1. Go to Window ➢ Render Globals... .

The Render Globals window opens.

2. Go to the various sections and set the options as shown below:

Notice that you have the options of setting different file extensions, file formats, resolutions. It is all up to you and how you plan to transfer your files to different media for reading. Make sure that whatever format, extension, and resolution you use are readable by your other media. And for testing images, a low resolution and low anti-aliasing level should be sufficient (see Figures 4-36 through 4-38).

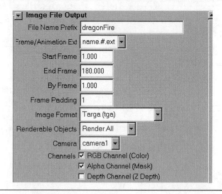

FIGURE 4-36   *Setting the image file output format*

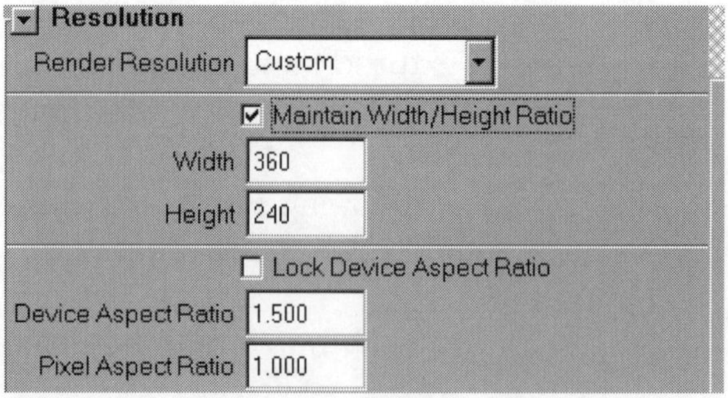

FIGURE 4-37   *The resolution setting*

FIGURE 4-38   *The quality setting*

3. Close the Render Global window when you are done.
4. Press F5 to go to the Rendering menu.
5. Go to Render ➤ (Save) Batch Render... -❏.

The Options window opens.

In Maya 2.0, you have the added option of rendering with more than one processor if you are working on a multi-CPU machine. This saves a considerable amount of time (see Figure 4-39).

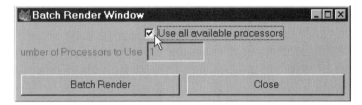

FIGURE 4-39   *Render with more than one CPU*

6. Click Batch Render.
7. Enter a filename and start your rendering.

Notice that in Maya 2.0, rendering scene files are all saved under a new directory called render. To render your scene from the command line, save the file and enter the command: Render –n 0 <filename.mb> in the appropriate directory where you save your files.

CONCLUSION

Congratulations on completing this first digital effects animation project! This project has given you the experience of working on a simple production project.

You should stop here and spend some time to recall what you have learned and ask yourself how you would approach the project again if you were to do a similar animation effect. If you did not get to the results you expected, do not get discouraged. Try again. Failure is part of the production cycle that every animator experiences. If you have successfully completed the project, it is time to ask yourself what are the five most unpleasant sights in your animation. Be critical of your work. You will learn the most by being objective. And it is almost always more comfortable to be criticized by yourself than by your director!

To have an idea of what you should have achieved, play the quicktime animation called chpt04.mov found on the CD-ROM. This shows you the animation of the project, the textured dragon, and the hand.

EXERCISE

1. The director decided that the dragon will come alive and will be moving its head as the fire is being emitted. Think of how you will animate the fire to accommodate the change. What problems might you encounter?
2. Based on what you learned here, apply the same method to create the fire effects of a torch fire, something similar to an Olympic torch fire. You should be able to get that without too much trouble.

5

THE DYNAMIC FIRE

INTRODUCTION

In this chapter, you will create a type of fire that does not burn or move in the usual way that you would expect. It will appear to have its own momentum and direction. Throughout the majority of its existence, it will not exhibit any characteristic typical of normal fire under the influence of natural forces, such as gravity. This kind of fire often occurs as a result of a sudden explosive reaction. It inherits the movement and momentum of its parent object and its life span is usually short.

PRE-PRODUCTION: UNDERSTANDING THE SCENARIO

TASK

- After successfully completing your first project assignment, you are now ready to tackle a different type of fire. The sketch for this project is shown in Figure 5-1.

FIGURE 5-1   *Sketch*

In this scenario, there exists a fantasy world where castles are built on a big turf of land. And each piece of land is layered with materials that defy the force of gravity. This gives the land and all its living entities the ability to remain steadily floating in the air. Each castle is self-contained. An invisible forcefield protects it from enemy attack.

Your task is to create the fire effects that result from the impact of a laser bomb on the forcefield. The movement of the fire is of particular importance. It should not be a hit-and-explode effect. Instead, the movement of the fire should convincingly reveal the existence of the spherical forcefield.

The entire fire effects should last about 1.5 seconds.

ANALYZE THE PICTURE

Carefully study the sketch in Figure 5-1. Think about how you will approach the problem. Make a list of all the questions that you have in mind, and try to provide the answers yourself. If your questions remain unanswered, you should seek clarification from your director, or make some educated assumptions based on your experience. Finally, if necessary, visit a nearby video store and rent some videos that have footages of the relevant effects that you have in mind. You should begin with a clear idea of what the entire fire should look like, including the timing.

APPROACHES

Now that you have done the previous assignment, you should feel more confident in solving more challenging and difficult problems.

The key part of this fire effect is the impact and movement of the fire. The usual way of creating impact is to use particle collision and let the dynamics solver animate and create the movement based on the properties of the dynamic bodies. There are no rules that say this will not work. However, a better approach to particle animation is always to try not to use the standard particle or dynamic system. It is not that such systems do not work well; they are simply not fast enough to implement. As explained in previous chapters, dynamic or particle systems are advanced systems that require a higher order of computational power. The employment of such systems often slows down your system and thus reduces your interactivity while increasing the rendering time.

In this project, the best method is to directly place an emitter at the point of explosion and control the particles through the emitter. As you will see later, there are some problems using this approach. However, the ease of control of the particle movement and direction will prove to be useful in the later stage.

The workflow model in this project is similar to the one in Chapter Four:

- Create a sphere to be used as reference.
- Create the explosion emitter.
- Adjust the various emission parameters.
- Adjust physical attributes of particles.
- Create shaders and adjust various shading parameters.
- Add layers of fine-tuning for the look and motion.

TASK

- If you have developed your own workflow model from the previous chapter, test your model here and see if it works under this new project.
- Have you planned how you will layer and composite your images?

PRODUCTION AND TESTING

Set a new project

1. Create a new project.
2. Enter Dynamic_Fire as the name of the new project and use the defaults for the rest of the options.

You will now load an image plane to be used as a reference for your animation. The image plane in this case will be your scanned-in sketch from above.

Create image reference

3. Select your persp camera.
4. Open its Attribute Editor.
5. Go to the perspShape tab.
6. Under the Environment Section, click on Image Plane ➤ Create (see Figure 5-2).

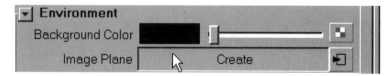

FIGURE 5-2   *Create an image plane*

An image plane is created and the Attribute Editor is updated with the image plane attributes.

7. Click on the folder icon button beside the Image Name (see Figure 5-3).

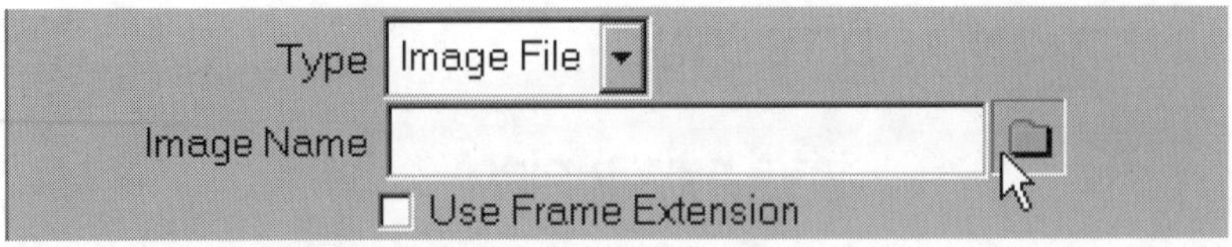

Type | Image File ▾

Image Name | [   ] 🗀

☐ Use Frame Extension

FIGURE 5-3   *Load in an image from the folders*

8.   Go to the CDROM drive and load in chpt05_sketch.tif
9.   Click on the Fit to Resolution Gate button to fit the
     image plane to the desired resolution (see Figure 5-4)

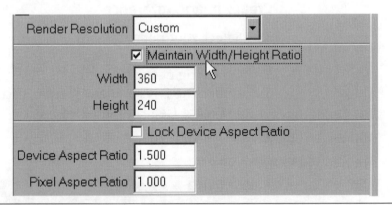

Render Resolution | Custom ▾

☑ Maintain Width/Height Ratio

Width | 360

Height | 240

☐ Lock Device Aspect Ratio

Device Aspect Ratio | 1.500

Pixel Aspect Ratio | 1.000

FIGURE 5-4   *Set the render resolution to the required aspect ratio*

If you need to use the image plane to precisely position
your objects in the scene, you have to ensure that the resolution that the image plane fits is in the same ratio that you are
going to render. For example, if the final images are supposed
to be 4000 × 3000, then set your render resolution size to a
ratio of 4/3.

In all the tutorials, a width/height ratio of 1.5 is assumed.

10. Open the Render Global... window.
11. Check on the Maintain Width/Height Ratio.
12. Set the resolution to 360 × 240 (see Figure 5-5).

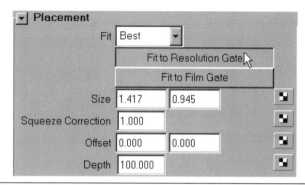

FIGURE 5-5   *Make sure that the image plane fits to the resolution gate*

From the image plane, you should get an idea of how and where you will place your objects in the scene. However, remember that for now it is not necessary to match exactly the look given in Figure 5-1. As long as the placement of objects and their relative distances are proportionally correct, you will still be able to match the camera look accurately most of the time in the later stage. It is important now to focus on maximizing the rendering so that your effects will occupy the maximum area of your image.

13. Go to the Image Plane Attribute, click on Display Mode, and choose None (see Figure 5-6). This will turn off your image plane. You will turn it back on at a later stage.

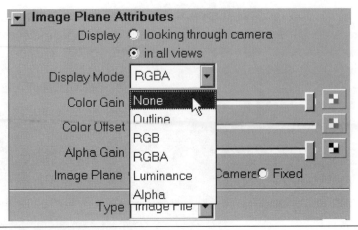

FIGURE 5-6   *Turn off the image plane display*

In the process of modeling or animation, it is often useful to create reference objects in the scene. Besides serving as visual references, the objects may serve as snapping points to precisely place your geometries. In Maya, the standard of snapping to grid, you are able to snap to curves, points, and viewplanes. These useful snapping tools will help you precisely place your geometries in the scene.

CREATE THE FORCEFIELD REFERENCE

You will first create a sphere that will serve as a guide for the forcefield.

1. Create a sphere from Create ➤ NURBS Primitives ➤ Sphere.
2. Scale the sphere by 8.0 along the X, Y, and Z axes.
3. Translate it to –8.0 along the Z-axis.
4. Rename the sphere as ForceField.
5. Template the ForceField by going to Display ➤ Object Components ➤ Templates.

Maya's user interface provides many options that are fully customizable based on the needs of individuals and projects. You should customize your hotbox, marking menus and hotkeys in a way that is optimized for your needs. Toggle between templates is one of the most commonly used functions. I have customized it with an Alt-t key. When customizing your preferences, remember that the objective is to speed up your workflow and spend more time focusing on your objects and scenes rather than searching for the menu bars. However, don't over-customize your preferences. This will cause you problem when you switch to working on another workstation, for example, to help solve a colleague's problem.

CREATE THE SOURCE AT THE CONTACT POINT OF EXPLOSION

You will now create an emitter that will be placed at the point of contact of the laser bomb and the forcefield. From there, you will set the various attributes of the particles and control how the particles will disperse and move.

Create the Emitter

You will create the emitter by creating a sphere and then detaching it into halves.

1. Create a sphere at the world origin.
2. Rotate it by 90 degrees about the X-axis.
3. Press F8 to toggle into the Component Selection mode.
4. Go to the component type Lines and make sure that isoparms is highlighted.
5. Select the middle isoparms of the sphere.

6. The isoparm will be highlighted in yellow.
7. Go to Edit Surfaces ➤ Detach Surfaces.
8. The sphere will be detached into halves.
9. Select the right half and delete it.
10. Rename the remaining sphere Fire_Sphere.
11. Transform the sphere to –1 for the translateZ.
12. Template the emitter.

What is the difference between detaching the sphere into halves and creating the sphere with the option of a 180-degree sweeping angle? In addition to using the option windows and detaching, Maya provides other ways of slicing surfaces, for example, trim and boolean. Detaching surfaces is a preferred method because a detached surface is still a valid NURBS object, whereas other methods, such as trimming, do not result in a valid NURBS object. As a result, if you trim a surface you will not be able to perform fillet on the surface. With the History On, when you detach the surface you will get a detach node as the input, together with the new detached surface. You can safely delete the detached input node if you do not intend to make use of the history information. Or when you detach an object, be sure to turn off the history.

Create the Particles

You will set the half-sphere you created as a surface emitter.

In Maya, in addition to using a surface as emitter, you are able to selectively choose from which part of a surface you would like to have particles emitted. (Refer to the manual for details.)

13. Select Fire_Sphere.
14. Press F4 to set to the Dynamics Menu.

15. Go to Particles ≻ Add Emitter.
16. At the Emitter Options window, enter E_Fire as the Emitter Name.
17. Set the rest of the parameters as shown in Figure 5-7.

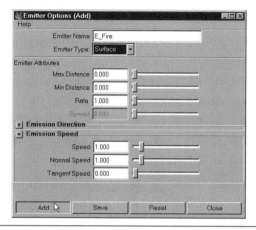

FIGURE 5-7   *Fire emitter settings*

18. Click on Add to create the emitter.
19. Close the Options window.

In Maya, the particle system is designed to be versatile. The separation of emitter and particle node allows you to have a single particle type but different emitters. This allows you, for example, to share common particle types but with different speed control.

20. From the Outliner Window, change the default name of the particle node, particle1, to particleFire.

FINE-TUNE THE FIRE MOVEMENT

Adjust the Rate of Emission

In a normal explosive reaction, the emission of fragments, fire, etc. is instantaneous, which means, you don't usually see the sequence happening as a continuous steady reaction. Instead, the reaction resembles more or less a normal distribution curve that is extremely skewed to one side. Figure 5.8 depicts an example of a possible graph.

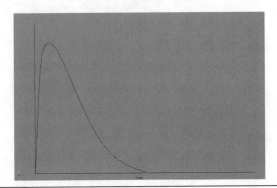

FIGURE 5-8   *A curve that depicts the emission rate*

Therefore, the rate of emission should be such that in the beginning of the reaction, the maximum number of particles is emitted. And in a split second, though depending on its scale, the particles will have traveled a great distance and begin to lose their momentum and start to disperse.

You will control the entire emission using a simple MEL script expression.

TASK

- Think of how you will write your expression to fulfill this scenario. Don't proceed until you have come up with an expression yourself. Don't worry if you're not yet familiar with writing expressions. You will become comfortable with writing expressions as you use this book. But first, you have to give yourself a chance to try.

1. Select E_Fire.
2. Open its Attribute Editor.
3. Under the Emission Attributes section, right-click on Rate, and select Create New Expression... .
4. Enter the following expression:

```
float $t = time;
float $explosionlength = 3.0;
if (($explosionlength/30.0) >= $t)
{
  $rate = 500; //# of particles per frame;
   E_Fire.rate = $rate*30;
}
else E_Fire.rate = 0.0;
```

5. Name the expression EmissionRate.

The rate of emission in Maya is per second. So, when the expression set the emission rate to be 500*30, it means that there will be 500 particles emitting in each frame, assuming you are using a standard of 30 frames per second. However, the rate of emission will sustain for a total of only 3 out of 30 frames, which is 0.1 second. After that, there will be no emission.

NOTE

There are several advantages to using seconds instead of frames as the standard unit of counting. This is particularly helpful when you are working on a project that you eventually will cut for different production. For example, if you work on a film production, the frame rate is 24 fps. However, if the production eventually cuts to NTSC video, which is based on 30 fps or 25 fps, you know that you have a minimum amount of changes because your animation units are based on per second and not per frame. Otherwise, you can imagine how much re-work would have to be done!

Adjust the Shape of Emission

When you play back the animation, you will notice that the shape of the particle movement resembles the exact curvature of the half-sphere. You will now work on reshaping the emission so that the particles appear to be more random and in all directions.

If your particles appear to be emitting in the opposite direction, go to Edit Surfaces ➤ Reverse Surface Direction. The surface direction will be reversed and the particles should be emitting in the right direction now. Another way to reverse the direction of movement is to change the normal value to –1.0.

NOTE

6. Select E_Fire.
7. From the Attribute Editor or Channel window, enter 1.0 as the Tangent Speed.
8. Play back the animation and you will notice that the particles are now emitted in all directions more randomly but uniformly.

By default, the surface emitter will emit particles in a direction that is normal to its surface. Setting a value for its tangent direction, will allow the particles to be emitted in a direction that is a result of both their normal and tangent values.

Adjust the Speed of Emission

The current particles do not display any dynamics. So, you will now increase the speed that the particles are emitted.

9. Select E_Fire.
10. Set the speed of the particles to 60.0.
11. Play back the animation and the particles now emit in a more dynamic manner.

Add the Air Resistance

You will now add in a dynamic resistant field to the particles.

12. Select particleFire.
13. Go to Fields ➤ Create Drag -❏.
14. Set the Drag Name to F_AirResist and set the Magnitude to 4.0 (see Figure 5-9).

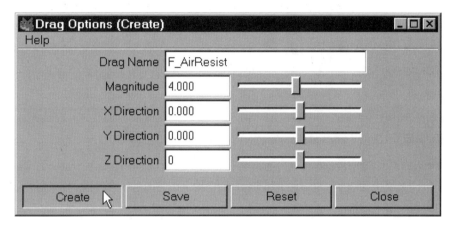

FIGURE 5-9 *Drag option settings*

15. Make sure that there is no direction set in either X, Y, or Z. This will allow the resistance to be in all directions.
16. Click Create to add the field to the scene.
17. Click Close to close the window.
18. This will add the F_AirResist field to the scene and connect it to the particleFire node.
19. Play back the animation. You should see the slowing down of the particles as they move further away from the emitter source.

*To manually link different dynamics together, you can go to
Window ➤ Animation Editor ➤ Dynamic Relationships... (see
Figure 5-10).*

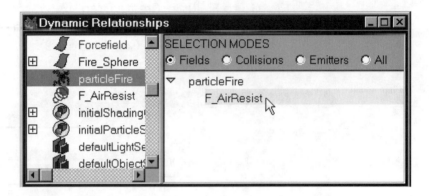

FIGURE 5-10   *The dynamic relationship window*

*When tuning for movement and other effects, unless your ani-
mation is simple and the playback from Maya is able to achieve
real time, it is hard to tell if the movement is exactly what you
want. This is especially the case for a novice animator. Therefore,
in order to test your animation movement, you can go to
Window ➤ Playblast... . Take note that playblast is display-
bound. That is, while Maya is playing and capturing the playblast
images, you cannot switch to other applications. If you do switch
to other applications, the correct images will not be captured.
On NT, if you have a default movieplayer, when playblast fin-
ishes, it will automatically launch the movieplayer and show the
images. And based on my experience on NT, it is almost always
better to use the movieplayer than the fcheck (see Figure 5-11).*

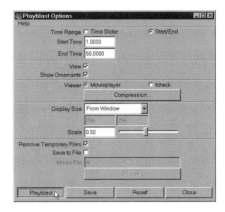

FIGURE 5-11   *Setting the movieplayer option on the playblast window*

Further Adjust the Shape of the Explosion

As you may notice, the general shape of the fire now is still pretty much like the circular explosion. That is not what you want. So, you're going to modify the original emitter. The emitter should conform more to the shape of the forcefield like the tip of the forcefield and not a semi-sphere itself.

20. Select Fire_Sphere.
21. Deform it by scaling along the Y-axis by 0.363. This is an arbitrary value and you should try changing to different values. Just remember that the idea is to break the semi-spherical shape so that it appears that the fire moves along the forcefield as it gets dispersed.

Adjust the Position of the Explosion

The problem now is that, upon impact, the particles are moving forward to the front and not backwards along the direction of the impact. So, you will have to translate the particles as they are emitted.

To translate the particles, you can set keyframe directly to the particle's translation values. However, it is always better to approach animation as a hierarchical concept. The concept of hierarchical animation is nothing new. Basically, you create more levels of hierarchy by grouping the objects. Each time you group the objects, the objects become the child of the new group. From there, when you need to animate the object, you can choose to animate the child node or the parent node, or any node in between them. Through this method of animation, you can hierarchically build complex animation. For example, to create a bouncing ball animation, you can create three hierarchies. One hierarchy handles all the translation values; another takes care of the rotation values; and the third handles the scaling values. In this way, when you need to fine-tune the animation, instead of, say, re-keyframing it, you can simply create offset values using the transform values at the higher or lower hierarchy. One important point is the order of hierarchy. Because transformation multiplication is not commutative—for example, rotation followed by translation is not the same as translation followed by rotation—you have to be careful which level is above or below the other.

22. Select particleFire.
23. Go to Edit ➤ Group to group the particle at the origin.
24. Select the new group created and rename it groupFire.

The next question now is how much to translate backwards. One way to do this is to keyframe the groupFire and translate it according to the movement required. An easier method is to translate automatically using an expression according to how much the particles move forward. The idea is to get the position of the center particle, and based on its position, set the negative translateZ value of groupFire. The center particle is chosen because it is the most unbiased position of the entire particle group.

25. Select particleFire.
26. Play the animation one frame at a time.
27. Immediately when the particles are emitted, stop the animation and pick the center particle. To pick the particle, go to Component Mode and make sure you are in Select By Points (Including Particles) Mode, and from the front view of the window, pick a particle that is closest to the center of the emitter.
28. Once the particle is selected, it turns from the default light-blue color to yellow.
29. Go to the Script Editor and view the command Echoed. You should see a command such as the following:

hilite particleFire ;
select -r particleFire.pt[1567] ;

30. Take note of the particle ID, in this case, 1567.

Another easier way of checking the particle ID is to switch the Particle Render Type to Numeric. You will be able to see every particle ID as they are emitted.

NOTE

31. Go back to select object mode and select groupFire.
32. Enter the following expression for the translationZ value of groupFire.

```
select particleFire.pt[1567];
float $temp[] = 'getParticleAttr -at position particleFire';
groupFire.translateZ = -1.0*$temp[2];
```

33. Change the name of the expression to fireMovement.

The expression first selected the particleFire, in particular the particle with ID 1567. This value of 1567 varies depending on how many particles are emitted. You are likely to get an entirely different particle ID.

The second statement attempts to get the position of particle 1567. Since the value is a set of floating numbers, the results are stored as an array.

The last statement simply assigns the Z values to the groupFire but in negative values.

34. Play back the animation and you should be able to see the particles emitted and at the same time moving backwards, as if it were a result of exploding at the center of the sphere.

35. To get a closer movement of the particles along the forcefield, set the particleFire's translateZ value to –1.0 (see Figure 5-12).

FIGURE 5-12   *Particles emitting and moving backwards simultaneously*

TASK

- Try out various other methods of controlling the particles and see if you can achieve the same results.

SET THE PHYSICAL ATTRIBUTES OF THE FIRE

You will have noticed from the playback that the particles appear to last forever. With your idea of how long the animation is, you will set the life span of the fire. But first, to have a better view of the particle, set the render type to Cloud.

Set the rendering type

1. Select the particleFireShape, and set the rendering type to Cloud.

Set the life span of the fire

TASK

- Based on your experience from the previous chapter and your understanding of the requirements, how would you set the life span of the particle? Based on a random value or per object?

2. Select particleFireShape, and add the LifespanPP attribute.
3. Enter the following Creation expression for particleFireShape:

```
float $Life = rand (1.5,1.5);
particleShape1.lifespanPP = $Life;
```

Set the size of the particles

4. Add the radiusPP attribute to particleFireShape.
5. Map a Ramp with the following input to the radiusPP (see Figure 5-13).

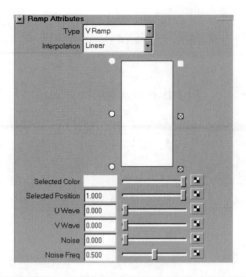

FIGURE 5-13   *The ramp attribute for the radiusPP*

POSITION	RGB VALUES
0.0	1.0,1.0,1.0
0.5	2.0,2.0,2.0
1.0	3.0,3.0,3.0

By default, when you map a ramp to the parameters such as radiusPP, the ramp's V value is used as the particle age input (see Figure 5-14). Therefore, based on the ramp values given above, as the particles get older, the radius will get larger and larger.

FIGURE 5-14   *Mapping the particle with ramp options*

6.   Enter ramp_radiusPP as the name of the ramp.
7.   Select particleFireShape.
8.   Click on the Current Render Type button and select Add Attributes For (see Figure 5-15).
9.   The additional attributes for Cloud Render type are added.

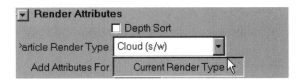

FIGURE 5-15   *Add the attributes for the cloud particle*

10.   Check on the Better Illumination box.
11.   Notice that there is also a Radius attribute added. This can be ignored because the radiusPP attribute has a higher priority.

CREATE THE LOOK

Create the fire shader

1. Create a particleCloud shader and name it particleFireSG and its material as particleFireM.

Assign the particle shader to the fire

2. Assign particleFireSG to particleFire.

Add a light source

3. Create a spotlight
4. Position the spotlight so that it covers the entire fire effect.
5. An example of the position is Translate: (48.566, 18.913, 49.153), Rotate: (—15.000, 40.800,0.0)

Bookmark the camera view

6. Tumble and rotate your camera to get the view that you want.

NOTE

A good way to tumble and rotate is to always tumble and rotate at your center of interest. To do so, make sure that the Tumble Tool option is set to the center of interest ➤ View ➤ Camera Tools ➤ Tumble Tool -❑. Another useful command is View ➤ Look at Selection. I have a hotkey set to the MEL command viewFit that allows me to very quickly bring the selected object right in front of the camera.

The transformation values of the camera I have is Translate values: (20.462, 3.701, 17.355), Rotate values: (–6.289, 37.217, 0.0)

Add the Transparency

You will make the fire quite transparent throughout and disappear towards the end.

7. Map the Life Transparency of particleFireM to the Ramp as shown.
8. Rename the ramp ramp_LifeTrans.

POSITION	RGB
0.0	0.9, 0.9, 0.9
1.0	1.0, 1.0, 1.0

Add the Blob Map

NOTE

When trying to map the particle to get the desired look, I prefer to always use grey-scale values for both the blob and transparency maps. As for the color information, I will usually leave them for the color map and the incandescence map. This guideline has served me well most of the time for most particle animation. However, you are encouraged to define your own method and guideline to generate your particles look. The map that I find useful for blob mapping is almost always a noisy or fractal function such as Brownian or cloud. Crater is always a preferred choice of 3D solid mapping whenever I need to create a noisy look. This is because it gives you the greatest control over the random nature of the map. However, this preference will definitely vary for different users.

9. Create a crater 3D texture.
10. Rename it crater_blobMap.
11. Map this crater_blob Map to the Blob map of particleFireM.

PARAMETERS	VALUES
Channel 1	(1.0, 1.0, 1.0)
Channel 2	(0.308, 0.308, 0.308)
Channel 3	(0.0, 0.0, 0.0)
Frequency	2.0
Shaker	1.5

NOTE

There are several advantages to using 3D texture. 3D texture allows you to easily change the texture within the world space. By altering the transform values such as scaling, translation, and rotation, you can create a wide range of different results that normal 2D UV texture cannot attain. You have already seen the usefulness of creating the fire effects with the help of simply translating the 3D texture. Although 3D texture is versatile, it does suffer from the problem of "swimming." That is, whenever you move your object, the texture will appear to be moving along the object rather than being fixed to it. This is due to the way that 3D textures are implemented in computer graphics. A way to solve this is to link the object to the 3D placement texture. However, this still suffers the same problem if your object is deforming and not transforming. In Maya 2.0, this problem is solved with the help of a reference object. You can go to the rendering menu and choose Create Texture Reference Object. Once the reference object is created, even if you deform the object, the 3D texture will appear to be deformed with it. (Refer to the manual for detailed instruction.)

12. Scale the texture by a factor of 3.0 along all its X, Y, and Z, axes.
13. Rotate the texture by (270, 0, 90).
14. Test-render the particle effects. You should be able to get quite an interesting look like the one in Figure 5-16.

In the expression, the rate of emission was 500. While testing for movement or rendering, you should substitute low values for high ones to get faster feedback and results. In the above rendering, you can get a similar look by using a value of 50 for example, instead of 500. Remember to template the emitter node before you render.

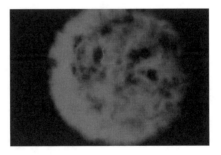

FIGURE 5-16 *A rendered image*

The values for transforming the texture placement node are arbitrary. You should experiment with various values to get the desired effects.

Add Color

This dynamic fire you're creating is different from the normal burning fire. In this fire effect, the color of the fire itself is one uniform value with a little variation on its hue. As the fire explodes and disperses, it doesn't have much time to evolve into a different color. For example, unlike some fire where you would see it turning smoky towards the end, the fire in this case exhibits little change in color as it expands and disperses. Of course this requirement is very much dependent on what you visualize or what your client or director wants. For the purpose of this exercise, assume that the color will not experience great change.

15. Create a Crater 3d texture.
16. Rename it crater_colorMap.
17. Map this crater_colorMap to the color of the particleFireM.
18. Set the crater values as shown in the following table:

PARAMETERS	VALUES
Channel 1	(1.0, 0.163, 0.0)
Channel 2	(0.171, 0.056, 0.0)
Channel 3	(0.843, 0.451, 0.0)
Shaker	1.5
Melt	0.0
Balance	0.0
Frequency	2.0

By default 3D texture mapping is based on the default parameter and there is no mapping based on the life span of the particle.

TASK

- The mapping is based on simple color information, which includes some kind of red and brown color. You should experiment with various color values to meet your requirements.

19. To emphasize the idea that the fire expands and disperses, set the keyframe for the 3D placement of crater_colorMap. At frame 1, its scale value is the default 1.0, but at frame 45, the 3D placement should be scaled 3.0 along all three axes (see Figure 5-17).

Keys				
	Time	Value	InTan Type	OutTan Type
0	1	1	spline	spline
1	45	3	spline	spline

FIGURE 5-17   *Keyframe values for the placement node*

By default, the keyframed animation curve is set to one of the standard functions: Spline. You can edit the preference so that whenever you keyframe, the standard curve used is Linear, Clamped, or Flat, for example. The preference can be set from Options ➢ General Preferences... and select the Animation tab (see Figure 5-18).

NOTE

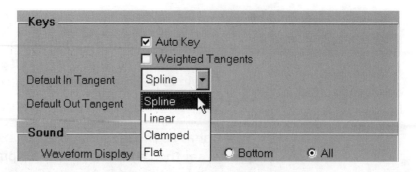

FIGURE 5-18   *The tangent options for the keyframe curves*

You can further edit your animation curve by using the Graph Editor, which can be opened from Windows ➢ Animation Editors ➢ Graph Editors... . If the attribute does not appear in the Graph Editor, click on the Select button at the bottom of your 3D placement, or whatever object's attribute editor (see Figure 5-19).

FIGURE 5-19   *Click on the Select button to display the animated attributes in the graph editor*

20.   Test-render a frame.

You should get an image similar to the one shown in Figure 5-20.

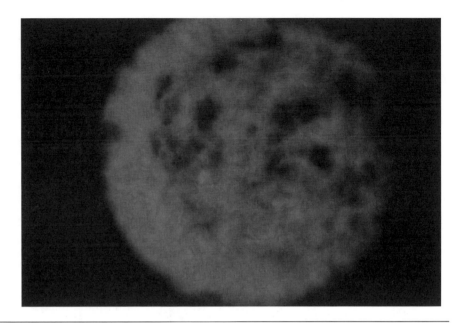

FIGURE 5-20 *A rendered image*

Add the Incandescence

When creating fire effects, you will almost always need to map its incandescence values.

21. Map the Life Incandescence of the particleFireM with a standard Ramp texture.
22. Rename the Ramp ramp_LifeIncand.
23. Set the entries of the ramp as shown (see Figure 5-21):

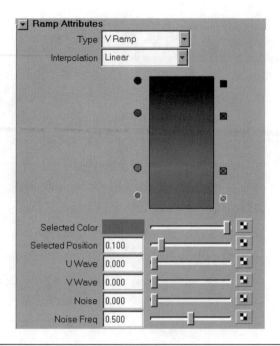

FIGURE 5-21   *Create the ramp texture for the Life Incandansance*

POSITION	RGB VALUES
0.1	1.0, 0.0, 0.0
0.31	1.0, 0.278, 0.0
0.725	0.518, 0.145, 0.0
0.97	0.0, 0.0, 0.0

FURTHER FINE-TUNE THE MOVEMENT

Add the Actual Forcefield

When you play back the animation you will notice that for some of the particles, the movements fall within the forcefield. Sometimes such small detail is not of great importance. However, in this case, no fire particles should be seen within the forcefield.

TASK

- What are the various ways to restrict the movement of the particles so that they do not enter the force-field region?

There are a few ways to restrict the movement of the particles. One obvious way is to use the reference forcefield sphere and make it a collision object so that the particles will collide with it. Another way is to use a Radial field to push any particles away from it. You can further restrict the Radial Dynamic field with the Maximum Distance option. The latter is the preferred method.

TASK

- List the pros and cons of using the collision method against using dynamic fields method to control the movement of objects, not necessarily particle objects.

1. Create a Radial Dynamic field with the options shown in Figure 5-22.

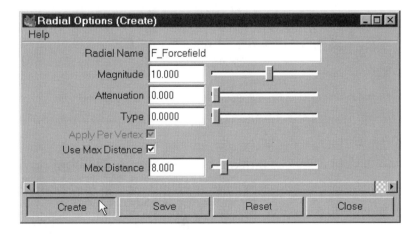

FIGURE 5-22   *Create a radical field*

Notice that the attenuation of the force is set to 0.0. That is to say, within a radius of 8.0, the forcefield is throughout 10.

2. Link the dynamic Forcefield with particleFireShape.
3. Select the dynamic Forcefield and translate it by 8.0 along the negative Z-axis. It should now be exactly at the center of the forcefield sphere.

TASK

- Try different values such as 500, or -10 for the magnitude. See if there is any difference in the way that the particles are being repelled away from the forcefield.

This value of 10 is arbitrary. As long as the values are able to sufficiently repel any particles in it, it will be enough. You should notice that too high a value will result in the particles being repelled away from the sphere with great force.

Create the Dispersion

So far the movement of the particles is able to convey the shape of the forcefield. The next challenge is to create the idea of the presence of the forcefield by dispersing the particles. The dispersion will be created with the help of the color transparency.

TASK

- Take some time to think about how you will control the dispersion of the fire. Do you add another dynamic force to push away the particles or do you make the particles disappear slowly using the transparency map? Or what other methods would allow you to have complete control over the movement of the particles?

The approach adopted to achieve this dispersion effect lies in the use of the condition node and the transparency mapping for the particles. The idea is to map the transparency of the particleFire based on a condition and vary the input of the condition based on animated ramp values. The ramp values will control how fast or slow the dispersion of the fire will occur.

4.   Create a Ramp texture.
5.   Name it Ramp_disperse.
6.   Set the Ramp Type to Circular Ramp.
7.   Set the ramp entries as follows:

POSITION	RGB VALUES
0.001	0.0, 0.0, 0.0
0.0	1.0, 1.0, 1.0

You will next introduce more noise to the ramp texture.

8.   Open the attribute editor of the 2D placement texture of Ramp_disperse.
9.   Set 0.1 for both NoiseUV values.

As mentioned, the idea of the dispersion is to control it using this disperse ramp. So, you will now animate the ramp position.

10. Set the keyframe position of the white color entry to the following values:

TIME	POSITION VALUE	IN/OUT TANGENT
5	0.0	Spline
15	0.25	Spline
48	0.5	Spline

11. Set the keyframe position of the black color entry to the values as shown below:

TIME	POSITION VALUE	IN/OUT TANGENT
5	0.001	Spline
15	0.5	Spline
48	1.0	Spline

12. Play back the animation and observe how the ramp changes as the animation plays.

NOTE

This ramp position control should move in accordance with the rate of movement of the particles. The movement should not be too fast or too slow. Otherwise, when the particleFire gets emitted, and the dispersion occurs, the animations will not blend together. They will appear to be out of sync. One way of testing movement for parameters such as transparency is to first map the texture as a color map. Because the color map will give you a visual and more accurate feedback, you will be able to interactively fine-tune your texture parameters. When you are satisfied with the parameters, you can then map the texture as a transparency map. Notice also that the time set for the position control is up to frame 48 but the animation that you are required to do is only up to frame 45 (1.5 seconds). When animating any parameters, it is always a good practice to create animation slightly beyond your required values. This is so that you can have better control over what happens at or towards the end of the animation. For example, the animation may sometimes seem to end abruptly if your keyframes are set to end exactly at the same time you expect the movement to end. This idea is analogous to one of the principles of character animation: overshoot.

In order for the ramp to correctly control the transparency of the particles, you will use a planar projection map.

13. From the Create Render Node window, create a planar project map (see Figure 5-23).

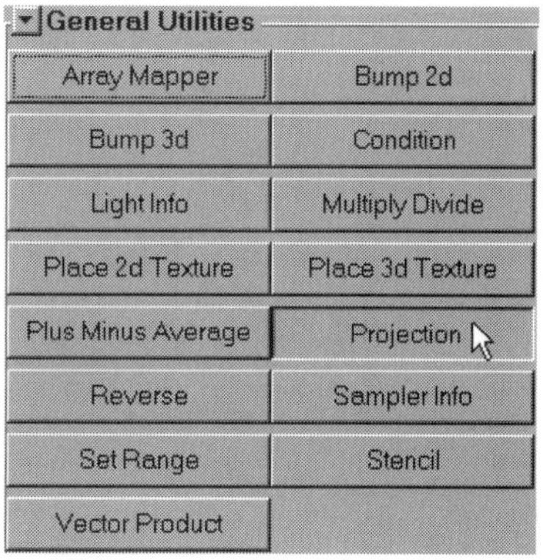

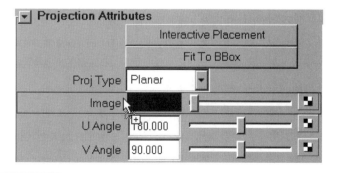

FIGURE 5-23 *Create a projection texture node*

14. Open the Attribute Editor of the projection map.
15. Drag and drop the Ramp_disperse into the map button beside the Image parameter (see Figure 5-24).

FIGURE 5-24 *Drag and drop a texture*

You will next create the Condition node that controls how the transparency for the particles will function.

16. From the Create Render Node window, click and create a Condition node (see Figure 5-25).

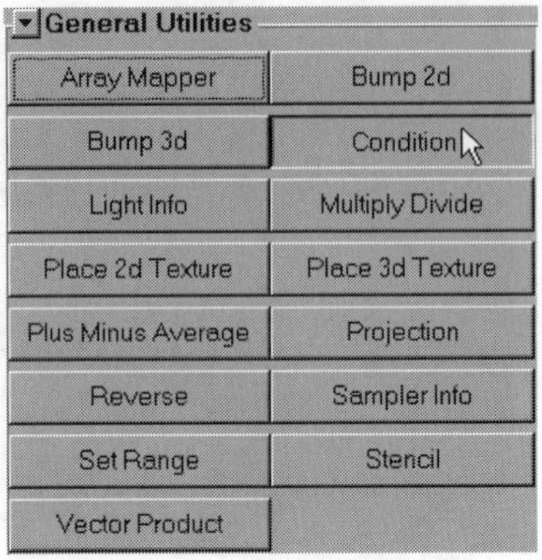

FIGURE 5-25   *Create a condition mode*

17. Open the Attribute Editor of the Condition node.
18. Set the first term value to 1.0.
19. Set the operation to be Greater Than.
20. Drag and drop the Projection node that you just created into the second term value. The alpha value of the Projection node is automatically mapped to this second term value.
21. Drag and drop the Projection node again into the Color 2 values. This time, the color value of the Projection node is automatically mapped to the Color 2 values.
22. Drag and drop your ramp_LifeTrans to the Color 1 values of the Condition node.
23. Finally, drag and drop the Condition node you created and map it to the transparency of particleFireM.

24. From the Multilister, go to Window ➤ Hypershade Highlighted.
25. The Hypershade window opens. You should get a network similar to the one shown in Figure 5-26.

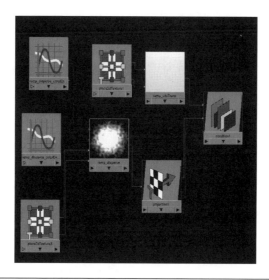

FIGURE 5-26   *A completed network*

26. To ensure that your projection is centered and properly mapping the entire particle shape, play back your animation to, say, frame 12.
27. Open the Attribute Editor of the Projection node.
28. Click on the Fit to Bbox button or you can also click on the Interactive Placement button to interactively place your Planar project.

FURTHER FINE-TUNE THE ANIMATION

When you test-render the animation, you will see that the fire still lacks dynamics. You will now further fine-tune the dynamics with the help of the 3D Placement node, the camera angle, and various other parameters. Remember that fine-tuning is an interactive process. The values obtained below are after several attempts. You should not take them as fixed answers but instead try out various values and parameters on your own as well.

Adjust the 3D Placement node

1.   Select the 3D Placement node of crater_blobMap.
2.   Set the X scale value to 1.0 and leave the rest of them at 3.0.

With the scaling of this Blob map crater texture, you will see that the particle appears more dynamic.

Adjust the Camera

Since you will be compositing the images, it is possible for you to make use of the extreme camera angle to produce the dynamics of the fire. This is a common practice of achieving effects that would otherwise be difficult to achieve. An important point to remember is that the camera perspective must match the rest of the objects in the scene when compositing them together.

3.   Select the persp. Camera.
4.   Open its Attribute Editor and set the Angle of View to 120.0.

This will create a wide-angle view You should try out different angle views.

Adjust the Incandescence Further

To create more noise and variation, the incandescence of particleFireM is edited as follows:

5. Select ramp_LifeIncand.
6. From its Attribute Editor, insert one color entry at position 0.003.
7. Keyframe the value of this new entry as shown below:

KEYFRAME	RGB VALUES
1	(1.0, 0.0, 0.047)
10	(1.0, 0.56, 0.0)

Adjust the intensity

8. Select particleFireM from the Multilister and open its Attribute Editor.
9. Set its Glow Intensity as an animated value as shown in the following table:

KEYFRAME	VALUES	IN/OUT TANGENT
1	0.4	Spline
20	0.3	Spline
45	1	Spline

ADD OTHER ELEMENTS TO THE SCENE

The elements presented below need not to be in the same scene as the fire particle effects. In fact, to create better flexibility, they should be created separately and composited together in the later stage.

In a typical strong impact, you can create a further emphasis on the impact by including a single frame or two of white. This would create the impression that a great amount of light is emitted from the impact with an instantaneous amount of white light emitted.

To add in this strong light effect, you will make use of the optical light.

Add the strong white light

1.   Create a point light source (see Figure 5-27).

FIGURE 5-27   *Create a point light source*

2.   Open the Attribute Editor of the point light.
3.   Under the Light Effects section, click on the map button beside the Light Glow (see Figure 5-28).

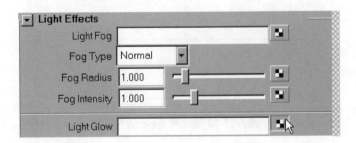

FIGURE 5-28   *Map the glow attribute*

4.   A default optical F/X light is created.
5.   From its Attribute Editor, animate its Glow Intensity (see Figure 5-29).

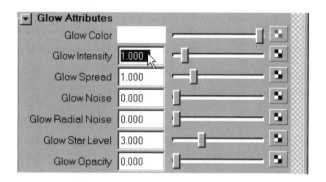

FIGURE 5-29   *Animate glow intensity*

You should animate the intensity such that the light emitted gives the impression of instantaneous emission. That is, in the beginning, the intensity of the light is high and rapidly drops to a low value eventually.

NOTE

A problem with using the glow optical F/X is that it is a post-production process and you are unable to create the perspective for the optical effects. Though light emits from all directions and therefore should appear to be somewhat spherical, it is still less than desirable to see the glow in a perfectly beautiful spherical shape. One way to solve it is to add noise to the effects. Another way is to render the effects as a separate layer and distort the shape during the post-production process. Whatever method you use, you should be aware of the process that the optical F/X is being created.

Further Emphasize the Forcefield

To further emphasize the presence of the forcefield, you can create a simple sphere and animate its transparency so that it will appear just when the laser hits the forcefield and disappear again when the impact and fire is over. I'll leave this as your exercise.

Create the Laser

At one time or another every animator has been asked to create laser effects. In Maya, to create a laser, simply create a cylindrical shape primitive and texture map it with an appropriate shader. The trick lies in mapping it with some glow effects. In Maya, not only can you create glow to the shader, you can even hide the cylinder primitive and render with just the glow (see Figure 5-30).

NOTE

When you create laser effects, a common mistake is to create a primitive that is too narrow and small. As mentioned in the introductory chapters, using primitives that are too small may create undesirable aliasing problems.

TEST-RENDERING

Test-render your animation. Refer to color plate 5. Compare your renderings with the fire effects. They should look similar.

FIGURE 5-30 *Toggle the hide source check box*

POST-PRODUCTION

In this project, you should have at least the following layers:

- Castle
- Fire effects
- Background of the scene
- Laser animation
- White light glow
- Spherical shape that emphasizes the presence of the forcefield

Using a composition software of your choice, further fine-tune the look of the fire so that each stage of the animation is clearly presented.

Play the animation movie chpt05.mov and compare your results with the movie file.

CONCLUSION

Having completed this chapter and the previous tutorial projects, you should have an idea how to create and control fire effects. Though these chapters provide an insight to create both a normal and dynamic type of fire, in most situations you may have to create fire effects that exhibit both characteristics discussed. What is important for you to learn here is not to consciously separate one type of effect from another. Instead, you should always try hard to integrate them. Remember, THINK (Try Hard to Integrate New Knowledge).

EXERCISE

1. In Maya 2.0, you have the built-in effects for creating particles that follow a flow of path (from Effects ➢ Create Flow). With the help of this function, create a dynamic fire effect that resembles the movement of fire along a pool of liquid.

2. Instead of compositing in layers, imagine that now you have to integrate all the animated fire effects (such as laser effects) into one scene file in Maya. This means that the fire effects will not start from frame 1. Instead, you have to shift your entire animation so that the first thing that happens is the laser coming in, followed by the impact, etc., before your fire effects start emitting. Attempt a shift of your animation. Which parameters you have keyframed need to change?

3. To conclude this chapter on fire, observe and think of a few real-life action movies that you know involved the use of different fire effects. Attempt to create them yourself.

UNDER AND ABOVE WATER

INTRODUCTION

Water is another commonly seen element in our daily lives. It is the element that can never coexist with fire. In fact, water is much more essential to living creatures than fire. Indeed, no living creatures are able to live without it.

However, as essential to life as it is, water has also caused the greatest destruction known to human history. It was written in the Book of Genesis that the same element that gave life to the living creatures was used to destroy them.

In the Chinese proverbs, there is a saying that goes like this: Di Shui Chuan Shi, which means each drop of water, tiny as it is, through persistency, can create a hole in the rock. This simple proverb sums up the smallness of each drop and yet the awful strength of water.

Creating realistic looking digital water has always been a challenging task for both the artist and technical director. At times, the image must convey the placid peace that water brings. But at other times, the images must convey the strength and awesomeness of water. Many graphics researchers have spent time in understanding the beauty of this simple H_2O molecule, hoping to create a perfect mathematical model that can duplicate this element. At present there are various theories and research such as the globular dynamics that attempt to describe the behavior of water. *Globular dynamics* is a technique for computing the interaction of particles with each other in a way that simulates the physics of fluids and foams. However, it will still be awhile before we can get to use them easily.

This and the next chapter attempt to bring insight into creating some digital water using Maya. The trick in creating realistic looking water is not really a trick. That is, despite all the development achieved so far in creating the ideal mathematical model of digital water, there does not exist a one-click solution for creating good-looking water. As varied as the forms of water, every new scene, and each new project will require careful planning and possibly even a new way, of creating the water. Though there exist some general equations and functions to create wavelike water, to actually be able to artistically direct the water as a character in a production scene still requires a wealth of artistic sense coupled with patience and skills.

FORMS OF WATER

From basic chemistry, you know that water is one of the most versatile elements that can take all three states of existence: solid, liquid, and gaseous. When it is below 4 degrees Celsius, it is in its solid state as ice; when it is above 100 degrees Celsius, it exists in the form of steam. And most of the time, you know that it exists in a liquid state.

Although water has no fixed shape, it does have a fixed volume. It is this flexible shape but constant volume that presents a challenging task to animators. Imagine having to create a scene where your character will interact with the water. Every interaction potentially will break the water up into its smaller form, which may take a completely different shape such as splashes or tiny droplets. But at the same time, the overall volume of the water must remain the same.

Along with its flexibility in taking any shapes and forms, water is able to reflect and refract light in many different ways. Hence, shading the water to the desired look presents another challenging tasks for even an experienced artist. At times, water looks opaque and white, like the white foams on the surface of the ocean. At other times, water looks transparent and creates various forms of caustic patterns when light shines through it.

This section on water creation will take you from creating under and above the water scene, to rain and splashes of water effects. This chapter will cover the water scenes and the creation of rain, while the next chapter will cover the creation of liquid splashes.

PRE-PRODUCTION: UNDERSTANDING THE SCENARIO

TASK

- In this project, you are tasked to first create an under water scene. Subsequently you are to create an above -water scene. The sketch of the scenes is shown below in Figure 6-1.

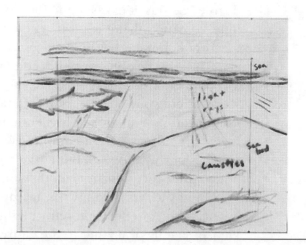

FIGURE 6-1   *Sketch*

In this project, it has not been decided yet how long this scene will last. The director requires that the scene look as convincing as possible. If the scene looks good, it will then be integrated with other characters in the scene. If not, the scene may be cut and replaced with alternative water shots.

NOTE

It is not uncommon to be working on a test scene in a production environment in which there is always an uncertainty if your work will be used in the final cut. It is everyone's hope that your hard work will be included ultimately in the final output. However, nothing is one hundred percent guaranteed. If your work were dropped eventually, you should not get discouraged. Failure does not mean you are not a competent animator, it just means that you have to try harder and possibly do things differently.

ANALYZE THE PICTURE

TASK

- Take some time to analyze the picture. Write down what you think constitutes an under water scene. Your questions should include the following:

- What is the color of the under water?
- What is the depth of the water?
- Where are the sources of light in the scene?
- How would you light your scene for under water?
- Will there be caustic effects?
- What are the other elements evident in an underwater scene?

By now, you should be used to creating a list of questions and answers. You should be able to analyze every detail of the scene and ponder how you would approach them.

Proceed to the next section only when you have given enough thoughts to the sketch and scenario.

APPROACHES

An underwater scene may look entirely different depending on the depth of the water. For example, the caustic effects are more likely to be present in shallow water than in deep water. And deep water normally is more milky and less illuminated as the only light source coming from above the water is dispersed and attenuated drastically through the water medium.

I've divided this underwater scene into the following elements:

- The water in its bluish color
- The seabed with the fungi and algae
- The caustic effects on the seabed
- The presence of dirt and particles

TASK

- Compare the above elements with the elements in your list.
- What other essential elements do you think should be present in an underwater scene?

PRODUCTION AND TESTING

Set a new project

1. Create a new project.
2. Enter Under_Water as the name of the project.

You will next create the waterbed of the scene.

Create the Seabed Model

In this scene, the seabed consists of mainly the uneven rock terrain. There are a few approaches to modeling it in Maya. For example, you can easily generate it with the help of the Sculpt Surface tool. Or, you can generate your desired terrain from a Terrain Generator program and import the data into Maya. And like any other model creation, you can also choose to slowly adjust the CVs, and edits points of the NURBS or polygonal surfaces. Whatever method you use, the main idea in generating terrain is to do one step at a time. In short, divide-and-conquer: from the overall shape of the terrain follow, the details necessary for other parts.

NOTE

Editing models by pulling CVs, and edit points is a very basic modeling approach. Before there were advanced tools such as sculpting and subdivision, being able to pull CVs and edit points was a skill that a lot of modelers learned to master. There are a few common methods of editing that will save you from seeing stars after pulling the CVs. You can, for example, make use of the Near and Far Clipping Plane of the camera to limit the number of CVs displayed. This will ensure that when you pick any points on one side of the object, the other side of the object will not be picked too. You can also make use of the Lasso Pick tool to pick any CVs within an arbitrary region that you draw. There is also a very useful MEL scripts from Alias Wavefront that allows you to select all the U or V span CVs based on one CV point that you select. The list of tricks can go on and on. What is important to note is to be innovative and creative in finding solutions to problems. See Figures 6-2 and 6-3 for an example of using clipping planes to limit the display information.

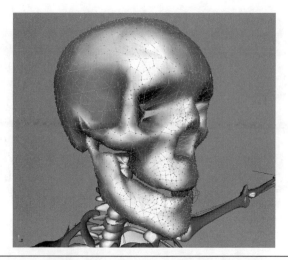

FIGURE 6-2   *A model displayed with default near and far clipping plane*

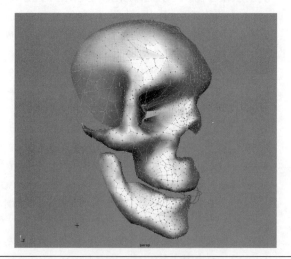

FIGURE 6-3   *Restricting the display by changing the far clipping plane*

For this seabed model, you will use the Sculpt tool to model.

3. Create a primitive NURBS plane.
4. Rename the plane seaBed.
5. From its channel box, set the Width to 50, and Length Ratio to 1.5. You may alter this value depending on the scale of the model that you are working on.
6. Set also its Patches U and Patches V values to 10 and 50, respectively. This will create more isoparms on the NURBS surface, thereby allowing you to add further surface detail using the Sculpt tool.

The Sculpt tool is based on the number of UV points on the surface. Therefore if you need to have more details, you will have to add more U or V spans. If you want to add details at only certain areas of the model and not the entire U or V spans, you are able to do so using the Subdivision Modeling tool. However, note that currently you have to convert the subdivision surface to polygonal mesh before you can render them out.

7. With the plane selected, go to Edit Surfaces ➢ Sculpt Surfaces Tool, and adjust the plane to look similar to Figure 6-5.

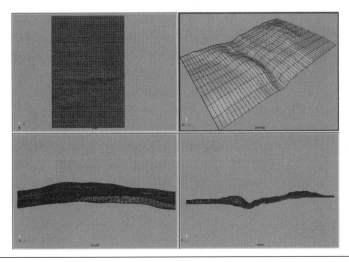

FIGURE 6-4 *The seabed model*

Create the Sea

You will now create the water surface.

8. Create a primitive NURBS plane.
9. Rename the plane Sea.
10. Set the width of the plane to 50, or the same value that you have set for the width of the seabed.

Translate the Sea so that it is about 10 units above the seaBed.

In the instructions that follow, the terms water and sea are inter-changeable.

Setting the Look Right

You will now check the models created through the look of the perspective camera.

11. Create a new camera.
12. Rename the camera Camera_UnderWater.
13. Set the camera as the current active view in the persp window by dragging and dropping it into the persp window from the outliner window.
14. Load chpt06_sketch.tif as the imageplane of the camera.
15. Adjust the camera so that the seabed and sea match the imageplane. If it does not, adjust the position of the seabed or the sea.
16. Set the Angle of View of the camera to 65. You should get a view similar to Figure 6-5.

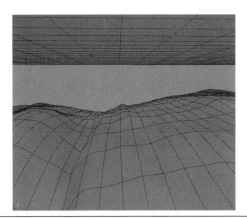

FIGURE 6-5   *Setting the right camera view*

You should have noticed that the entire model of the seabed is only partial. It does not extend all the way to the far clipping plane. Remember that what really counts is the look of your final pictures. Whether the entire models and scenes that you worked on are able to plug-and-play into another project is of secondary importance. In fact, in many production projects, it is not uncommon to see that a scene that is working beautifully in this shot will display defects if you change the shot to a different angle. Your job is to make the best picture within your available time and resources constraint. In realizing a shot, camera perspective plays a crucial role, especially when you have other characters that you will eventually integrate into a complete scene. Often, a mismatch of camera perspective will result in a badly composed image. To successfully match a digital image with other characters that are not created together within the shot, such as a real person, you are likely to need more than one view of the shot to correctly integrate them.

TASK

• What will you do if the camera were to move into the region not covered by your model? Do you recreate the entire model and scene?

CREATE THE ELEMENTS OF THE SCENE

Create the Sea Particles

One of the essential elements that give an underwater scene its look is the tiny impurities that you often seen moving randomly. Be it tiny living organisms or simply impurities, such particles are important to make your underwater scene look convincing. However, depending on the lighting of your scene, such tiny particles may not be visible at all times. In this project, you will make them conspicuously visible.

1. Press F4 to switch to the Dynamics menu.
2. Go to Particles ➤ Particle Tool -❑.

   The Particle Tool option window opens.

3. Enter particleSea as the Particle Name.
4. Set the various options as shown in Figure 6-6.

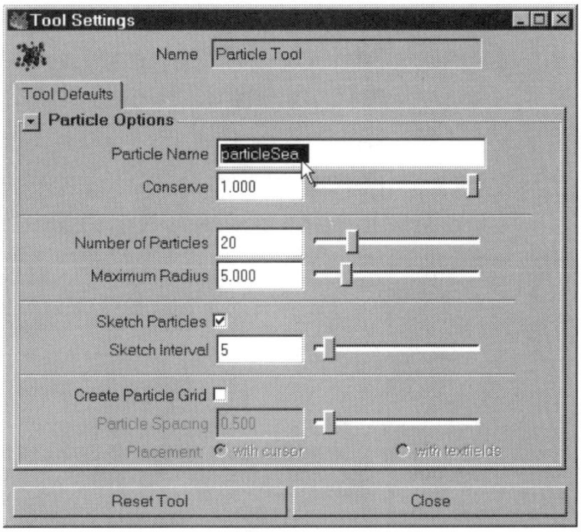

Tool Settings

Name | Particle Tool

Tool Defaults

Particle Options

Particle Name | particleSea
Conserve | 1.000

Number of Particles | 20
Maximum Radius | 5.000

Sketch Particles ☑
Sketch Interval | 5

Create Particle Grid ☐
Particle Spacing | 0.500
Placement | ⦿ with cursor   ○ with textfields

Reset Tool   Close

FIGURE 6-6   *Creating particle using the particle tool*

5.   Click Close to close the option box.
6.   With the help of the four different window views, click to create the particles so that they appear in front of the camera.

Remember that what is important are the particles that appear around and in front of the camera. Do not spend time creating particles that are way beyond the view of the camera. If you are not familiar with using the Particle tool, try out a few clicks first. If you make a mistake on your click, you can always use the Delete key to delete your click. The normal Undo using the default "Z" key does not work with the Particle tool.

7.   Press Enter when done.
8.   Open the Attribute Editor of particleSea.

9. Set the Particle Render Type to Cloud (s/w).
10. Click on the Current Render Type button beside the Add Attributes For.
11. Set the radius to 0.1 and the Surface Shading and Threshold to 0.0.
12. Click to check ON the Better Illumination box.

Your view from the perspective camera should look similar to Figure 6-7.

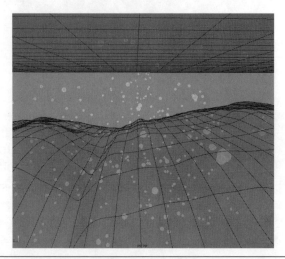

FIGURE 6-7   *Particle's distribution viewed from the camera*

13. When you get the view you desire, bookmark the camera view.

Animate the Particles

You will now add the random movement of the particles with the help of a turbulence function.

14. Make sure that you are under the Dynamics menu.
15. With particleSea selected, go to Fields ➤ Create Turbulence -❑.
16. Set the options as shown in Figure 6-8.

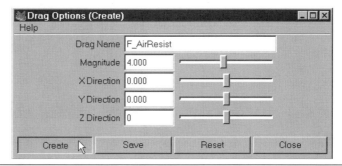

FIGURE 6-8   *Create the turbulence field*

This will link the particleSea particles with the turbulence field.

17. Play back your animation.

You should see your particles moving in a random direction based on their influence of the turbulence function.

18. If necessary, adjust the magnitude of your turbulence function to achieve the randomness that you desire.

Create the Depth

In an underwater scene, visibility is always very limited. This is due to the dispersion of light by the many particles in the sea. When there is no light, there is no visibility.

You will now create the sense of depth of the sea as you look through the camera. To do this, you will need the help of the environment fog.

19. Open the Render Globals window.
20. Click on the Render Options section. In the earlier version of Maya, this was the Special Effects section.
21. Click on the Map button besides the Environment Fog (see Figure 6-9).

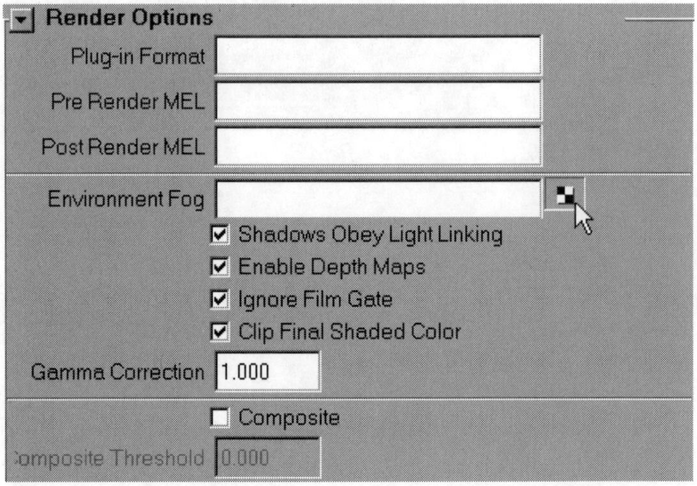

Render Options	
Plug-in Format	
Pre Render MEL	
Post Render MEL	
Environment Fog	
	☑ Shadows Obey Light Linking
	☑ Enable Depth Maps
	☑ Ignore Film Gate
	☑ Clip Final Shaded Color
Gamma Correction	1.000
	☐ Composite
Composite Threshold	0.000

FIGURE 6-9   *Mapping the Environment Fog*

The default environment shading group, material, and light are created (see Figure 6-10).

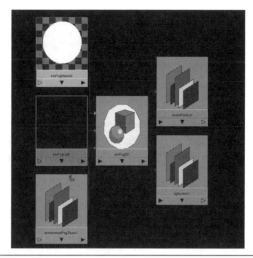

FIGURE 6-10 *The default environment fog nodes connection*

22. Open the Attribute Editor of envFogMaterial.
23. Set the parameters as shown below:

PARAMETERS	VALUES
Color	(0.298, 0.361, 0.365)
Density	0.05
Color Based Transparency	ON
Fast Drop Off	ON

FINE-TUNE THE SCENE

Fine-tune the Depth

You will now fine-tune the scene by adding more depth.

TASK

• Think about the ways to add in more depth to the water scene, such as mapping the envFog color.

Currently the scene will be rendered into the Far Clipping plane. A way to add depth is to just use the fog to create the sense of depth. However, a better way is to create a simple plane that is near enough to be seen but far enough to give the impression that it is the depth of the sea and not a plane.

With the plane serving as the background, you can also alter its color to create better variation on the water depth.

1. Create a new NURBS plane.
2. Rename it sea_BG.
3. Set the parameters as shown below:

PARAMETERS	VALUES
Width	22
Length Ratio	5
Patches U	1
Patches V	1

4. Transform the plane with appropriate parameters so it sits at the back as a BG. The following parameters were used for my scene. (see Figure 6-11):

PARAMETERS	VALUES
Translate	−56.0, 7.0, −4.82
Rotate	0, 0, 90
Scale	1.1, 1.0, 1.0

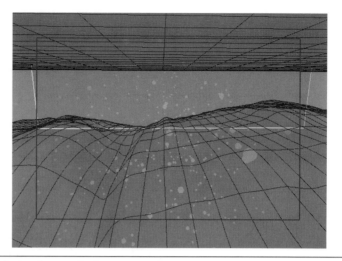

FIGURE 6-11 *Placing the background plane correctly*

When you create the BG, be aware of any animation that you may need to accommodate. For example, if you have a fish swimming from the far end and slowly appearing in the milky water, then your BG must be able to accommodate it.

Fine-tune the Environment Fog

With the BG added, you will now adjust the environment fog so that the depth is properly set.

5.   Open the Attribute Editor of envFogMaterial.
6.   Set the parameters as shown in Figure 6-12.

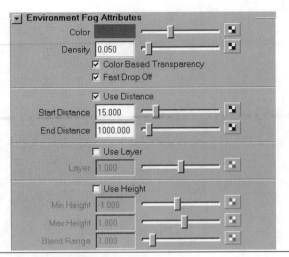

FIGURE 6-12 *Setting the environment fog attributes*

In Maya, the environment fog by default will fill the scene from the Near Clipping plane to the Far Clipping plane. Therefore, to restrict the coverage of the environment fog, you can set the distance and height with the appropriate values. Notice that the distance set above does not cover from the beginning of the camera to the end at the location of sea_BG. It is often insufficient to create a sense of depth by strictly following the starting and ending values. Instead, you can create a greater sense of depth by making sure that those in front are clearer and start the fog only at a later distance.

Add in a Temporary Light Source

Currently the scene is illuminated entirely by the envFog light. You will add in a temporary direction light to illuminate the scene. This light will be used for fine-tuning the materials. The lighting of the entire scene will be properly set up later.

7.   Create a directional light source
8.   Name it seaLight_1.
9.   Position the light source so that the scene is properly illuminated.

Color the BG

You will now adjust the color of the BG. It is important to note that in order for the BG to blend well with the scene, you should make sure that the color changes of the BG are gradual.

10.   Create a default Lambert shader.
11.   Name the shader backgroundSG.

TASK

•   What are the things to note for the BG to blend with the scene?

For the BG to blend with the scene, the color change at the edges should follow the curvature of the model.

12.   Click on the Color map button and map a Ramp texture to the color.
13.   Set the color of the ramp as shown below:

COLOR ENTRY POSITION	RGB VALUES
0.0	0.22, 0.424, 0.694
0.210	0.10, 0.13, 0.611
0.345	0.325, 0.325, 0.732
0.770	0.226, 0.337, 0.699
1.0	0.223, 0.427, 0.698

14. Also set the Ramp Type to U Ramp and the U Wave value to 0.165.
15. Assign the backgroundSG to sea_BG.

You should get a BG scene similar to Figure 6-13.

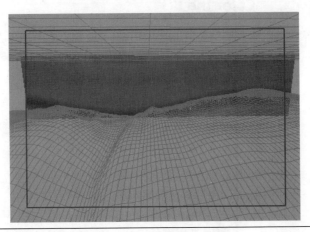

FIGURE 6-13   *The background plan with wave-like ramp mapping*

When rendering the scene, the edges of the ramp may not be obviously clear. However, it is often these subtle hints that add values to your imagery.

NOTE

Color the Seabed Using IPR

You will now add the rendering details of the seabed. This time you will adjust the details with the help of the Interactive Photorealistic Rendering (IPR). IPR provides interactive fine-tuning of shaders. It is particularly useful when all that you need is to create and tune your shaders to the desired values.

16. Create a Blinn shader.
17. Name it seaBedSG and seaBedM for the shading group and material, respectively.

18. Assign this to the seaBed model.
19. Go to Render ➤ IPR Render Into New Window... .

The IPR window opens and starts the first IPR rendering (see Figure 6-14).

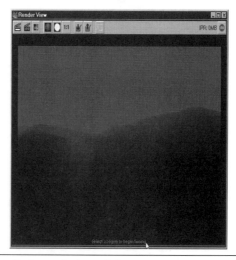

FIGURE 6-14 *Interactive Photorealistic rendering of the scene*

20. To start the interactive rendering, select any region of the render window.
21. The selected region will start to render immediately.

As the rendering is updating the IPR window, you can now adjust any parameters of the scene and they will immediately be updated. The entire process is fully interactive. And the images updated are completely photorealistic.

The IPR can be updated in several ways. For example, you can drag and drop new shaders to the seabed, or you can bump map on the shader.

Following is an example of the rock shader that I created for the seabed. You should feel free to create your own shaders with a different look and feel.

22. Map a 2D Mountain texture to the color attribute of the Blinn shader (see Figure 6-15).

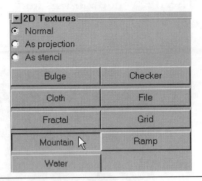

FIGURE 6-15   *Create a mountain texture node*

23. Set the attributes of the Mountain texture as shown in Figure 6-16.

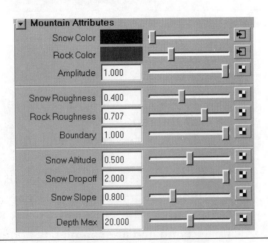

FIGURE 6-16   *Setting the mountain texture attributes*

24. The snow color attribute of the Mountain texture is mapped to a standard 2D fractal texture (see Figure 6-17).

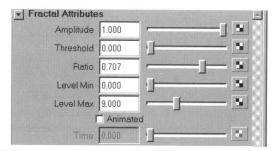

FIGURE 6-17 *The default 2D fractal texture parameters*

25. The rock color attribute of the Mountain texture is mapped to another similar standard 2D fractal texture except that the color offset is created with the following green values: 0.121, 0.257, 0.121.
26. Map the Bump Mapping of seaBedSG to another standard 2D fractal texture.
27. Set the Eccentricity of the seaBedSG to 0.7.
28. Test-render your scene. You should get an image similar to the one in Figure 6-18.

FIGURE 6-18 *Rendered image of the scene*

ADD MORE ELEMENTS TO THE SCENE

Basic Lighting

Lighting in an under water scene is rather different from the normal lighting in animation. Underwater, light tends to get attenuated faster than normal. This is because of the denser water medium and the various tiny particles that help scatter the light. When under water, everything tends to look more blurry. Your vision is further impaired by the goggles or underwater camera lens. Thus, in an under water creation, nothing appears sharp.

1. Select seaLight_1.
2. Set the light Intensity to 0.62.
3. Translate the light so that it points horizontally to the left.
4. Create another directional light.
5. Name this light seaLight_2.
6. Set the intensity to 0.50.
7. Translate the light so that it points horizontally to the right.

The following table shows the lights' transformation values that I use.

LIGHT	INTENSITY	TRANSLATE	ROTATE	SCALE
SeaLight_1	0.62	(0.0, 9.38, 0.0)	(0.0, 0.0,0.0)	(1, 1, 1)
SeaLight_2	0.50	(0.0, 9.38, 0.0)	(0.0, 180,0.0)	(1, 1, 1)

Create the Caustics

One of the obvious clues that the scene is shot in underwater is the caustic effects. *Caustics* are caused by the subtle variation in intensity as light gets reflected and refracted from different surfaces. Examples of caustics are the light patterns that you often see on the bottom of a swimming pool, and the light that gets focused through a glass or clear plastic bottle of liquid.

Creating accurate caustics effects is an ongoing research topics. Several attempts have been made to use ray tracing or radiosity to accurately simulate the caustic effects. However, these illumination models do not appear to be promising. At present, one of the most notable results of simulating accurate realistic caustic effects is by Henrik Wann Jensen using Photon maps. Other ways of achieving caustic effects are through the generation of caustic maps. The caustic maps are then applied to the geometrical model. While creation of caustic maps may not be physically correct, this can produce very realistic results.

Maya provides great flexibility in creating different shaders. However, to be able to achieve realistic looking shaders for animated caustic effects in Maya is still a difficult process. What you'll be creating here is a simple, and straight forward method of faking a caustic effects. If your production requires a realistic caustic effects, it is still a good suggestion to write your customs code to generate this. There are several papers in the past, including those from Jos Stam of Alias Wavefront that explain how to create very realistic caustic maps. They are good resources for your reference.

TASK

- What other clues are essential to reveal to the audience that this is an underwater scene?
- Think about what method you would use to create good looking caustic effects. Remember that for most production purposes production, the caustics need not be physically accurate; it is more importantly that they look convincing.
- If necessary, save your file at this time and create a new scene with a simple plane to test your idea of creating caustic maps.

In this project, you will make the caustics appear on the seaBed model. The basic idea is to create a variation of intensity and map it onto the Specular color of the seaBedSG. The variation of intensity is easily created and controlled with a Ramp textured.

8. Create a Ramp texture.
9. Name it ramp_Caustics.
10. Also name its 2D Placement Texture node as place2dTextureCaustics.
11. Set the ramp with the follow entries and values:

ENTRY	RAMP POSITION	RGB VALUES
0	0.09	0, 0, 0
1	0.210	0, 0, 0
2	0.275	0.535
3	0.315	0
4	0.410	0
5	0.455	0.162
6	0.510	0
7	0.645	0
8	0.705	0.115
9	0.770	0
10	0.870	0
11	0.930	1.034
12	0.965	0

12. Set the Ramp Type as Circular Ramp.
13. Set the Noise to 0.203 and its Noise Frequency to 1.0 (see Figure 6-19).

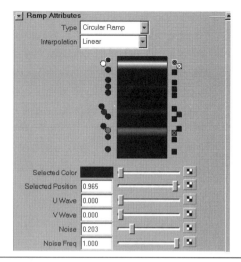

FIGURE 6-19 *The caustic ramp set up*

NOTE

Each entry of the ramp can be read from the Script Editor. So, to check what is the current entry number of the selected ramp, simply refer to the Script Editor. If the selected entry number is not shown, from the Script Editor, go to Edit ➤ Echo All Commands. Note that each entry can be randomly moved around, so, do not assume that entry 0 is always the one at the lowest end of the ramp. Besides using ramp, decent results for caustics can also be obtained by using Leather 3D Texture or the Brownian 3D Texture. You may also try using Crater 3D Texture node together with the help of the Sampler Info node.

Animate the Caustics

After creating the caustics, the next challenge is to animate it so that the movement reveals the characteristic of caustics. To create a single caustic maps is not difficult. However, to be able to create one, animate convincingly, and render with the look of real caustic effects is the biggest challenge.

The following expressions and animation are highly subjective. It is a result of several hours of trial and error and is entirely dependent on your particular scene and requirements. Therefore, you should take the following expression and keyframe values as a point of reference and set your own values. When I first created this tutorial, there was no IPR, and this was truly a render-and-see. With the help of the IPR, you should be able to get your results much faster.

The following instructions are based on the assumption that the ramp entries are entered according to the order given above. The idea is to rotate the placement of the ramp to create a periodic caustic pattern, and at the same time vary the color values of the ramp to create a variation of intensity on the specular map of the shader. They are presented without simplification. You should be able to easily simplify the expression further.

1. Open the Attribute Editor of place2dTextureCaustics.
2. Right-click on its Rotate Frame parameter and select Create New Expression.
3. From the Expression Editor, enter the expression given below.
4. Name the expression expressionCaustics.

```
float $t = time;
float $eleven, $eight, $five, $two;
float $NEW_reduction = 0.5;
$eleven = 0.5 + 0.75*(noise($NEW_reduction*2*$t)+1.0);
$eight = 1.0*(abs(noise($NEW_reduction*1.5*$t)));
$five = 1.0*(abs(noise($NEW_reduction*2*($t+0.5))));
$two = 0.0 + 2.5*(noise($NEW_reduction*1.5*$t)+1.0);
$eleven *= 1.0;
$eight *= 0.4;
$five *= 1.0;
$two *= 0.3;
ramp_Caustics.colorEntryList[11].colorR = $eleven;
ramp_Caustics.colorEntryList[11].colorG = $eleven;
ramp_Caustics.colorEntryList[11].colorB = $eleven;
ramp_Caustics.colorEntryList[8].colorR = $eight;
ramp_Caustics.colorEntryList[8].colorG = $eight;
ramp_Caustics.colorEntryList[8].colorB = $eight;
```

```
ramp_Caustics.colorEntryList[5].colorR = $five;
ramp_Caustics.colorEntryList[5].colorG = $five;
ramp_Caustics.colorEntryList[5].colorB = $five;
ramp_Caustics.colorEntryList[2].colorR = $two;
ramp_Caustics.colorEntryList[2].colorG = $two;
ramp_Caustics.colorEntryList[2].colorB = $two;
place2dTextureCaustics.rotateFrame = 1.5*sind (4*30.0*$t);
```

Notice that the expression contains not only the instructions to rotate the Caustic Placement node, it also contains instructions for the control of the ramp texture entries. Depending on your habits, you may create several expression entries to control different things. However, I find it easier to manage and control when I have only one or two expressions than to have to open and browse through several expressions.

5. Render a few key frames of the scene.

You should see different images based on the different caustic effects on the seaBed.

Create the Sea Shading

You next task will be to create the under water surface of the sea.

TASK

• List the characteristics of an underwater sea surface.

6. Create a Blinn shader.
7. Name it waterSG and name the materials waterM.
8. Map the Color parameter of the shader to a Ramp shader.
9. Name the ramp as ramp_Water.
10. Name its 2D Placement node place2dTextureWater.
11. Set the parameter of the ramp as follows:

POSITION ENTRY	RGB VALUES
0.455	0.0, 0.14, 0.230
0.59	1.0, 1.0, 1.0
0.760	0.076, 0.088, 0.276

12. Set the Noise of the ramp to 0.459.
13. Set the noise frequency to 1.0.
14. Map a standard Water texture to the Bump Map of waterM.
15. Name the Water texture bump_Water.
16. Set the parameters shown in Figure 6-20 for bump_Water.

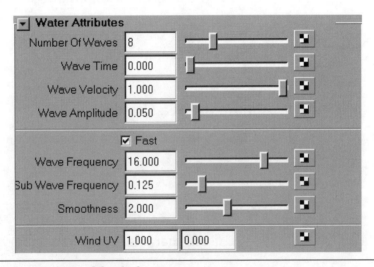

FIGURE 6-20   *The water texture used for the bump map*

17. Set waterM's Eccentricity to 0.70.

In order to create the highly reflective shining water surface, you will need the help of the glow function shader. If you have done the creation of the laser in the previous chapter, you should be familiar with this.

18. From the Special Effects section of waterM, set the parameters shown in Figure 6-21.

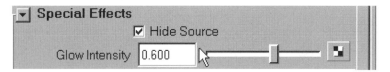

FIGURE 6-21   *Creating the water surface by adding glow and hiding geometry*

19. Do a test-render.
20. You should get a picture similar to the one shown in Figure 6-22.

FIGURE 6-22   *A rendered image with water surface*

You will notice a distinct line running across the water surface. This is because the Sea geometry extends beyond the sea_BG geometry and the glow is showing through the sea_BG geometry. This is not necessarily an undesirable effect because it is often natural for you to see surfaces with distinct color or reflection.

If you stand carefully looking at a real horizon, you will also notice that there also seems to a distinct line that runs across the surface of the sea. This is a natural effect because of the great depth and distance of the horizon. Thus the line here will serve to convey also the distance and depth of the underwater sea surface.

However, if this line is undesirable, you can always blur it during the post-production process or simply shorten the Sea geometry.

Animate the Sea Shading

Your next task will be to create the animation of the water surface. Remember that the water surface movement must match the movement of the caustics. Though they need not be physically correct, they should look convincing.

21. Select place2dTextureWater.
22. Set the U value of the Translate Frame with the following expression. (see Figure 6-23):

FIGURE 6-23   *Setting expression for the U translate value*

Place2dTextureWater.translateFrameU = 0.05*$t;

You may also simply insert this line in expressionCaustics. This is my preferred way since I can keep all expressions as one.

23. Test-render the scene using IPR.
24. Play back your animation one keyframe at a time, and you should see the updates in IPR. This gives you an idea of the movement of your water surface with the caustic movement.

If you do not see the update of the glow effects for your water shader, make sure that the Update Shader Glow is set ON (see Figure 6-24).

NOTE

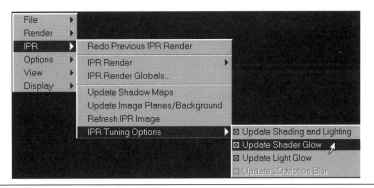

FIGURE 6-24 *The fine-tuning option of IPR*

Create the Light Rays

You will next create the effects of the light rays shining through underwater. The light rays are a result of the light interacting and passing from the water surface.

Among all the light sources available in Maya, spotlight is the most versatile light source to create these light effects.

25. Create a spotLight source.
26. Name it spot_Sunrays.
27. Transform the light source so that it looks down at the water surface.
28. The transform values that I've used for spot_Sunrays are shown below:

TRANSFORMATION	VALUES
Translate	1.76, 36.25, –4.6
Rotate	–815.5, -73.19, 722.91
Scale	1.34, 1.34, 2.87

To create the visibility of the rays, you will create a light fog effect.

TASK

• What are the points to notice when creating the light rays?

29. Open the Attribute Editor of spot_Sunrays.
30. From the Light Effects section, click the Map button beside the Light Fog (see Figure 6-25).

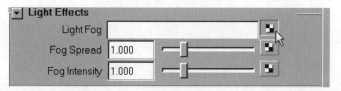

FIGURE 6-25 *Mapping the Light Fog attribute*

A default cone-shaped lightFog is created.

31. Name the lightFog lightFog_Sunrays.
32. Check on the Fast Drop Off button (see Figure 6-26).

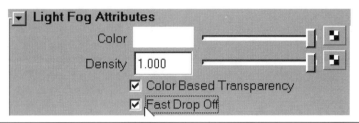

FIGURE 6-26   *Turning on the Fast Drop Off option*

33. Set the Cone Angle of spot_Sunrays to 120.0.

As the lightFog is linked to the spotlight, setting the cone angle will also change the size of the lightFog cone.

Unlinking the Light Rays

By default, any light created in a scene will automatically be added as part of the list of default lights. This default set of lights is usually the one responsible for the lighting of the entire scene. If you do not want any particular light to be within the default set of light, simply uncheck the Illuminates by Default check box in the Light Attribute Editor.

To directly edit the default light list, from the Rendering menu (F5), go to Lights ➢ Light Linking ➢ Light-Centric (see Figures 6-27 and 6-28).

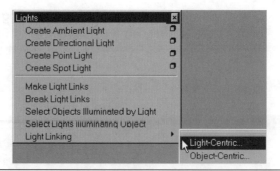

FIGURE 6-27   *Controlling the linking lights*

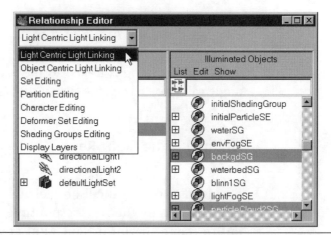

FIGURE 6-28   *Relationship editor settings*

The Relationship Editor that opens allow you to selectively link and unlink different light and objects together. In addition, you are able to edit and view various other relationships besides the Light-centric relationship.

34. From the Attribute Editor of spot_Sunrays, uncheck the Illuminate by Default checkbox.

This will ensure that spot_Sunrays will not offset the light setup that you have previously created. However, lightFog_ Sunrays will remain visible when you render.

Animate the Light Rays

The points to be careful about when creating the light ray is to ensure that the light rays will blend together with the caustics and the surface water movement so that they will all appear to be from one single source.

Currently, the lightFog appears to be one blocky light source. You will map it so that the rays of light will appear and that it will animate well with the entire scene.

35. Open the attribute editor of spot_Sunrays.
36. Go to the Light Effects section.
37. Drag and drop ramp_Caustics to the Fog Intensity.

This will automatically map the alpha value of the ramp_Caustics to the fog intensity.

The advantage of directly using this ramp_Caustic texture is that the animation of the ramp will apply to both the caustics effects as well as the light rays of the fog. Thus, solving your problem of having to reanimate the fog texture and ensuring that they are synchronized with the entire scene.

38. Test-render a few keyframes and you should notice the subtle presence of the light rays, with the caustics, and the water surface movement.

Color the Particles

39. Create a new Particle Cloud shader.
40. Name the shader particleSeaSG and the material particleSeaM.
41. Set the Color of particleSeaSG with the following RGB values: 0.276, 0.280, 0.231.

42. Set its Density to 5.0. and leave the rest as defaults.
43. Assign the shading group to particleSea.

RENDERING

Go to Render Globals and set the necessary resolution for rendering.

Test-render you scene. Your rendering results should resemble. Figure 6-29. Refer also to color plate 6 for a color image.

FIGURE 6-29   *A rendered image of the scene*

POST-PRODUCTION

Render your sequence of images. Composite your images with other elements of the sea, such as some fish. You may use the fish models available from the accompanied CD.

Your layers of rendering may include the following:

- Particle impurities
- Seabed layer
- Sea surface layer
- BG layer
- Sunlight rays layer.
- Caustics layer

Fine-tune the various layers as needed.

Go to the CD and play the movie file chpt06_U.mov. Compare your results to the movie file.

ABOVE WATER SCENE

In this section, you will be exploring the creation of an above-water scene. Creating water wave effects is one of the most common animation tasks. However, to create good water effects requires a great deal of patience and trial and error. Water waves that look good in one shot may not be useful in other shots. However, the process and experience of the creation will certainly help you in future water effects work.

The best way to create realistic looking water waves is to first go watch a real water-ocean movement. Though the movement of the water, waves are similar, but the results may be entirely different. The appearance of the water surface is largely dependent on the light interaction with the reflective surface of the sea. Water waves may look entirely different on a bright day than on a dark gloomy day. In this exercise, you will create a water wave for gloomy weather.

Start a new scene

1. Save your previous section work and start a new scene.

Create the water geometry

2.   Create a NURBS plane
3.   Name it waterWaves.
4.   Set its Width to 50, Length Ratio as to 2, Patches U to 8, and Patches V to 16.
5.   Translate the waterWaves to (9.33, 0.0, 2.18).
6.   Position your camera so that it looks towards the horizon (see Figure 6-30).

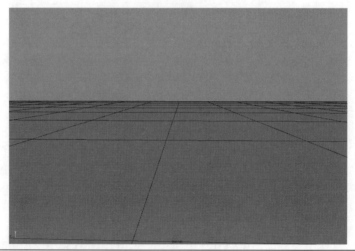

FIGURE 6-30   *Setting the camera for an above the scene view*

Create the Water Shader

Generally, to create a decent-looking water shader, you will need to layer various shaders. Each layer of shader will take care of different highlights of the water waves. In this example, you will layer just two shaders, one for the general ocean waves, one for the high light of the ocean foam. However, for your production needs, you should attempt to create the shader, by slowly building up one layer at a time, adding details when you need to.

Create the base water shader

7. Create a Blinn shader.
8. Name it waveBaseSG and waveBaseM, respectively for the shading group and the materials.
9. Assign the Blinn shader to geometry waterWaves.
10. Set the color of the Blinn shader with the RGB values as (0.082, 0.184, 0.255).
11. Set the Diffuse to 0.60.
12. Set its Specular Roll Off value to 0.1.

To create the waves of the ocean, you will map a displacement to waveBaseSG.

13. Create a standard Water texture node.
14. Name it displacementWater.
15. Set the various parameters of the water attributes as shown in Figure 6-30.

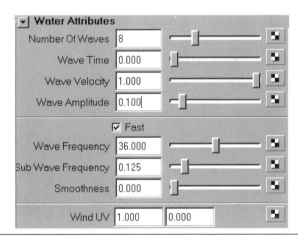

FIGURE 6-31 *Setting the water attributes*

16. Drag and drop displacementWater to the Displacement Material of waterBaseSG (see Figure 6-32).

Shading Group Attributes

Surface Material	waterBaseM
Volume Material	
Displacement Mat.	

FIGURE 6-32 *Drag and drop the water texture as the displacement shader*

A default displacement and a bump2D node are created and connected to the waveBase shader.

In Maya, a displacement mapping consists of two parts, the physical displacement of the geometry, and the detailed bump mapping of the geometry. Therefore, the Bump Mapping attribute of waveBase shader is also mapped with the displacementWater texture.

You will now add more subtle details to the shader by mapping the specular color.

17. Map a standard 2D fractal texture to the Specular Color of waveBase shader.
18. Open the Attribute Editor of the 2D Placement node of the fractal texture
19. Set the Repeat UV values to 10 and 4, respectively.

The last thing to set for the shader is to map an environment texture for its reflected color.

20. Open the Attribute Editor of waveBaseM.
21. Click on the Map button beside Reflected Color.
22. Click to Create an Env Sphere texture (see Figure 6-33).

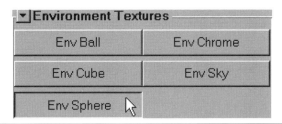

FIGURE 6-33   *Create an environment sphere texture node*

23. From the Environment Sphere Attribute Editor, click and map a Ramp texture to its Image attribute (see Figure 6-34).

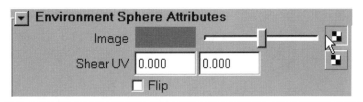

FIGURE 6-34   *Mapping the image attribute of the environment sphere*

24. Set the Ramp attributes to the values as given below. Leave the rest of the attributes as the defaults.

RAMP ENTRY POSITION	RGB VALUES
0.0	0.129, 0.231, 0.298
0.310	0.235, 0.4, 0.463
0.435	0.439, 0.439, 0.431
0.528	0.591, 0.591, 0.514
0.736	0.403, 0.509, 0.671
1.0	0.076, 0.127, 0.263

Create the foam shader

25. Create a Lambert shader.
26. Name it foamSG and foamM for its shading group and material, respectively
27. Set the Color attribute of the material as RGB (0.579, 0.623, 0.650).
28. Set the Diffuse value to 0.907.

You will now create a fractal noise texture to be used as the random nature of the foam.

29. From the Create Render Node window, click and create a Color utility, Rgb to Hsv (see Figure 6-35).

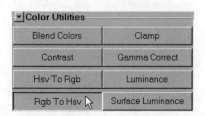

FIGURE 6-35 *Creating a RGB to HSV Color Utilities*

30. Name this color utility noiseCreation.
31. Also create a standard Ramp texture and a 2D Fractal texture.
32. Name the Ramp ramp_Trans and the Fractal texture noise_Input.
33. Open the Attribute Editor of noiseCreation.
34. Drag and drop the noise_Input to its In RGB attribute (see Figure 6-36).

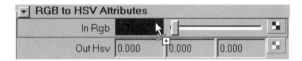

FIGURE 6-36 *Drag and drop to map the RGB attribute*

35. Go to Windows ➣ General Editors ➣ Connection Editor... .
36. Load noiseCreation on the left of the Connection Editor.
37. Load ramp_Trans on the right.
38. Map Out HSV H to U coord.
39. Map Out HSV V to V coord (see Figure 6-37).

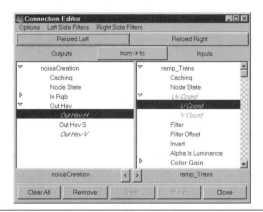

FIGURE 6-37 *Connecting different attributes using the connection editor*

40. Edit the ramp_Trans to the values shown below:

POSITION	RGB VALUES
0.223	(0.996, 0.996, 0.996)
0.341	(0.685, 0.685, 0.685)
0.451	(0.996, 0.996, 0.996)

41. Finally, drag and drop the ramp_Trans texture to the Transparency attribute of foamM.

You should now see the noise nature of the foam.

Create the layer shader

42. Create a layered shader (see Figure 6-38).

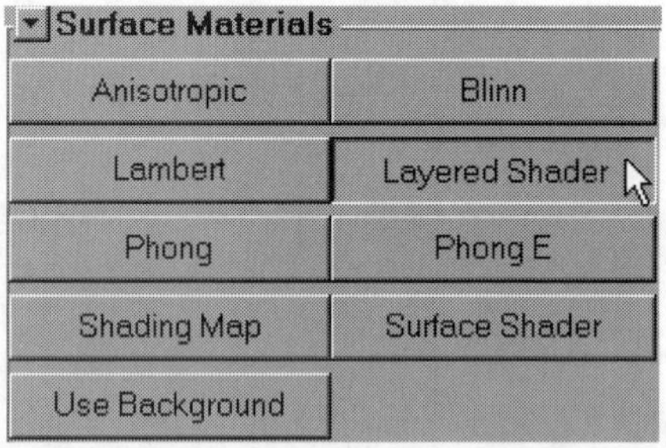

FIGURE 6-38   *Create a layer shader shading group*

43. Name it layeredWaveSG and layeredWaveM for both the shading group and materials, respectively.
44. Open its Attribute Editor.
45. Drag and drop foamM to layeredWaveM.
46. Drag and drop waveBaseM to layeredWaveM.

The final layer shader should look similar to Figure 6-39.

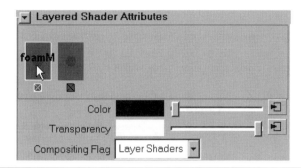

FIGURE 6-39 *The layer shader result*

47. Assign layeredWaveSG to the geometry waterWaves.

Animate the Base Water Shader

When using the water texture of Maya, you can easily create wave movement by procedurally controlling the various attributes.

48. Select the displacementWater node.
49. Keyframe the Wave Time attribute to the values given.

You should alter the values as according to your needs (see Figure 6-40).

Keys	Time	Value	InTan Type	OutTan Type
0	1	0	spline	spline
1	90	0.05	spline	spline

FIGURE 6-40 *Keyframe values of the wave time*

In a similar manner, you can animate your foam shader by simply keyframing the fractal position or the ramp_Trans position. I'll leave this as an exercise for you to practice.

Render the Scene

Set up your own light source and test-render your scene. You should get an image similar to the one in Figure 6-41. You should notice that the water still appear to be periodic. That is, the waves patterns seems regular. You are encouraged to further fine-tune the patterns by mapping more layers of shaders.

FIGURE 6-41 *A test rendered image of the above water view*

CONCLUSION

In this project you have created both an under water and an above-water scene. These two examples should give you an idea of what to look out for when creating similar scenes for your productions.

From the CD, play the animation of chpt06_Above.mov. Compare the results of the wave movement with that of yours. Remember that just as there exists calm and smooth waves, there exist stormy waveforms. Always be sure what the requirements are and create the animation according to your needs.

EXERCISE

1. Play chpt06_UA.mov. Based on your work for the above- and under water scenes, create an animation that combines both of them. Notice that in the chpt06_UA.mov, the bottom of the bottle below the water level appears to be fuzzier.

2. Comment on the caustic patterns created for the under water scene. Based on what you understand from the introductory chapters about ray tracing and radiosity, explain why it is not possible to create a realistic-looking caustics map.

7

HOT SPLASHES!

INTRODUCTION

C reating effects of fluids, and making them interact within themselves or with other characters is one of the toughest animation jobs. In the previous chapter, you created the effects of waves and water scenes using simple geometry and shaders. However, in creating effects of fluid movement, such as splashing water, pouring liquid, and spraying fountains, it is almost inevitable that you will use the particle system. In addition, to control the movement of the fluid, you are likely to need the help of the particle collision system. Therefore, creating interacting fluid animation often requires greater processor power and a lot of trial and error.

This chapter is a follow-up to the previous chapter. Here, you will further experiment with the creation of common water effects animation, such as creating splashing liquid, rain, and ripples.

PRE-PRODUCTION: UNDERSTANDING THE SCENARIO

TASK

- In this project, your task is to create the effects of hot liquid splashes shooting out from a volcanic mountain. The scene is purposely set during dawn so that you will create the detail of the splashes and make them conspicuous (see Figure 7-1).

There are a few requirements for this animation:

1. Because this is a simple scene, you are required to make the animation more interesting for the audience. You have to exercise your creativity to decide how to make the animation more interesting instead of just simply animating the shooting out of the liquid.

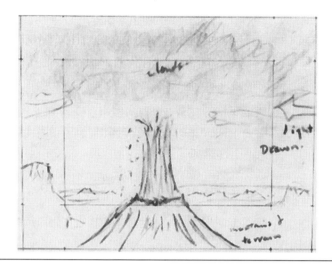

FIGURE 7-1 *Sketch*

2. The movement of the liquid should be entirely controllable. For example, if the director wants to change the height of the splashing at a certain point in the scene, your animation should be editable to accommodate it. If the movement must synchronize with the background music, you should have precise control over the height and scale of the splashing.
3. The movement must be random and natural.

For this animation, you are required to create the mountain model. You are also required to present techniques for generating rain and ripples for further production study.

ANALYZE THE PICTURE

TASK

• Again, take some time to analyze the picture. Imagine that this is a real production task given to you, and write down the factors and parts that you foresee might be difficult to handle.

- Go through the process of planning and think about how you would create the animation using the various methods of particle generation in Maya. Pay particular attention to the emphasized requirement of being able to control the splashing quickly and easily.

APPROACHES

You should have noted a few points to consider based on the requirements. When creating the emission of the splashes, the volume of emission must be scalable. That is, if the mountain crater is changed to a larger or smaller opening, you should have built the control to alter the volume of the splashes emitted.

You will use the surface emitter to create the splashing animation. Next, you will use a texture to control the patterns and shapes of emission. Finally, you will fine-tune the animation using expression control and dynamic fields.

PRODUCTION AND TESTING

Set a new project

1. Create a new project.
2. Enter Splashes as the name of the project.

Set up the scene

3. Create a new camera object.
4. Set this new camera as the default perspective viewing window.

Creating the Mountain

There are various ways of creating mountains, depending on the scale required for your scene. For example, if you need only a single mountain, like the one in this scene, you can quickly create a geometry and add various details through the normal method of texturing and geometry editing. However, if you are required to create a scene where a large part of the scenery is mountain range and ridges, it will require an entirely different approach. In Chapter Ten, you will be introduced to creating the latter example. But for now, you will generate a simple stand alone mountain.

5. Go to Create ➢ CV Curve Tool.
6. From the Front View window, create a simple outline of a mountain.
7. With the curve created, go to Surfaces ➢ Revolve.

A NURBS geometry is created based on revolving the curve about the default Y-axis. If the geometry created seems out of shape, ensure that you have revolved the curve about the vertical axis.

8. Edit the geometry created by editing the CV points of the curve.
9. Name the geometry as mountain.

NOTE

In Maya 2.0, you have the added option of generating the revolved surface as a subdivision surface, in addition to the standard NURBS and polygonal surfaces. When creating curves with the CV tool, you have the option of creating different degrees of curves. The default of degree 3 is the most commonly used option since it is the easiest to control and provides great flexibility. You should try to avoid using any higher degree curve because although they provide greater flexibility, they are more costly to compute. In Maya, there are fundamentally two ways of

creating curves: using edit points (EP) or using control vertices (CV).
Topologically, there is no difference in the curves generated using CV
or EP tools. The only difference is that NURBS curves always pass
through their edit points, while control vertices are vertices that con-
trol the shape of the curve but are not necessarily on the curve itself.

When you are satisfied with the general shape of the mountain, you should delete its history so that you can add details to the geometry.

10. Select mountain.
11. Go to Edit ➢ Delete by Type ➢ History.
12. The history information of the mountain is deleted.
13. Delete the generation curve.
14. Edit the mountain to your desired detail
     (see Figure 7-2).

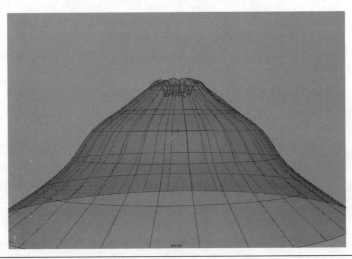

FIGURE 7-2   *A simple mountain geometry*

1. *The five elements of nature as represented by the five platonic stones*

2. *From Left to Right—Render with radiosity and raytracing using BMRT, Render with raytracing using BMRT, Render with default Maya Renderer.*

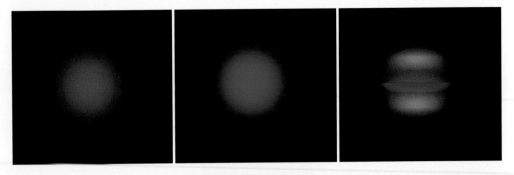

3. Color changes from red (Left) to blue (Middle) when mapping particle Life Color attribute using the default ramp texture. Color remains the same (Right) throughout the particle's life-span when mapping the Color attribute.

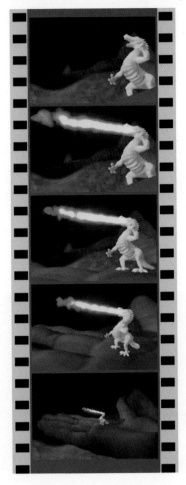

4. A common type of fire effects.

5. *A dynamic fire effect in action.*

6. *Under and above the water animation
   seen with caustics and rain effects.*

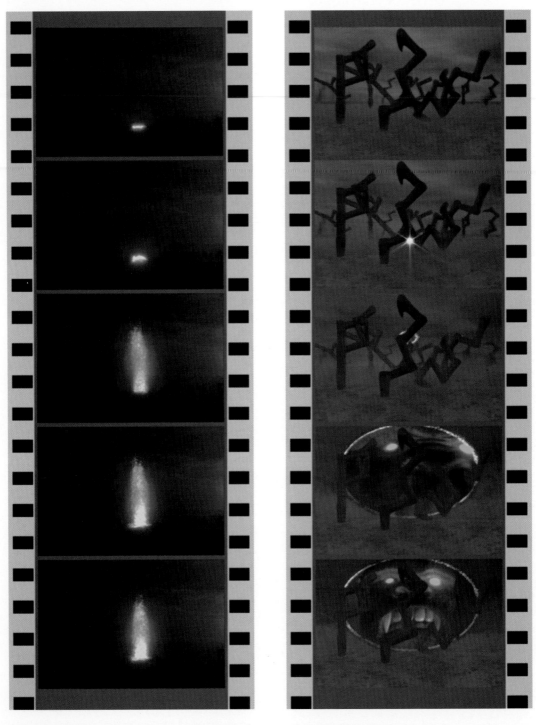

7. *Hot splashes of liquid moving under the influence of gravity and colliding with surfaces.*

8. *Subtle air particles existing in the form of dust and sand.*

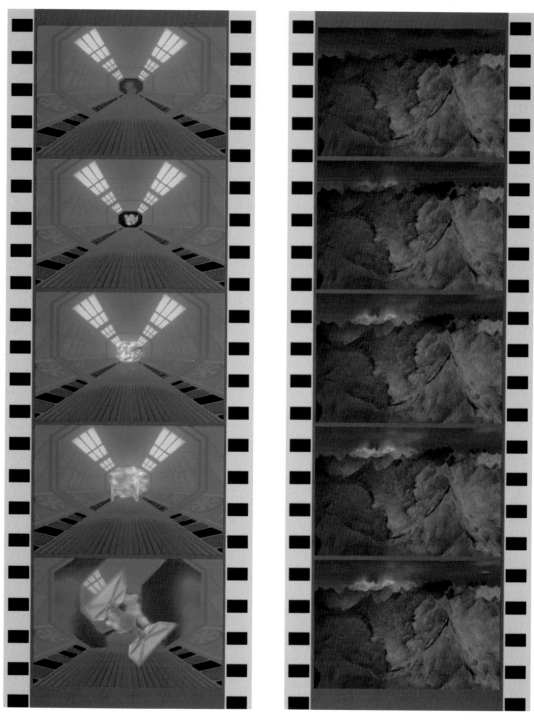

9. *Typical explosion effects with cumulus volume.*

10. *Making earth and terrain using fractal based shader and displacement map.*

11. *Examples of the primitive shapes created using the plug-in on the CD.*

12. *An example of soft and rigid body dynamics in action.*

13. *Controlling the movement of the school of fish using a control system created entirely using MEL.*

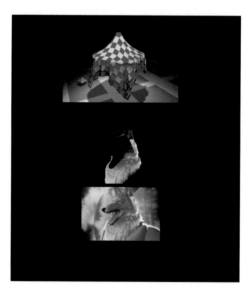

14. *Examples of animation created using the advance modules, Maya Cloth and Maya Fur.*

15. Lighting a scene. From top to bottom—the key light, located at the front provides the main source of illumination, the lights from both the sides add in the diffuse atmosphere, while the back light fills up the scene by removing the harsh shadows.

In Maya, the construction history is of particular importance and usefulness, because, for example, you can easily control and animate the various shapes of objects through the history of simple curves or other geometry. However, one important point to remember is that the computation of construction history can sometimes be very expensive. This is especially the case if you have substantial animation on an object based on its parent's construction history. And when you save a scene with large history information, and subsequently load the scene again, the history will be computed while loading. Thus, a heavy scene with a large amount of construction history information may be very slow in loading. If you do not need to edit or control using the history, turn it off before you create any new object. Deleting the history can also be done through the Hypershade or Hypergraph. In the preceding example, when you delete the history of the mountain, you should see from the Channel Box that the input information called revolve1 is disconnected from the creation function (see Figure 7-3).

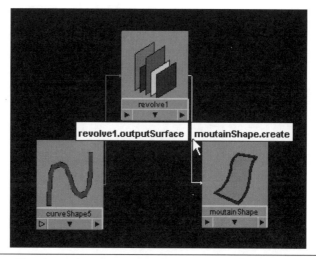

FIGURE 7-3   *Viewing an object input/output connection from the Hypershade window*

It is often useful to use the Hypergraph or Hypershade to check your scene connection whenever you suspect that the performance appears to slowdown unusually. At times certain information such as node connections were made but were not disconnected even though they appear to be absent from the scene or outliner window.

Texture map the mountain

15. Create a Blinn shader.
16. Name the shading group and material mountainSG and mountainM, respectively.
17. Map the Color attribute of mountainM to a 3D Rock texture (see Figure 7-4).

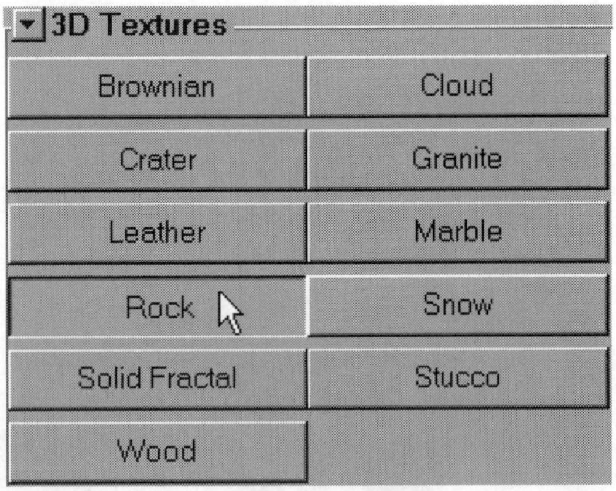

▼ 3D Textures	
Brownian	Cloud
Crater	Granite
Leather	Marble
Rock	Snow
Solid Fractal	Stucco
Wood	

FIGURE 7-4   *Create a Rock texture*

18. Set the attributes of the rock texture as follows (see Figure 7-5):

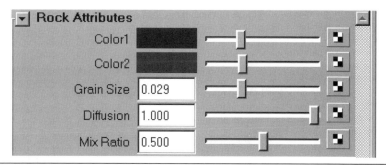

FIGURE 7-5   *Setting the rock texture attributes*

PARAMETERS	RGB VALUES
Color 1	0.280, 0.104, 0.0
Color 2	0.3, 0.236, 0.147

19. Map the Bump Mapping attribute of moutainM with a standard 3D Crater texture.
20. While leaving the rest of the attribute set to default, set the Shaker value to 10.0.

Add Detail to the Mountain

Generally, a mountain has large vertical cracks that flow from the top down. This is the logical result of the force of gravity. To create these lines flowing down the mountain, you can scale the 3D placement texture of the Crater node.

21. Select the 3D placement texture node of the Crater.
22. Scale the node along the vertical Y-axis by 6.759.

This is an arbitrary value; you should try out various values that suit your scene.

23. Assign the Crater texture to the mountain.
24. Set up a simple lighting and test-render the scene.

You should get an image similar to the one shown in Figure 7-6.

FIGURE 7-6   *A rendered image of the mountain*

CREATE THE SPLASHES

TASK

• Make sure that you have an idea of how to approach this animation before you read further. Compare the approach presented below with your ideas.

Create the emitter plane

1. Create a NURBS Plane.

2.   Name it splashObj.

This NURBS plane will be used as the emitter of the splashes.

3.   Transform the mountain so that the plane sits at the mouth of the mountain.

The plane that I used for the scene is set with the following parameters (see Figure 7-7):

ATTRIBUTES	VALUES
Width	1.5
Length Ratio	1.0
Patches U	4.0
Patches V	4.0

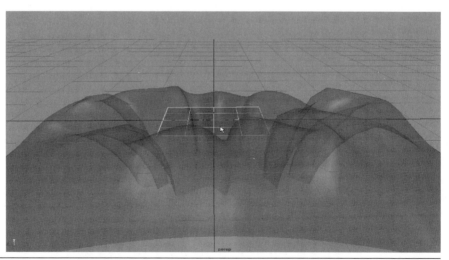

FIGURE 7-7   *Placing the emitter plane in the center of the mountain*

Remember that it is always easier to transform non-particle or non-emitter objects in the scene than to transform the particle object itself.

NOTE

4. Layer, template, and hide the mountaln.

You will now create the splashes.

Create the emitter

5. Select the plane.
6. Set the plane as a surface emitter with the following options shown in Figure 7-8.

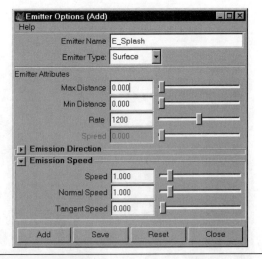

FIGURE 7-8   *Creating the splash particle emitter*

7.   Enter E_Splash as the name of the emitter.

Play back your animation and you should see the default particles emitting from the plane in a uniform, steady manner (see Figure 7-9).

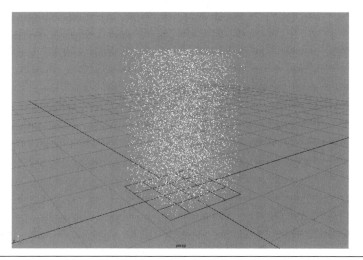

FIGURE 7-9   *Uniformly emitted splash particles*

8.   Rename the default particle to particleSplash.

Control the Emission of Particles

There are several ways to fine-tune and control the particle's emission and movement; through the use of expressions or a ramp that controls the position, velocity, acceleration, and mass.

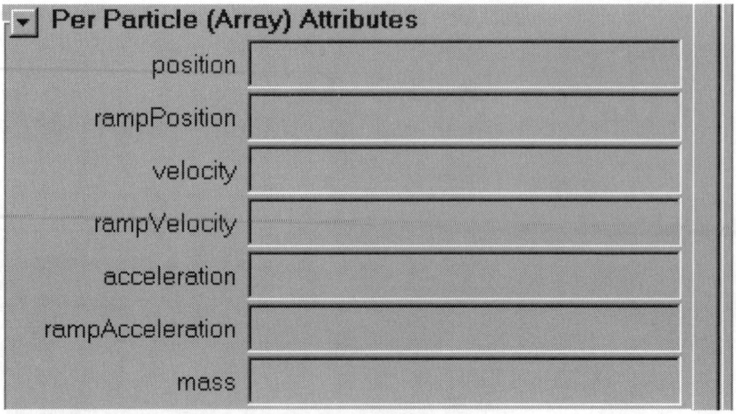

FIGURE 7-10 *Various attributes available for control at the per particle level*

Or with the help of dynamic forces. In Maya 2.0, you have an added method of controlling the rate of emission of the particles and color with the help of the textures (see Figures 7-10 and 7-11).

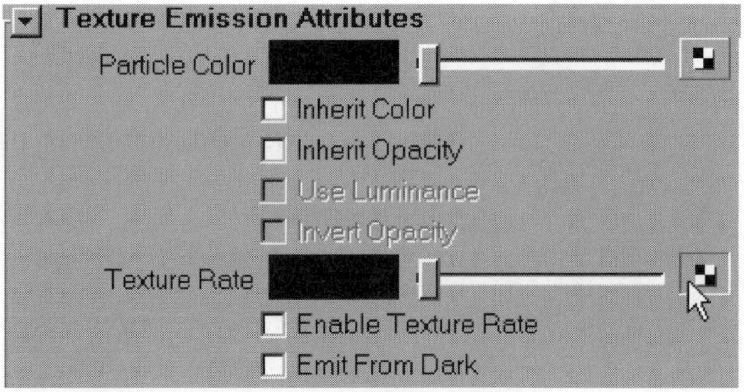

FIGURE 7-11 *Controlling particle emission with the help of textures*

These methods of controlling particles are straightforward and intuitive. In this project, however, you will not use any of these methods. Instead, you will learn to write your own expression that reads a ramp alpha texture value and sets the velocity of the particles based on the texture values.

Don't be afraid of writing your own MEL scripts to control different aspects of particles. They are not difficult. In fact, you may realize that writing your own MEL scripts to do certain functions is faster and more efficient than using the standard mapping functions available.

You will first create the ramp texture that will be used as the height patterns of the splashing.

9. Create a Ramp texture.
10. Name it ramp_Splash.
11. Name its 2D placement texture node placement2DSplash.
12. Set the ramp texture with the following attributes:

ENTRYNUMBER	POSITION	RGB VALUES
0	0.0	0.2, 0.2, 0.2
1	0.1	0.18, 0.18, 0.18
2	0.2	0.5, 0.5, 0.5
3	0.22	0.45, 0.45, 0.45
4	0.3	0.7, 0.7, 0.7
5	0.32	0.65, 0.65, 0.65
6	0.4	0.495, 0.495, 0.495
7	0.5	0.65, 0.65, 0.65
8	0.6	0.5, 0.5, 0.5
9	0.65	0.55, 0.55, 0.55
10	0.7	0.383, 0.383, 0.383
11	0.8	0.3, 0.3, 0.3
12	0.82	0.25, 0.25, 0.25
13	0.9	0.71, 0.71, 0.71
14	1.0	0.15, 0.15, 0.15

13.   Set the Noise attribute to 0.1.

This ramp is derived based on the height of the splash. Whenever you create a ramp to control velocity, position, etc., you should first design the ramp by simply sketching its general shape that you would want it to take (see Figure 7-12).

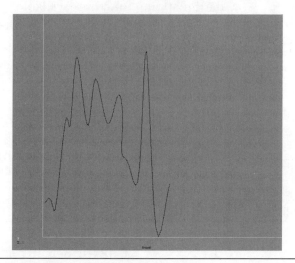

FIGURE 7-12   *The desired patterns of the splashy particles*

14.   Open the Attribute Editor of particleSplash.
15.   From the Per Particle (Array) Attributes section, right-click on the velocity attribute and choose Create New Expression… (see Figure 7-13).

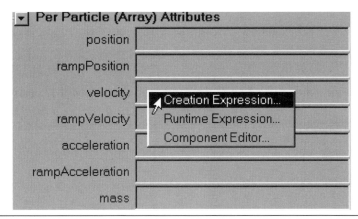

FIGURE 7-13 *Setting the velocity attributes with the help of the expressions*

16. Enter the following expression:

```
string $placenode = "placement2dSplash";
string $tex_val = "ramp_Splash.outAlpha";
float $dynamics = 0.5;
vector $tmp = particleSplashShape.position;
float $x = $tmp.x;
float $z = $tmp.z;
float $map_x;
float $map_z;
 // Remap the x and z into u and v values.
 // Remap function. Assuming the size is 1.5 unit square.
$map_x = ($x + 0.75)/1.5; //normalize
$map_z = ($z + 0.75)/1.5;
setAttr ($placenode + ".uCoord") $map_x;
setAttr ($placenode + ".vCoord") $map_z;
float $offset = getAttr ($tex_val);
float $vy = $offset + rand (4.0,6.5);
float $vx = 0.0 * noise (time);
float $vz = 0.0 * noise (time);
particleSplashShape.velocity = <<$vx, $dynamics*$vy, $vz>>;
```

This expression first samples each particle's position as it is generated. And since the width of the emitter plane is 1.5 and it is placed at the origin, the particle position will return a value within the range of negative 0.75 to positive 0.75. Therefore, the position values are remapped into the range or of 0.0 to 1.0–. From here, you can directly sample the ramp texture values based on this value. (Remember that a default ramp is mapped as UV values of 1.0 unless you changed the values.) The ramp texture value obtained is then used as an offset value to alter the vertical velocity of the particles. As a result, the particles will move in a way that depicts quite closely the exact shape of your ramp texture.

With this simple expression, you can easily control the way that you want the splash to animate by simply animating the ramp values.

17. Play back the particle animation and you should see that as you play further, the particle's position gets closer and closer to the ramp patterns that you set.

In Maya 2.0, there is an easy way of getting the UV values of an emitted particle. You can simply turn on the Need Parent UV checkbox to get the UV values of the particle. You are encouraged to try using this function.

NOTE

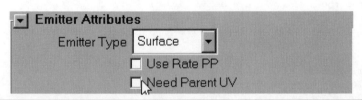

FIGURE 7-14   *Getting the UV values of the particles*

Animate the Emission of Particles

You will now animate the emission of the particles by animating the ramp_Splash texture. To do so, you may choose to animate the ramp values by keyframing or any other means. The idea is to vary the ramp color values and if you would like, the ramp entry positions, so that you are able to create a natural variation of the ups and downs of the splash movement. In order to achieve the ease-of-use factor, you will control the entire ramp entry values using an expression. This should not be anything new since you have already tried controlling ramp values using an expression in Chapter Six.

I used the expression below to control the ramp values of ramp_Splash. Do not be concerned with all the details of the function variations. They are of no value to you quantitatively. Instead, based on your understanding that the intensity of the ramp values control the height of the splash, you should write your own expressions.

The expression below is a result of much trial and error. It contains the usual calls to simple functions such as rand and noise. These functions have already been introduced to you in previous chapters.

```
float $seven, $thirteen, $six, $ten;
$seven = 0.2*(noise (time) + 1.0 )+ rand (0.5,0.7) ; //The BIG peak
$thirteen = 0.2*(noise (time) + 1.0 )+ rand (0.4,0.6) ; //Another SMALL peak
$six = 0.2*(noise (-1*time) + 1.0 )+ rand (0.3,0.5) ; //Next to the BIG peak
$ten = 0.12 + 0.25*(sind (3*time*30) + 1.0); //The valley between the 2 peaks
ramp_Splash.colorEntryList[7].colorR = $seven;
ramp_Splash.colorEntryList[7].colorG = $seven;
ramp_Splash.colorEntryList[7].colorB = $seven;
ramp_Splash.colorEntryList[13].colorR = $thirteen;
ramp_Splash.colorEntryList[13].colorG = $thirteen;
ramp_Splash.colorEntryList[13].colorB = $thirteen;
ramp_Splash.colorEntryList[6].colorR = $six;
ramp_Splash.colorEntryList[6].colorG = $six;
ramp_Splash.colorEntryList[6].colorB = $six;

ramp_Splash.colorEntryList[10].colorR = $ten;
ramp_Splash.colorEntryList[10].colorG = $ten;
ramp_Splash.colorEntryList[10].colorB = $ten;
```

Set the lifespan of the particle

18. Add a lifespanPP attribute for particleSplash.
19. From the Expression Editor, set the lifespan to 2.3 seconds.

```
particleSplashShape.lifespanPP = 2.3;
```

20. Your expression should be set as Creation.

The lifespanPP attribute controls the height of the splash. If you set a longer lifespan, the splash will last longer before the particles die. So, change the lifespan of the particles according to the height and length of your animation.

NOTE

Fine-tune the Movement

You will now further fine-tune the movement of the splash with the help of the dynamic fields.

21. Create a Gravity field with the parameters shown in Figure 7-15.

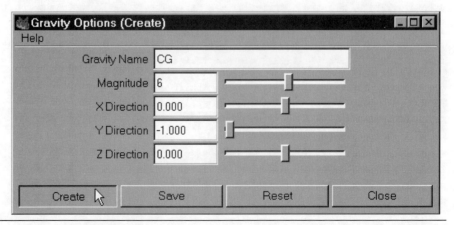

FIGURE 7-15 *Create a gravity field*

22. Name the field CG.
23. Link the field to particleSplash.
24. Play back the animation.

You will notice that the particles appear to be falling down when they reach reasonable height.

TASK

- What are the parameters that you created previously in your expression that allow you to control the height of the splash?

25. Go to the Expression Editor.
26. Edit the particleSplashShape expression and change the $dynamic variable to a value such as 1.2.
27. Play back the animation.

The value of 1.2 is again dependent on your requirement. You should adjust this $dynamic value accordingly.

Create the Anticipation Movement

TASK

- What details would make the movement of the splashes more interesting?

To make the animation more interesting, you will introduce a simple animation principle, anticipation.

There are twelve well-known Disney principles of character animations. Each provides interesting guidelines in helping you to generate great character animation. However, many of them are not only applicable to character animation but to all types of animation and movement. To read more about the principles of animation, a recommended book is "The Illusion of Life: Disney Animation." The principles of character animation can be applied to many other types of animation such as effects animation. Each kind of animation has its own timing, movement, anatomy. Though they may not exist as a form of physical character, the application of the principles are the same. However, it is important to remember that the Disney principles of character animation are simply guidelines. They should not be taken as rules that have to be followed strictly. In any animation creation, you should always define your own world and own style. Many Japanese anime actions do not follow the principles of Disney animation. However, they are equally, if not better, presented in their own styles.

To create the anticipation of the splash shooting from the mountain, you will first create a small movement, followed by a pause, and subsequently a fast shooting out of the splash.

You will control this movement with the help of the CG dynamic field that you have just created.

28. Open the Expression Editor and edit the particleSplashShape expression to include the following expression:

```
if (time*30.0 < 40.0)
{
CG.magnitude = 20;
}
else
{
CG.magnitude = 6;
}
```

29. Play back the animation.

You should see that the splash creates the effect of anticipation by first moving up slowly, then pausing, and then shooting up after the 40th frame.

To further emphasize the anticipation effects, you will control the life span of the particles so that towards the 40th
frame, most particles will have died. This creates the illusion
that the emission is going to stop. However, after frame 40, the
emission will resume with even greater strength.

30. Open the Expression Editor again, this time, combine
the previous lifespanPP expression with the CG
expression to get the following combined
expression:

```
if (time*30.0 < 40.0)
{
CG.magnitude = 20;
particleSplashShape.lifespanPP = 1.8*sind(6*time*30);
}
else
{
CG.magnitude = 6;
particleSplashShape.lifespanPP = 2.3;
}
```

NOTE

*Notice again the use of the sine function to control and create
the effects that you want. The purpose of the sine function is to
help control the life span of the particles when each of the them
is created. The result towards the end of the 40th frame is that
most particles are dead or dying.*

Setting the Turbulence

You will now add turbulence to the movement of the particles.

31. Create a turbulence dynamic force.
32. Link the turbulence force to particleSplash.
33. The turbulence should be set to the parameters shown in Figure 7-16.

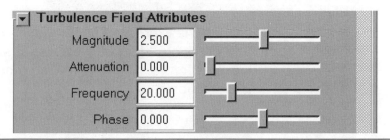

FIGURE 7-16   *Setting the turbulence field attributes*

Add More Dynamic Forces

For better control and to create more interesting animation, you should create more dynamic force fields. In this project, I've added other dynamic forces such as Radial and Vortex. The purpose of these forces is to create the dispersion effect so that the particles will not move up and fall down exactly in a predictable manner. I'll leave it up to you to create additional forces to make your animation movement more interesting.

NOTE

In Maya, to see the influence of a dynamic force, go to Modify ≻ Transformation Tools ≻ Show Manipulator Tool. From there, when you pick any of the dynamic forces, you are able to view information such as the attentuation values. In addition, you can simply drag and manipulate the values in real time (see Figure 7-17). This Show Manipulator Tool is also very useful when you need to control and view other information, such as deformation controls for character animation.

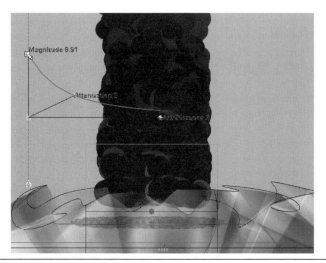

FIGURE 7-17 *Using the Manipulator Tool to view the dynamic field influence*

Set the physical attributes

34. Open the Attributes Editor of particleSplashM.
35. Set the Particle Render Type to Cloud (s/w).
36. Click the Current Render Type button.
37. Check ON for the Better Illumination checkbox.

38. Add the Dynamic Attribute radiusPP.
39. Map the radiusPP attribute with the following ramp entries:

POSITION	RGB VALUES
0.0	0.120
0.330	0.08
0.680	0.05
0.995	0.05

CREATE THE SPLASHING LOOK

Create the particle shader

1. Create a particleCloud shader.
2. Name it particleSplashSG and its material particleSplashM.
3. Assign the shader to particleSplash.
4. Map the Life Color attribute of particleSplashM to the following Ramp attribute.
5. Name this ramp ramp_LifeColor.

Notice that to create variation of the color values, one of the ramp entries is mapped again. You should experiment with your own mapping values.

POSITION	VALUES
0.0	Map again
0.255	0.86, 0.02, 0.0
0.45	1.0, 0.45, 0.183
0.610	0.607, 0.607, 0.607
0.790	1.0, 0.373, 0.0
0.865	0.793, 0.784, 0.661

6. Leave the rest of the values as default and re-map the Ramp entry of position 0.0 to a new ramp with the following values:

POSITION	VALUES
0.0	1.0, 0.747, 0.0
0.510	1.0, 0.397, 0.0
1.0	1.0, 0.0, 0.0

7. Set the Noise value of this ramp to 1.0.
8. Set its V wave as 0.632.
9. Go back and select particleSplashM.
10. Map the Life Transparency attribute of particleSplashM to the following values:

POSITION	VALUES
0.0	0.5, 0.5, 0.5
0.235	0.266, 0.266, 0.266
1.0	0.105, 0.105, 0.105

11. Go back again to open the attribute editor of particleSplashM,
12. Set the Glow Intensity to 0.70,
13. Set the Noise to 0.523,
14. Set the Noise Frequency to 0.1,
15. Leave the rest of the attributes at their default values.

Test-render

Add a simple spotlight and test-render the scene. You should get an image similar to the one shown in Figure 7-18.

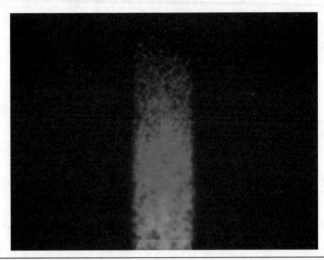

FIGURE 7-18   *A rendered image of the splash*

While you are testing the render result of a particle effects animation, it is often better for you to play back and animate the particle in the Point Render Type mode and render in your chosen Cloud or other Render Type mode. This will ensure that you have interactive feedback and can save you considerable time. To quickly switch between these different Render Types, simply use a MEL script. An example of the script is as shown here:

```
//change to points
setAttr particleSplashShape.particleRenderType 3;
//change to Cloud
setAttr particleSplashShape.particleRenderType 8;
```

The various render type id is as shown here

PARTICLE RENDER TYPE	TYPE ID
MultiPoint	0
MultiStreak	1
Numeric	2
Points	3
Spheres	4
Sprites	5
Streak	6
Blobby Surface (s/w)	7
Cloud (s/w)	8
Tube (s/w)	9

CREATE THE PARTICLE COLLISION

Create the Collision

You are now ready to make the particles move and collide with the mountain.

To create the collision for both the splash and the mountain, you will make the mountain a collide object.

1. Untemplate your mountain object.
2. Select the mountain object.
3. Go to Particles ➤ Make Collide -❏.
4. Set the options to the ones shown in Figure 7-19.

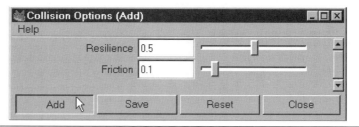

FIGURE 7-19 *Setting the collision options*

This will create the mountain object as a collide object.

Link the Collision

You have to link the collide object with the appropriate particles in order for them to have collisions.

5. Open the Dynamic Relationship Editor.
6. Connect mountain geometry with particleSplash (see Figure 7-20).

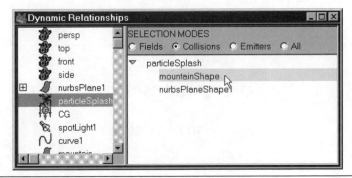

FIGURE 7-20 *Connecting the mountain with the particles for collision using the Relationship Editor*

7. Play back the animation and you should see that the particles will now collide with the mountain.

In creating particle collision, you can always use a simpler geometry to replace the larger geometry. The simpler geometry could be templated and not rendered at all. This trick will save considerable time, especially when you have a large geometry for collision detection. An example is seen in Chapter Eleven.

Creating New Particles

In Maya, you can have control of normal frictional or bouncing collision effects, and you can also generate new types of particles when collisions occur. This added control is particularly useful when you would like the particles to change properties after the collision occurs.

This is achieved with the Particle Collision Events.

8. Create a new particle.
9. Name this particle particleSplashCollide.
10. Set the Particle Render Type to Cloud (s/w).
11. Set the particle with a normal life span of 0.5.
12. Create a radiusPP attribute for the particle.
13. Map the radiusPP value with a standard Ramp texture.
14. Set the Ramp texture with the following values:

POSITION	RGB VALUE
0	0.08
0.7	0.08
1	0.03

15. Assign the same shading group particleSplashSG to this particleSplashCollide.

Create the particle collision event

16. Go to Particles ➤ Particle Collision Events.... .
17. Enter the Set Event Name as Splashevent (see Figure 7-21).

FIGURE 7-21 *Setting the collision event name*

18. Set the event with the values shown in Figure 7-22.

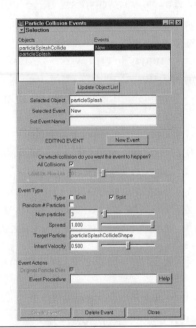

FIGURE 7-22   *Setting the collision event parameters*

This will ensure that when a collision event occurs, three new particles will be split as a result and each of these new particles is of the type particleSplashCollide.

Create Another Collision

In addition to the collision of the particle with the mountain, the NURBS plane splashObj is also made as a collision object. This is because of the way that the mountain geometry is created. (See the earlier Figure 7-2.) If your mountain geometry is without any hole in the middle, you can skip this part.

19. Select the splashObj geometry.
20. Make it also a collide object as mountain.
21. Set the values for the collision as shown below:

PARAMETERS	VALUES
Tesselation Factor	200
Resilience	0.6
Friction	0.1

22. Connect this object with the particles.

Connect All Collisions

23. Go to the Dynamic Relationship Editor.
24. Ensure that SplashObj, particleSplash, particleSplashCollide, and mountain are all connected to each other.

RENDERING

Rendering small particles such as splashing effects generally does not require very high anti-aliasing and motion blur. This is because of the nature of the particles that are to be presented. Rendering with motion blur will blur off the details of the splashing effects for the animation. You will likely end up with little or no visible details of the tiny splashes.

You should experiment with rendering a frame of the above animation with motion blur and high-quality anti-aliasing and compare the results with no motion and medium-quality anti-aliasing.

Go to the CD and playback the animation chpt07.mov. You should have an animation similar to it.

To end this section on water effects, you will further experiment with the creation of rain and ripple effects.

RAIN EFFECTS

Create the rain particles

1. Start a new scene.
2. Create a simple NURBS plane.

This plane will be used as the surface emitter to generate the rain particles.

3. Scale the plane accordingly to the size that you want for your sky.

The scale that I have is set to the width of the plane set to 15.0.

4. Name the plane Sky.
5. Create a new particle object using the plane as the surface emitter.
6. Name the particle particleRain.
7. Set the surface emitter of the rain with the parameters shown in Figure 7-23.

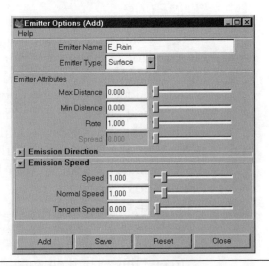

FIGURE 7-23　*Setting the rain emitter options*

NOTE

Similar to the creation of a large terrain model, you should not be bothered with making a huge sky that will generate the physically correct amount of rain particles. As long as when you render, the rain appears to fall from the whole area of the sky, that is sufficient.

Set the physical attributes of the rain particles

8. Open the Attribute Editor of particleRain.
9. Set the Current Render Type to Tube (s/w).
10. Set both the radii of the Tube attribute, Radius 0 and Radius 1, to be 0.04.
11. From the Expression Editor, set the Tail Size to be a random value between 1.0, and 5.0. using the rand( ) function:

```
particleRain.tailSize = rand (1.0, 5.0);
```

12. Create a lifespanPP attribute for the particle.
13. Set the lifespanPP to vary between 2.0 to 3.0 using the random function.

Accelerate the rain

14. Play back your animation.

The movement of the rain appears to be rather constant. In a typical rain effects, like any other object falling under the influence of gravity, the object will gain velocity as it falls. Therefore, you will add in the acceleration for the rain. There are two ways to control the acceleration. One way is to animate the acceleration or velocity attribute of the particles. Another way is to create and link a Gravity dynamic field.

Below is an example of the gravity field values set to link the rain. You should change the values according to the speed and setup of your entire scene.

Shade the rain

15. Create a new particle shading group.
16. Name the shading group particleRainSG and its material as particleRainM.
17. Set the Color attribute of the shading group with the RGB values of 0.73, 0.895, and 1.0.
18. Assign the shading group to the rain particles.
19. Map the Transparency attribute of the shading group with a ramp texture.
20. Set the ramp texture with the following values:

POSITION	RGB
0.0	0.872, 0.872, 0.872
0.109	0.233, 0.233, 0.233
0.953	0.326, 0.326, 0.326
1.0	1.0, 1.0, 1.0

21. Set the other attributes of particleRainM with the following values:

DENSITY	1.0
Noise is	1.0
Noise frequency	0.15.

Test-render

22. Set up a simple lighting for the scene.
23. Test-render the rain effects.

24. You should get an image similar to the one shown in Figure 7-24.

FIGURE 7-24 *Setting the gravity to pull down the rain*

Lighting a scene with rain requires careful consideration. This is because all rain is illuminated by natural lighting, which has always been a challenge for most lighting artists. In this example, the rain is illuminated simply by a single light source. However, you will be able to make the rain more interesting by employing different layers of light for the rain. For example, nearer to the camera, you may want the rain to exhibit some reflection characteristics while further away, you can make the rain dimmer.

TASK

- Based on what you learned in the introductory chapters, try illuminating the rain with just the backlight or sidelight. Compare the results of illuminating the rain from other angles.

Making the rain collide

You can make the rain more interesting by creating collision events for the rain when it hits the ground.

25. Create a NURBS plane.
26. Make the plane a Collision object with the following parameters:

Resilience	0.5
Friction	0.0

When the rain hits the ground, you can create a new particle type.

27. Create a new particle.
28. Name it particleRainCollide.
29. Set the particle as a Cloud (s/w) Render Type.
30. Set the new particle type with the following parameters:

Life span	0.3
Lifespan 0.3 Radius	Radius 0.04

Shade the Collide Rain Particles

Create a new shading type for particleRainCollide.

31. Create a Particle Shading group.
32. Map its Color attribute with the RGB values: 0.482, 0.591, and 0.661.
33. Set its Density to 0.5.
34. Set its Noise to 1.0.
35. Set its Noise Frequence as 0.15.
36. Set the same Transparency Ramp type for its Transparency attribute as above.

Test-render Rain Collision

Based on the instructions above, make the necessary connection for the collision events for the rain. Create the necessary setup. Render the rain animation and composite the results.

TASK

* Imagine that the camera moves forward in a scene. Create an effect such that the rain will hit the camera and create small splashes on it as the camera moves.

RIPPLE EFFECTS

In Maya, creating ripples is easy using the water texture. By layering several layers of the water texture, you are able to create random ripple effects. And using simple expressions, you can coordinate the rain with the creation of ripples.

In this example, you will experiment with the creation of the ripple effects using a simple plane.

1. Create a simple NURBS plane.
2. Create a shader. Any type of shader will do.
3. Map a water texture to the Color attribute of the shader.

In this example, you are experimenting with the creation of ripples using the Color attribute. However, the same method can be applied to using the Bump Mapping attribute, or even the Displacement mapping of the shader.

NOTE

4. Set the water attribute section of the texture to the values shown in Figure 7-25.

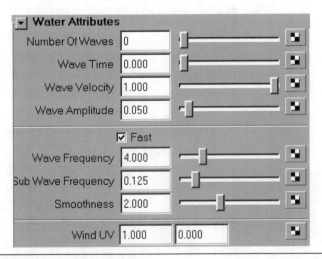

FIGURE 7-25 *Water attribute texture settings*

5. Under the Concentric Ripple Attributes, set the following parameters:

PARAMETERS	VALUES
Ripple Time	Expression Control
Ripple Frequency	Any value within the range of 60–90
Ripple Amplitude	Expression Control
Drop Size	Any value within the range of 0.04–0.2
Ripple Origin	Expression Control
Group Velocity	Any value within the range of 0.15–0.3
Phase Velocity	Any value within the range of 0.3–0.5
Spread Start	0.008
Spread Rate	Any value within the range of 0.03–0.1

6. Map the Color Offset attribute of the water texture to another new water texture.

7. For this new water texture, set the various parameters as the same or similar to the previous water texture.

8. Continue to map the Color Offset attribute of each new water texture. To have sufficient ripples for a scene, a layer of 7-8 water textures is sufficient.

9. The actual ripple animation is then easily achieved with a simple expression that randomly sets the parameters such as Ripple Time, Ripple Amplitude, and Ripple Origin.

An example of the expression is as shown next. This expression is similar to the expression that is available from Alias Wavefront's 3DCD if you purchase the PowerAnimator software.

```
global float $ripple_speed = 0.5;
water1.rippleTime = fmod ((((3+frame)*0.1)*$ripple_speed),1);
water1.rippleAmplitude = 10*(1-fmod ((((3+frame)*0.1)*$ripple_speed),1));
water1.rippleOriginU = ( ( sin ( ( floor ( ( ( ( 3 + frame ) * 0.1 ) * $ripple_speed ) ) * 0.66 ) ) * 0.23 ) + 0.5 );
water1.rippleOriginV = ( ( cos ( ( floor ( ( ( ( 3 + frame ) * 0.1 ) * $ripple_speed ) ) * 9.2 ) ) * 0.24 ) + 0.5 );
water2.rippleTime = fmod ( ( ( ( 10 + frame ) * 0.14 ) * $ripple_speed ), 1 );
water2.rippleAmplitude = 10*(( 1 - fmod ( ( ( ( 10 + frame ) * 0.14 ) * $ripple_speed ), 1 ) ));
water2.rippleOriginU = ( ( cos ( ( floor ( ( ( ( 10 + frame ) * 0.14 ) * $ripple_speed ) ) * 8.25 ) ) * 0.3 ) + 0.5 );
water2.rippleOriginV = ( ( sin ( ( floor ( ( ( ( 10 + frame ) * 0.14 ) * $ripple_speed ) ) * 0.91 ) ) * 0.3 ) + 0.5 );
water3.rippleTime = fmod ( ( ( ( 16 + frame ) * 0.08 ) * $ripple_speed ), 1 );
water3.rippleAmplitude = ( 1 - fmod ( ( ( ( 16 + frame ) * 0.008 ) * $ripple_speed ), 1 ) );
water3.rippleOriginU = ( ( cos ( ( floor ( ( ( ( 16 + frame ) * 0.08 ) * $ripple_speed ) ) * 3.2 ) ) * 0.25 ) + 0.5 );
water3.rippleOriginV = ( ( sin ( ( floor ( ( ( ( 16 + frame ) * 0.08 ) * $ripple_speed ) ) * 1.11 ) ) * 0.25 ) + 0.5 );
water4.rippleTime = fmod ( ( ( ( 22 + frame ) * 0.11 ) * $ripple_speed ), 1 );
water4.rippleAmplitude = ( 1 - fmod ( ( ( ( 22 + frame ) * 0.11 ) * $ripple_speed ), 1 ) );
water4.rippleOriginU = ( ( cos ( ( floor ( ( ( ( 22 + frame ) * 0.11 ) * $ripple_speed ) ) * 11.52 ) ) * 0.35 ) + 0.5 );
water4.rippleOriginV = ( ( sin ( ( floor ( ( ( ( 22 + frame ) * 0.11 ) * $ripple_speed ) ) * 8.111 ) ) * 0.35 ) + 0.5 );
water5.rippleTime = fmod ( ( ( ( 5 + frame ) * 0.13 ) * $ripple_speed ), 1 );
water5.rippleAmplitude = ( 1 - fmod ( ( ( ( 5 + frame ) * 0.13 ) * $ripple_speed ), 1 ) );
water5.rippleOriginU = ( ( sin ( ( floor ( ( ( ( 5 + frame ) * 0.13 ) * $ripple_speed ) ) * 0.66 ) ) * 0.3 ) + 0.5 );
water5.rippleOriginV = ( ( sin ( ( floor ( ( ( ( 5 + frame ) * 0.13 ) * $ripple_speed ) ) * 9.118 ) ) * 0.3 ) + 0.5 );
water6.rippleTime = fmod ( ( ( ( 1 + frame ) * 0.11 ) * $ripple_speed ), 1 );
water6.rippleAmplitude = ( 1 - fmod ( ( ( ( 1 + frame ) * 0.11 ) * $ripple_speed ), 1 ) );
water6.rippleOriginU = ( ( sin ( ( floor ( ( ( ( 1 + frame ) * 0.11 ) * $ripple_speed ) ) * 2.3 ) ) * 0.3 ) + 0.5 );
water6.rippleOriginV = ( ( cos ( ( floor ( ( ( ( 1 + frame ) * 0.11 ) * $ripple_speed ) ) * 4.2 ) ) * 0.3 ) + 0.5 );
water7.rippleTime = fmod ( ( ( ( 3 + frame ) * 0.11 ) * $ripple_speed ), 1 );
water7.rippleAmplitude = ( 1 - fmod ( ( ( ( 3 + frame ) * 0.11 ) * $ripple_speed ), 1 ) );
water7.rippleOriginU = ( ( cos ( ( floor ( ( ( ( 3 + frame ) * 0.11 ) * $ripple_speed ) ) * 0.6 ) ) * 0.3 ) + 0.5 );
water7.rippleOriginV = ( ( sin ( ( floor ( ( ( ( 3 + frame ) * 0.11 ) * $ripple_speed ) ) * 0.9 ) ) * 0.3 ) + 0.5 );
```

10. From the companion CD, play the animation movie file, chpt07_r.mov. You should get similar results when your animation is rendered.

CONCLUSION

In this section of water effects, you have learned the general technique of creating water waves, splashes, rain, and ripples. These techniques are general. You should creatively combine them to create your own effects animation. Remember that each water effect will always require different consideration.

EXERCISE

1. Apply what you learned here to create a simple scene of a spraying fountain. Think about it to be able to build controls for the speed, direction, etc. of the water in the fountain.
2. Play back the animation, chpt07_w.mov, from the CD. Create a similar pouring of water effect.
3. Create a rain effect such that the particles falling nearer to the camera have a smaller tube radius than those farther away. Compare the results that you get when the rain is all generated with the same radius particle. Compare the results again with the different illumination methods that you tried for the rain.

EXPLOSIONS

INTRODUCTION

Air is a form of gaseous element. This makes it a suitable object to be simulated using the particle system. Unlike the other elements that you have seen so far, you are more likely to feel the presence of air than to see it. Besides being able to taste it, you can feel the presence of air with your other four senses: you can smell it when someone is wearing perfume; you can touch it when wind blows on you; you can hear it roaring when it comes as a storm; and you can see it when it exists in a larger form of particles such as steam or clouds. Perhaps some day the computer on your desk will have the added capability to simulate your senses of touch and smell; for now, you will focus on creating air particles that will stimulate sight.

In this chapter, you will create a common type of air effects: *explosion!* In general, an explosion occurs as a result of a chemical reaction. When an explosion occurs, a huge amount of heat is produced. This heat is normally conspicuously displayed as a form of fire and flames. The sudden and violent expansion of gases also generally results in cumulus smoke. In addition, a thundering noise is dissipated.

TASK

- Sound requires a medium to travel. Usually, the medium is air. And in outer-space, there does not exist any medium, only a vacuum—nothing but enormous empty space. Have you ever wondered why, when an explosion occurs in outer-space, you can always hear that loud noise, in those sci-fi movies such as Star Trek?

PRE-PRODUCTION: UNDERSTANDING THE SCENARIO

TASK

- In this project, you will work on a futuristic scene. The sketch of the scene is shown in Figure 8-1.

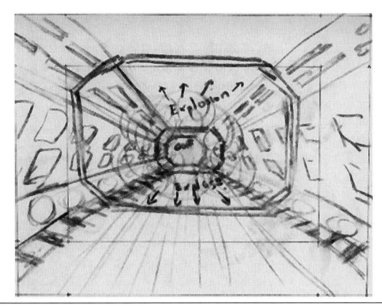

FIGURE 8-1   *Sketch*

This cut is a chasing scene, which takes place in a launching tunnel within a space station. An unexpected war broke out in the space region 277. A squadron of Red force spacecraft invaded the region, setting off alarms and producing an imminent counter attack by the Green forces.

This cut will begin with an explosion that is a result of two hyperlasers brushing against each other. This happens right in front of a tunnel. The camera will shoot from there. Red forces flew into the launching tunnel in an attempt to evade an attack by the Green forces. The entire scene will take about four seconds.

In this project, you'll create the explosion effect and the entire chase sequence. Because the scene is set within a tunnel, the explosion must flow along the tunnel towards the camera. You should create controls for the rate that the explosion evolves towards the camera. Therefore, when it is required that the explosion moves faster along the tunnel, your animation must be able to accommodate the change easily.

TASK

- Study the given sketch carefully. As usual, think about the list of questions that you have in mind. Seek answers from the director or do some research into similar work.

ANALYZE THE PICTURE

The challenge of creating explosions is many-fold. One challenge lies in creating the dynamic fast movement. Consider the movement of smoke or steam particles where the movement is generally turbulent and under the influence of gravity. The explosion is very characteristic in nature. It is fast. And depending on the situation, and how you place your D4 explosive or other explosive charges, there are many different shapes that it can take. On the other hand, steam, fog, and smoke have very general movements that you can use in most situations. But explosions are completely dependent on the situation. There is very little similarity in terms of the shapes and forms that different explosions can take. However, the color and evolution of the smoke particles are similar in nature. They all move in an upward and outward radial manner.

The following elements are essential to creating a believable explosion:

- Production of noise
- Heat
- Violent expansion of gases
- Sudden speed and force
- Noise from internal energy
- Shock wave
- Shattered debris

TASK

- Before you do anything in this tutorial, I suggest you look up some footages of explosion. This is because though you may have seen many explosion scenes from the big screen, it is unlikely that you have observed enough for the tutorial. For example, I've seen over 1000 animated explosions, both realistic and cartoon-type, to have a basic grasp of the anatomy of explosions.

APPROACHES

The challenge in most explosion animation is to convey the strength of the explosion. If it is a simple volumetric spherical explosion, the effects could be created quite easily with the help of high-volume audio and strong flash lights. And therefore more time can be spent focusing on shading the particles. However, in this scene, for the additional requirement of the explosion movement, the approach of using normal explosion creation may need to be revised.

In the companion CD, all the animation movie files are without audio. As in any motion picture, audio is one of the most important elements in creating a scenario. Imagine seeing a wind effect without hearing the windy sound, seeing an explosion without getting bombarded by the loud audio, and seeing splashing water without hearing the familiar "splash" sound. The difference is beyond written description.

These are the steps to create the required explosion animation:

Set up the shooting angle and camera. Explosion is random in nature. And typically a good-looking explosion will turn ugly and uninteresting when you change your view. Therefore, deciding how far away you will be when viewing the explosion, from what angle, what kind of lighting, etc, are all fundamental questions that you must address before creating the effects.

Create the explosion. This stage is similar to deciding where you would want to place your explosive charges in a real live action setting. Often explosions are created with a great deal of exaggeration. In a Hollywood setting, a car can explode with such an immerse strength that you wonder what kind of engine the car had. However, in film, anything that creates an impact and captivates the audience will work. Hence, digitally, you will decide where the explosion particles are to be emitted.

In this project, you will simplify the animation by having only one source of emission. However, to create a much more varied form of explosion, you should have a few particle emitters placed at different positions. By coordinating the timing of the emissions, you will be able to create various interesting explosion effects.

Direct the explosion. In this particular project, with the help of an expression, you will control the particles so that they will move in a physically correct manner, and at the same time towards the camera in a controlled way.

Create the explosion look. This is the stage of rendering the explosion to the desired look. For the random nature of its movement, rendering a digital explosion to a desired look has always been a big challenge for many visual effects artists. Though many methods and tricks have been developed to create a good-looking digital explosion, nothing comes close to the real ones. This includes the method presented here.

Create the motion path spacecraft. When the explosion effects are created, you will experiment with the motion path animation of Maya and include a simple spacecraft for the animation.

Add secondary animation. In creating character animation, there are primary and secondary animations. An animation created without secondary movement lacks believability.

For example, if you are creating the animation of a character jumping up and down, the jumping movement is the primary movement. However, merely making the character jump up and down does not make your animation anywhere close to a believable one. What is needed are the secondary motions. These secondary motions result from the primary animation. In this example, you can enhance the believability by, say, making some dust effects when the feet hit the ground, and making the camera shake a little at the same time.

For the purpose of this project, only a simple shaking of camera movement during the explosion will be created. However, you should attempt to add as many secondary and subtle animation details as possible. You may, for example, make shattered pieces of glass flying.

PRODUCTION AND TESTING

Create a new project for this tutorial

Create a new project

1. Create a new project with the default settings.
2. Name the project Tunnel_Explosion.

You will create a simple tunnel as a stand-in model for the real tunnel.

Create the tunnel

3. Go to Create ➤ CV Curve Tool -❑.

The Tool Settings window opens.

4. Set the curve degree one (see Figure 8-2).

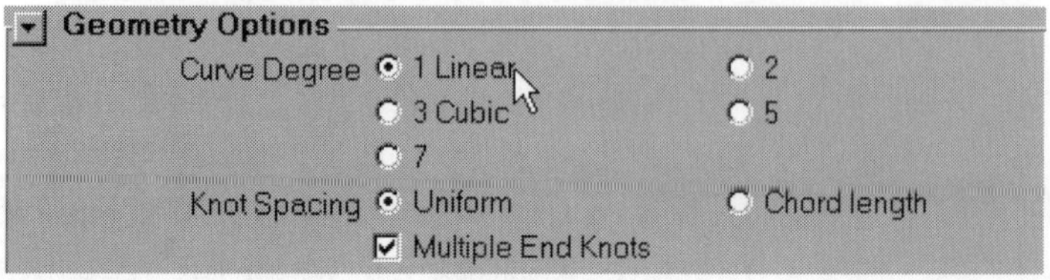

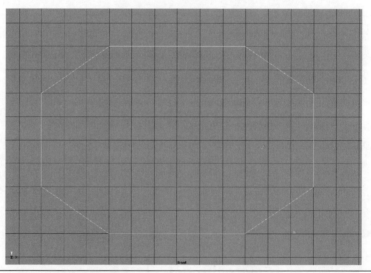

FIGURE 8-2   *Setting the curve creation option to degree one*

5. From the Front View window, create a curve as shown in Figure 8-3.

FIGURE 8-3   *The tunnel profile curve*

6. Press F3 to switch to the Modeling menu.
7. Further duplicate the curve and translate it along the Z-axis with a value of 40.0.
8. Using the function Surfaces ➤ Loft, create the tunnel as shown in Figure 8-4. Scale the tunnel if necessary.
9. Name it Tunnel.

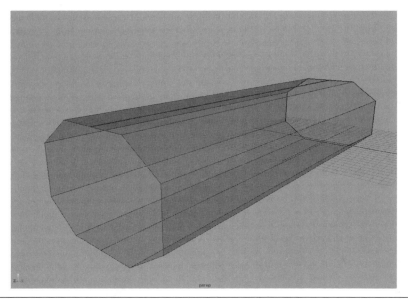

FIGURE 8-4 *Using Loft tool to create the tunnel*

Setting the camera view

10. Create a new camera.
11. Set the camera attributes to values similar to the following:

PARAMETERS	VALUES
Translate	0.022, 2.125, 39.770
Angle of View	96

To create the illusion of depth, it is common to use a wide angle of view.

NOTE

CREATE THE EXPLOSION

Prepare the shape of the emitter

1. From the Front View window, create a curve as shown in Figure 8-5.

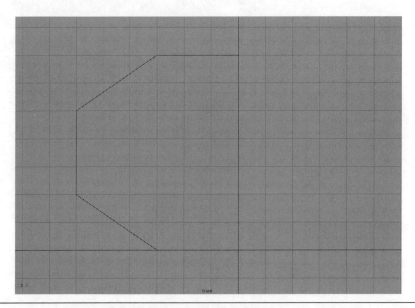

FIGURE 8-5   *Creating the profile of the emitter shape*

2. With the curve selected, go to Edit ➤ Duplicate -❏.

   The Duplicate Options window opens.

3. Duplicate the curve with the scale value as set in Figure 8-6.

   This will mirror and create another side of the curve

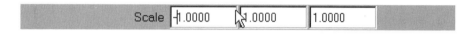

FIGURE 8-6   *The mirror method: duplicating by scaling along the negative X axis*

4. Loft the curves to create a simple surface.
5. Rename the loft surface Explosion_Surface.

   This surface will be used as the particle emitter.

6. Delete the history.
7. Scale the surface in X, Y, and Z axes with a value of 0.169.

Create the surface emitter

8. Press F4 to switch to the Dynamics menu.
9. With Explosion_Surface selected, go to Particles ➤ Add Emitter -❏.
10. Create the surface emitter with the following parameters shown in Figure 8-7.

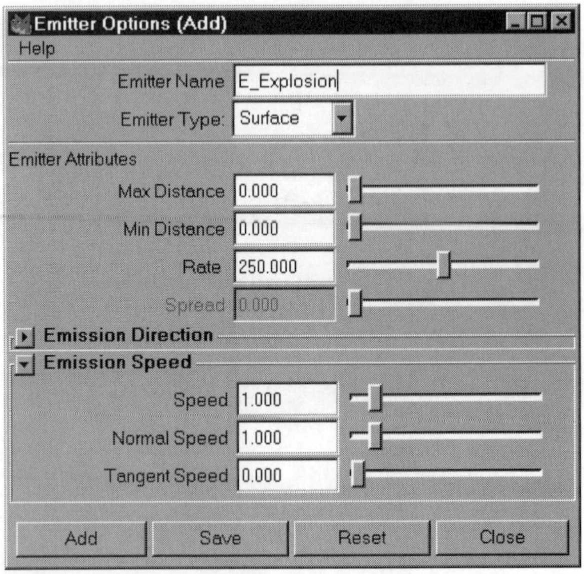

FIGURE 8-7   *Setting the Explosion Emitter option*

11. Template the surface Explosion_Surface.
12. Rename the emitter particleExplosion.

Increase the speed of emission

13. Play back the animation. If the particles are in reverse direction, reverse the surface normal of Explosion_ Surface or set the normal Speed of E_Explosion to –1.

You will now increase the speed of emission.

14. Open the Expression Editor and enter the following expression for the attribute E_explosion:

E_Explosion.speed = 20*time;

In creating emission of particles, there are several approaches. Here the emission is controlled entirely by the emission speed of the emitter. Another method of controlling emission is to have zero emission speed for the particles but create dynamic forces to control the speed and acceleration of the particles. That is to say, when the particles are born, they are without any initial speed. The subsequent speed that they attain is through the influence of the dynamic fields. Each of these methods is useful. You should experiment with different ways of controlling particle emission and speed.

Spread the Emission

To create a general explosion shape, you will spread the explosion emission. You will achieve this with the tangent values of E_Explosion and its Min and Max Distance attributes.

15. Select the Tangent attribute of E_Explosion and set the keyframe values shown in Figure 8-8.

Keys		Time	Value	InTan Type	OutTan Type
0		1	1	spline	spline
1		25	1	spline	spline
2		32	0.3	spline	spline

FIGURE 8-8 *Keyframe values of the tangent attribute of the emitter*

The keyframe values are set so that in the beginning of the explosion, the particles will generally spread out in a spherical manner. However, as time passes, you will channel more particles towards the camera since most sides of the explosion are covered by the particles in front.

16. Under the Emission Attribute section of E_Explosion, set the Max Distance attribute to 1.0. This will ensure that particles are created within a range of 0.0 to 1.0 radius.

The Max and Min Distance values should be set in accordance with the rate of emission and the particles radius etc. A too wide range will result in gaps visible between the particles.

NOTE

Set the particle physical attributes

17. Select particleExplosion
    a. Set the particles as Cloud (s/w) Render Type.
    b. Add the attributes for the Current Render Type.
    c. Set and check ON for the Better Illumination.
18. Add the dynamic attribute of lifespanPP.
19. Add the dynamic attribute of radiusPP.

TASK

• Based on your experience from the previous tutorials, how would you set the radius and life span of the particles?

20. From the Expression Editor, set lifespanPP and radiusPP to the following Creation expression:

particleExplosionShape.lifespanPP = rand (1.0,4.0);
particleExplosionShape.radiusPP = 1.1;

Controlling the Particles

To control the movement of the particles, you will use two methods: the **dynamic field** and **expression controls**.

Create the Drag Field

You will first create an air resistance to the movement of the particles.

1. Create and link a Drag field with the options shown in Figure 8-9 to the particles.

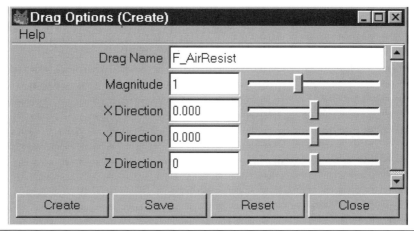

FIGURE 8-9 *Create a drag field as the air resistance*

2. Play back the animation and you should see a slow down of the particles

EXPRESSION CONTROL

Figure 8-10 illustrates the movement of the particles. In the beginning, the particles are emitted from the emitter. As they travel, they lose their momentum due to air resistance or other resistance to their motion. At the same time, when more internal explosion occurs, other inner particles will push through these slowed-down particles and carry on the explosion to a further distance.

The following expression is written to create such effects. In the expression, the velocity vector of the particle is obtained. Based on the velocity of the vector, you create a simple temporary vector that is 0.001 unit less in the Z direction. A cross product of the original vector with this simple temp vector will result in a new sideways vector. This processing of computing and creating a new sideways vector will result in the particles moving in the manner similar to that as shown in Figure 8-10.

Simultaneously, as the older particles are undergoing rotation in their velocity direction, the new particles are being emitted with greater velocity (remember the emission speed expression above). As a result, the entire motion would depict quite closely the actual required animation of the explosion expanding and moving forward towards the camera.

In addition, as the explosion evolves, the radius of the particles is also enlarged to depict the real life similarity of explosion expansion.

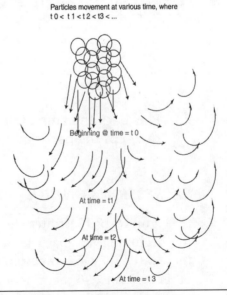

FIGURE 8-10 *The movement of the particles at various time stages*

3. Select particleExplosion and enter the following expression as its Runtime expression:

```
vector $pos = particleExplosionShape.position;
if (0.05*$pos.z > 1.0)
particleExplosionShape.radiusPP = 0.05*$pos.z;
float $DTOR = 0.01745
if ((particleExplosionShape.lifespanPP ñ particleExplosionShape.age ) < 1.5)
{
float $theta = 5.0*$DTOR;
vector $vel = particleExplosionShape.velocity;
vector $tmp = <<$vel.x,$vel.y,$vel.z-0.001>>;
//Take note that I use minus instead of the multiply because
//multiply will result in the negative values of the
//vector and the whole thing will be +/-,+/-.
//vector $tmp = <<$vel.x,$vel.y,$vel.z*0.5>>;
vector $axis = cross($vel,$tmp);
vector $new = rot($vel,$axis,$theta);
particleExplosionShape.velocity = $new;
}
```

NOTE

You can change the angle at which the particles change direction by altering the degree of rotation $theta. You can also change when you want the change of direction to occur by editing the if statement above.

Shading the particles

4. Select particleExplosion.
5. Keyframe the Surface Shading attribute with values shown in Figure 8-11.

Keys	Time	Value	InTan Type	OutTan Type
0	1	0.1	spline	spline
1	90	0	spline	spline

FIGURE 8-11   *Keyframe value for the Surface Shading*

NOTE

In the beginning of the explosion, the particles should be prominently displayed with distinct clear lines of crack between each volume of explosion. As the particles are closer to the camera, they appear to be more dispersed and fuzzy and therefore the lines of cracks between them are no longer obvious. The particles closer to the camera appear to be more dispersed and fuzzy and therefore the lines of cracks between them are no longer obvious. Hence, the shading of the particles approaches zero. Figure 8-12 shows the difference between a complete surface shading (= 1.0) value, no shading value (= 0.0), and a half shading value (0.5). Notice that when the shading value of the cloud particles is set to full (= 1.0), the result of the rendering is essentially the same as Blooby Surface (s/w) Shading. Note also that when the surface shading is 1.0, the use of Lambert or Phong or another shading method for the Surface Material will generate particles with different results. You should try out various different settings with the different surface materials. By default, whenever a new Particle Cloud shading group is created, no surface material is mapped. When rendering without the surface material, the result is the same as having surface shading equal zero. A warning is normally displayed when you render particles without surface material.

TASK

- Test the different Render Types (s/w) for the particles with different software shading values. (see Figure 8-12a–8-12e.)

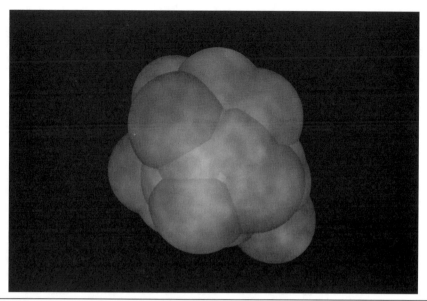

FIGURE 8-12a *Shading with the Blooby particle type*

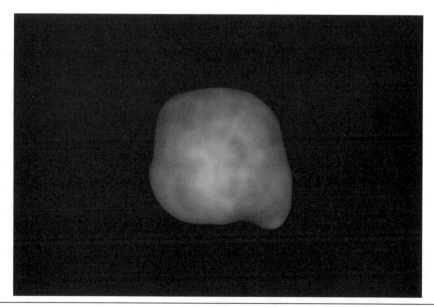

FIGURE 8-12b *Controlling the mat-clay look of the blooby surface with the help of its threshold value*

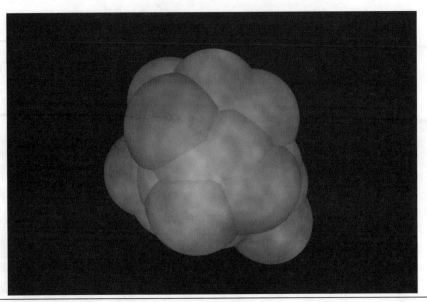

FIGURE 8-12c *Cloud particles created with a surface shading of 1.0*

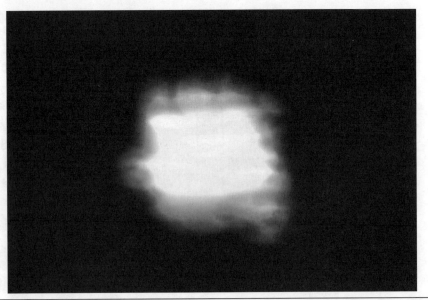

FIGURE 8-12d *Cloud particles creased with no surface shading (0.0)*

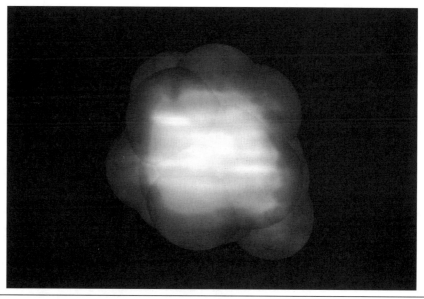

FIGURE 8-12e *Cloud particles with a surface shading of 0.5*

Create a cloud particle shader.

6. Name the shading group particleExplosionSG and the material particleExplosionM.
7. Assign the shading group to particleExplosion.
8. Map its Color attribute with a ramp texture.
9. Name the ramp texture ramp_Color.
10. Set the ramp with the following entry values (see Figure 8-13):

POSITION	RGB VALUES
0.0	1.0, 0.231, 0.0
0.120	0.0, 0.0, 0.0
0.22	1.0, 0.184, 0.0
0.480	0.964, 0.455, 0.0
0.555	0.829, 0.829, 0.829
0.675	1.0, 0.231, 0.0
0.865	0.323, 0.107, 0.0

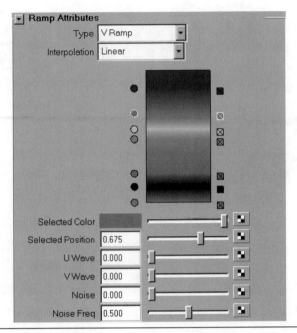

FIGURE 8-13   *The ramp color texture attribute*

11. Set the Repeat UV values of the placement node to (0.5,0.5).

TASK

- What is the result if you were to map the Life Color instead of the Color attribute?
- The ramp is mapped with the V Type. Try out other Ramp Types such as Circular Type. You should also be able to get very interesting results.
- Test out different values for the placement 2D values to get different mapping results.

12. Map the Transparency attribute of particleExplosionM to a texture ramp.

13. Set the ramp with the following entries:

POSITION	RGB VALUES
0.0	0.8, 0.8, 0.8
0.605	0.9, 0.9, 0.9
1.0	1.0

To represent the various stages of the explosion evolvement, you will animate the Glow Intensity of the particle shader.

14. Set the Glow Intensity of particleExplosionM with the values shown in Figure 8-14.

	Time	Value	InTan Type	OutTan Type
0	75	0.125	flat	flat
1	90	0.05	flat	flat
2	100	0.025	flat	flat

FIGURE 8-14   *Keyframe values of the glow intensity attribute*

A problem with mapping the color and transparency of the particles with a standard ramp is the regular pattern that each particle exhibits. The regular patterns are even clearer when the particles are closer to the camera. Hence, to break the regular patterns, you will increase the noise values as follows.

15. Set the Noise, Noise Frequency, and Noise Aspect to various values such as 0.5.

TASK

- Think of other methods of breaking the regular patterns when you map the color or transparency attributes of the shader with a 2D placement texture such as a ramp.

16. Map a Stucco 3D texture for the Blob Map attribute of particleExplosionM (see Figure 8-15).

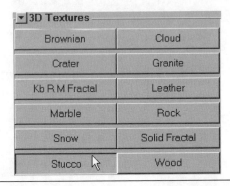

FIGURE 8-15　*Create a Stucco texture*

17. Name the Stucco texture blob_Stucco.
18. Edit blob_Stucco with the following values:

ATTRIBUTES	RGB VALUE
Shaker	20.0
Channel	1.0, 1.0, 1.0
Channel	0.37, 0.37, 0.37

SETTING THE LIGHTING

Light setup in explosion scenes is an extremely important process. In an explosion, a vast amount of light energy is emitted. Most of this energy is conspicuously displayed as a sudden flash of light, or glowing balls of fire. These obvious lights are not too difficult to control and create. However, what is difficult to present is the interaction of the various light sources bouncing off clouds of smoke, both internally and externally. This is partly due to the fact that most global illumination methods practiced are not able to fully simulate the actual volumetric nature of explosions. Therefore, in digitally simulated explosions most of the tricks lie in layering different parts of the explosion and carefully adjusting the layers to achieve the desired results.

In this explosion project, you will attempt to create two forms of light effects: the inner self-shadowing light effects, and the normal external illumination on the explosion volumes.

Inner Light

To create the inner glowing effects of explosion (i.e., inner light) you must create a point or volume light and center it around the explosion volume. The light is then animated with the movement of the explosion. In addition, the particles are rendered with an animated glowing intensity. The overall effects created would then be able to disperse as if the light is generated internally from the explosion.

External Light

To create more random light effects on the volume of explosions, a fractal noise is mapped to the external light intensity. This would create a varying degree of light intensity shining on the explosion. The overall effects would be more interesting than using a simple light with uniform intensity.

NOTE

At present, volume light is not implemented in Maya. However, if you have access to other software applications such as Alias PowerAnimator, RenderMan, or even the shareware BMRT, you will be able to create the effects of volume light. You can then combine the volume light effects by carefully designing your layouts and scenes.

Create the lighting

1. Create a point light source.
2. Transform the light source so that it is right at the center of the particleExplosion. Ensure that the light source is pointing straight towards the camera.
3. While leaving the other attributes as default, animate the color attribute of the light source as shown in the following table.

	RGB Color
FRAME 70	(1.0, 1.0, 1.0)
FRAME 80	(1.0, 0.373, 0.0)

The idea of the keyframe values is to alter the color of the explosion as time passes. You are encouraged to try out various color values at different keyframes based on your scene.

4. Create a spotlight source
5. Transform the spotlight source so that it is pointing at the emitter.
6. Set the various attributes of the light source as shown in Figure 8-16.
7. Map a standard fractal texture map to the light intensity of the spotlight.

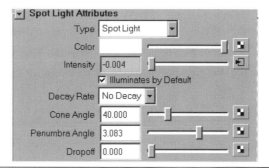

FIGURE 8-16 *Setting the spotlight attributes with a default fractal map*

Test-render

8. Test-render a selected frame of the animation.

You should get an image similar to the one shown in Figure 8-17.

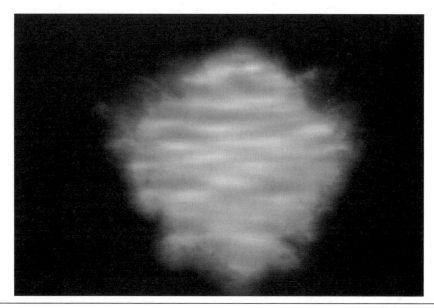

FIGURE 8-17 *A test rendered image*

NOTE

Depending on how you set up your explosion scene, an explosion may sometimes exhibit thick cumulus black smoke of particles. This effect can be achieved with the help of simple shadowing of the particle volume. However, at times when the shadows are not sufficient, you will have to create another layer of particle emission that is rendered with dark black shadings. When this layer of dark particles is carefully mixed with the bright orange-looking particles, they will be able to create an overall natural looking explosion effect. Figure 8-18 shows the images created with the added layer of black particles. This layer of black particles is an exact duplication of the particleExplosion except the shading group used is of complete black color. Compare this image with Figure 8-17.

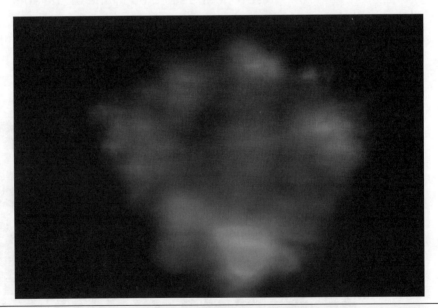

FIGURE 8-18   *A test rendered image with the black particles*

Setting the Collision Event

Since the explosion occurs within the tunnel, there will be particles hitting and bouncing off the walls of the tunnel. Instead of loading the actual complex tunnel model, you will simplify the animation with the use of the stand-in tunnel model for the collision.

9. Select Tunnel
10. From Particles ➤ Make Collide, make the tunnel a collision object.
11. Test the movement of the particles.
12. Ensure that the collision of the particles is natural.

TASK

*   Use the Collision Event method to experiment with the collision and the generation of the particles.
*   Bear in mind that if the animation does not make any visible difference with the collision set on, you should turn collision off. It will save you substantial computational time to turn off collision detection.

NOTE

In setting a scene, the choice of color for the scene is greatly influenced by the theme that you want to depict. In this scene, I have chosen to use a great deal of bluish color to create feelings of the cool nature of the metallic tunnel structures. You should feel free to use any theme and color to create your sets. However, you should pay particular attention to the interaction of the color of the explosion and the entire theme of the scene.

The complete tunnel model is not available on the companion CD. You will have to create it yourself. However, similar to the castle models that you saw in the previous chapter, this tunnel model was created without taking into account its reusability. In other words, it looks good in this angle, but it is pretty useless if your angle of view changed. You should be able to create such a one-time model quickly using the primitives in Maya.

THE SPACECRAFT ANIMATION

You will now create the animation for the spacecraft using motion path. In Maya, the motion path tool is simple and straight forward to use. Compared to the normal method of keyframe animation, motion path animation provides you with immediate feedback action and the path taken of the character. In addition, with the help of the graph editor, you can subsequently edit the path and change the speed and acceleration of the motion.

Create the motion path

1. Create a curve using the normal curve tool.
2. Edit the curve so that the path will follow the way you want the spacecraft to move (see Figure 8-19).

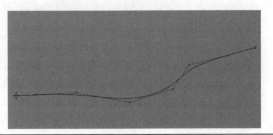

FIGURE 8-19   *Create the path curve using the CV tool*

3. Name the curve path.
4. Go to File ➢ Import and import an aircraft or space-craft model from the companion CD.
5. Translate the spacecraft model so that it is centered at the origin.
6. Group the model with the options shown in Figure 8-20 (center at the origin).

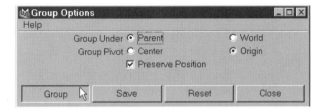

FIGURE 8-20 *Options for grouping the objects*

7. Name this node space_top.
8. Select the parent of the model (see Figure 8-21).

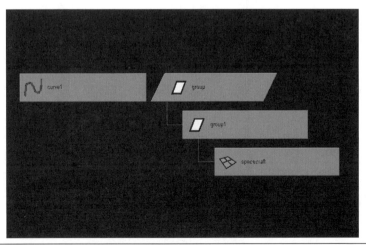

FIGURE 8-21 *Hierarchical order of the spacecraft model*

In Maya, whenever you click to select an object of the scene, the lowest leaf node is always picked. You can cycle up or down the hierarchy of the nodes with the arrow keys on your keyboard. This cycling method works whether you are in hypergraph, hypershade, outline, or the camera view window.

9. Shift select the path curve.
10. Go to Animate ➤ Paths ➤ Attach to Path -❑.

    The option window opens.

11. Set the options shown in Figure 8-22 for the motion path.

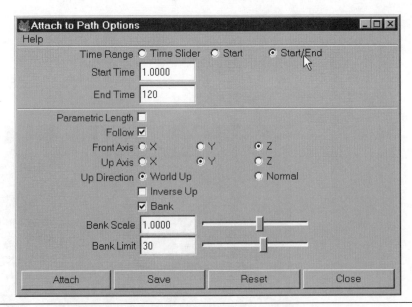

FIGURE 8-22   *Setting the motion path option*

12. Click create.

The motion path is created (see Figure 8-23).

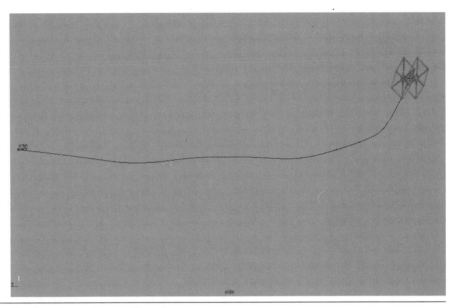

FIGURE 8-23 *Setting the motion path option*

A banking value of 30 is usually sufficient for you to create a nice turning of the spacecraft. Any higher value may create a wobbly effect when the spacecraft turns.

NOTE

13. Play back the animation. You should see the spacecraft moving along the motion path.

Fine-tune the Path Animation

There are generally two approaches to editing the path animation for your spacecraft. One approach is to edit the animation directly using the Graph Editor. Another is to edit using the hierarchy setup that you have just created.

Graph editor

14. Select the parent node of the space craft space_top.
15. Open the Graphic Editor from Window(Animation Editors ➤ Graph Editor.

The Graph Editor opens (see Figure 8-24).

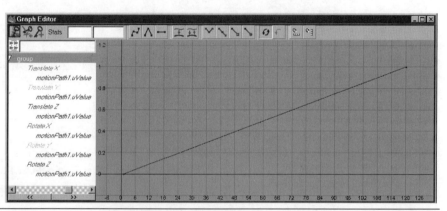

FIGURE 8-24   *A default linear graph of the motion path*

16. From within the Graph Editor, go to View ➤ Show Buffers Curve.

This will allow you to view the previous graph curve while you edit the curve to its new values (see Figure 8-25).

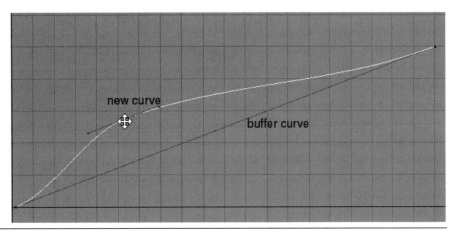

FIGURE 8-25 *Adjusting motion curves with the buffer turned on*

You will now edit the curve so that the spacecraft moves at a generally constant speed when it first enters the tunnel and starts speeding up when it tries to beat the gate before it closes.

17. From the Graph Editor, activate the Insert Keyframe Tools.
18. Using the middle mouse button, click anywhere along the curve where you want to control the movement. You should create an extra point near the middle and one near the end.
19. Click to activate the Move tool of the Graph Editor.
20. Adjust the curve so that it resembles Figure 8-26.

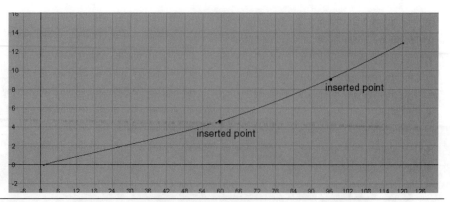

FIGURE 8-26 *Adjusted motion path curve*

NOTE

The use of the Graph Editor to control the motion path is straightforward. The tangent, i.e. gradient, of the curve resembles the velocity of the object. Thus, to move the object backwards, simply edit the curve so that the tangent goes into a negative value (see Figure 8-27).

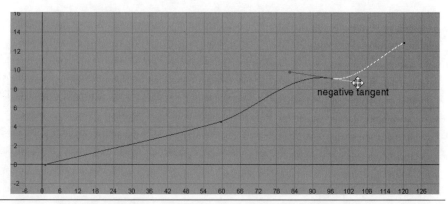

FIGURE 8-27 *Create a negative tangent to make the spacecraft move backwards*

TASK

- What does the curve shown in Figure 8-28 do to the spacecraft?

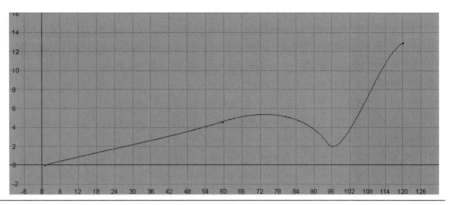

FIGURE 8-28 *Can you describe the animation created with this motion path curve?*

Hierarchical method

When creating motion curve, it is a common practice to first create a few layers of hierarchy before you use the top parent to set the desired motion path. This is especially important when you have a complex character on motion path and need to fine-tune the movement. For example, if you have decided that you would like to have the spacecraft flying slightly off the axis, simply set a rotation value at the lower level of the hierarchy and the spacecraft will fly in a slightly off-axis direction. Without this hierarchical structure, you would have to regroup the objects with the appropriate pivot points. In addition, the resulting animation might go completely haywire. This is due to the fact that transformation matrices are never commutative. This concept was discussed in Chapter 5.

In addition to creating offset values, you are also able to create subtle animation by simply keyframing the lower hierarchy nodes. For example, if you are required to make the spacecraft wobble a little when it is hit by the shock wave of the explosion, you can simply keyframe the appropriate transformation nodes of the lower hierarchy. Without this hierarchy, if you try to edit the motion path to create the wobbling effects, you may realize that your curve may not have enough edit points to achieve it.

SECONDARY ANIMATION

As explained above, secondary animation is a very important concept. You will create the secondary animation by shaking the camera. However, you should explore further the creation of other details.

Make the camera shake

1. Select the camera node.
2. Open the Expression Editor and enter the following expression:

    ```
    persp.translateY = 21.0 + 1.1*(linstep(0,5,time))*sin(10*time);
    persp.translateZ = 0.0 + 1.1*(linstep(0,5,time))*cos(10*time);
    ```

3. Play back your animation and you should see the camera jittering.

NOTE

If you test-render your animation with the complete detail model of a tunnel, you may realize that you are faced with some serious aliasing problems. This is a common problem of rendering small objects with small shivering movement. One way to solve this is to increase the tessellation of the entire models that makes up the tunnel. However, that would unnecessarily increase the computation time. Therefore, to solve this problem, since it is merely a camera movement, you can simply render at a slightly larger resolution size and with the help of simple composition, animate the composition frame according to how you want the camera to shake. This approach through composition has the added advantage of enabling the control of the jittering at post-production. The main disadvantage is that you have to render a slightly larger frame size for your animation (see Figures 8-29, 8-30, and 8-31).

FIGURE 8-29   *Render with a larger frame resolution*

FIGURE 8-30 *Jitter the view area to create the shaking camera effects*

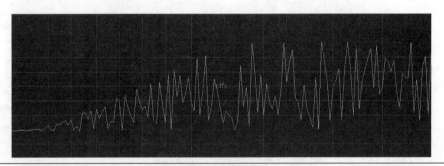

FIGURE 8-31 *The noise pattern used to jitter the camera node*

Rendering

Rendering an explosion requires careful consideration. The details of an explosion are often lost if you render the scene with multi-pixel or other filtering methods. In fact, the aliasing problem may be a blessing in disguise when rendering an explosion animation. Therefore, most of the time a medium-quality rendering is good enough to create explosion effects.

Test render a few frames of your animation and compare your results with the color plate 9.

POST-PRODUCTION

In this production, you should have at least the following layers:

1. The tunnel layer, where you render a detailed model of the tunnel.
2. The explosion layer, where you render only the explosion particles. Note that you must have the stand-in tunnel model present to set the collision.
3. The spacecraft layer, where you animate the spacecraft with the help of the motion path.

Play back the animation, **chpt08.mov.** You should get a similar results to this movie.

CONCLUSION

In this chapter, you learned how to create an explosion. You should now be comfortable controlling different aspects of explosion effects. In the next chapter, you will learn to create more subtle air effects.

EXERCISE

Test your skills with the following additional animation exercise:

1. Using motion path, animate another spacecraft chasing the first one.
2. As the second spacecraft catches the first one, animate its collision against the wall of the tunnel and the explosion as a result of the collision.
3. Create a typical mushroom explosion effects.
4. Research and create a shock wave effects. You can further emphasize the shock wave effects with the help of the glass shattering etc.
5. Add fire effects that you learned in the previous chapter.
6. Do a camera animation with the camera following behind the spacecraft.

9

MAKING DUST
AND CLOUDS

INTRODUCTION

There are two basic types of air particle effects; one that is visible, with obvious edges and color, and another that is less visible, without clear boundaries defining its existence. In the previous chapter, you saw an example of the former type, explosion. In this chapter, you will see an example of much more subtle air effects, *dust*.

Although this example focuses on dust effects, with some simple tweaking the methods and approaches illustrated here, will allow you to create other similar subtle air effects such as steam, smoke, and fog. In addition, you will also be introduced to creating various *cloud* effects, using a procedural approach, a geometrical approach, as well as a particle system approach.

When creating subtle air effects, you must be aware of two important elements: *turbulence* and *lighting*. The turbulence element affects how your particles travel and get turbulated along their path. Their animated movement will reveal the relative weight of the particles and their physical properties. Though the particles are subtle and small, the lighting element has tremendous effect on the final imagery. The scattering of the light and the presence or absence of the particle self-shadowing will affect the mood of the scene.

PRE-PRODUCTION

Figure 9-1 shows the sketch required for your work. The scene is set in a beyond-the-world environment where blocks of tree-like structures are enacted above the ground. A light moves slowly upwards. As it moves, the dust and sand became unsettled and the sky gets darker. Towards the end of the scene, the light disappears slowly and the gate to another part of the world opens.

TASKS

- Your main task is to produce the subtle presence of the sand and dust effects. What is important here is the establishment of the mood as the light travels upwards and the gate to the fantasy opens. Your effects add to the mysterious ambience of the scene.

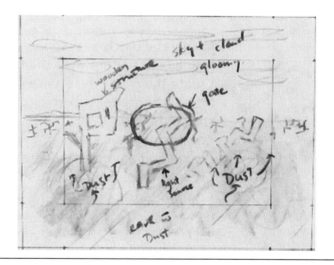

FIGURE 9-1   *Sketch*

In addition, you are required to model the wooden blocks present in the scene as well as the opening of the gate. The entire cut will last for about 5 seconds.

ANALYZE THE PICTURE

TASK

- Think about how you would create the model of the wooden blocks.
- What dynamic fields would you use to control the turbulence of the air particles?

- How would you separate the rendering into different layers and composite them?

APPROACHES

The scene is divided into the following individual layers. Each layer is modeled and animated separately. They are composited together at the end of the production.

1. Model the block of shapes.
2. Model and texture-map the ground.
3. Create the dust effects with movement.
4. Model the scene with an appropriate lighting to create the mood.
5. Create and animate the moving light.
6. Create and animate the gate.
7. Create the background clouds.
8. Composite the different parts of the scene.

PRODUCTION AND TESTING

Create a new project

1. Create a new project with the default settings.
2. Name the project Dust_Cloud.

TASK

- As you can see in the sketch (see Figure 9-1), the blocks of shapes are fairly rectangular in nature. What are the appropriate modeling approach and tools that you would use to model them? Take note that there are several shapes, of similar structure, but with slightly different orientation and branches.

The blocks of shapes in the final animation were in fact created using an *L-system* that I wrote using MEL. An L-system is a procedural modeling system that is particularly appropriate for creating models such as trees and leaves. For this section, whatever method you employ, you should consider the following factors:

Create the blocks of shapes

- The blocks of shapes are are not animating.
- There are sharp edges and angles.
- The shapes are all similar with some alteration in their angles and size.

Based on these factors, a polygonal modeling approach may be more efficient and productive.

3. Press F3 to switch to the Modeling Menu.
4. Go to Create ➤ Polygon Primitives ➤ Cube.

A polygonal cube is created at the origin.

5. Press F11 to activate the hotkey to select the polygonal faces.
6. Click on the top polygon face.
7. Go to Polygons ➤ Extrude.

The Manipulator tool should appear as shown in Figure 9-2. If you do not see it, go to Modify ➤ Transformation Tools ➤ Show Manipulator Tool.

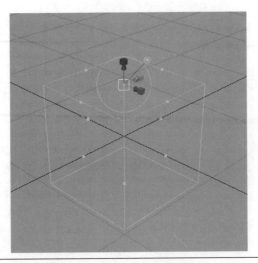

FIGURE 9-2   *Polygonal modeling with the help of the Manipulator Tool*

8.   Select Manipulator tool and extract the face upwards (see Figure 9-3).

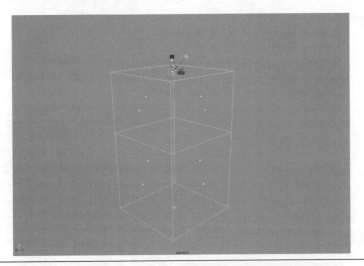

FIGURE 9-3   *Extruding the polygonal faces with the help of the Manipulator Tool*

9. Keep repeating the process of picking and extruding different polygonal faces.
10. An example of the shape that you may end up with is shown in Figure 9-4.

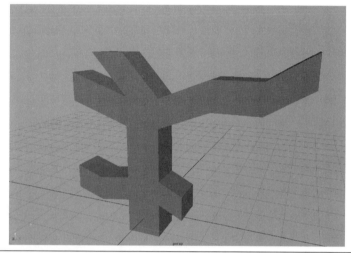

FIGURE 9-4 *An example of the tree-like structure model*

11. When you are satisfied, select the polygonal object that you have just created.
12. Go to Edit Polygon ➢ Smooth -❑

The Polygon Smooth Option window opens.

13. Enter 2 for the value of Divisions and click on Smooth (see Figure 9-5).

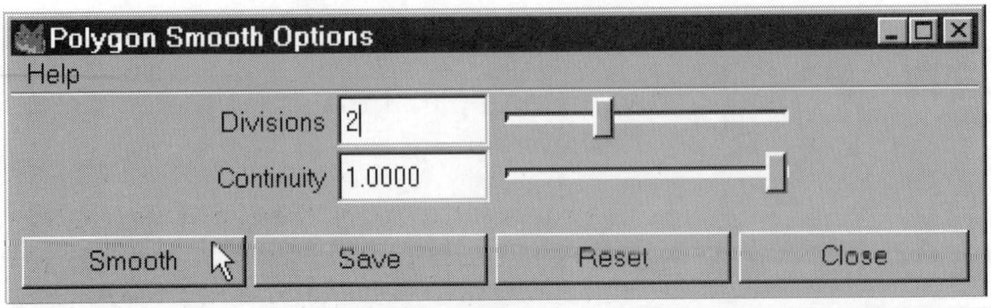

Polygon Smooth Options

Help

Divisions 2

Continuity 1.0000

| Smooth | Save | Reset | Close |

FIGURE 9-5   *The smoothing options for polygonal models*

14. The polygon is smoothed and a figure similar to the
    in Figure 9-6 is created.

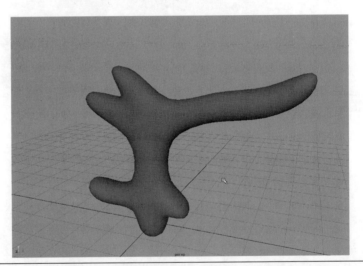

FIGURE 9-6   *The tree-like structure after smoothing*

15. Repeat the above process and create as many differ-
    ent sets of the block of shapes as desired.
16. Save the shapes. You will import them into the scene
    later.

Create the Ground Plane

TASK

- You have already created at least one kind of ground: the seabed in Chapter Six. Now, what do you think are the important things that you should consider when creating a simple geometry like a floor for the scene in this chapter?

When creating a ground plane for your scene, there are several basic but crucial factors that you have to consider:

- What is the angle of view and will the camera be moving? If so, the ground plane has to be sufficiently large so that when you animate the camera, you don't see the edge of the ground.
- Will there be a displacement map on the ground plane? If so, you have to ensure that there are sufficient details of the UV spans on the geometry of the plane. If there are not enough CVs, no matter how detailed your displacement map, you will not get the desired details.

1. Create a new scene.
2. Go to Create ➢ NURBS Primitives ➢ Plane.

A plane is created at the origin.

3. Rename the plane to ground.
4. Set the ground geometry information as shown in Figure 9-7.

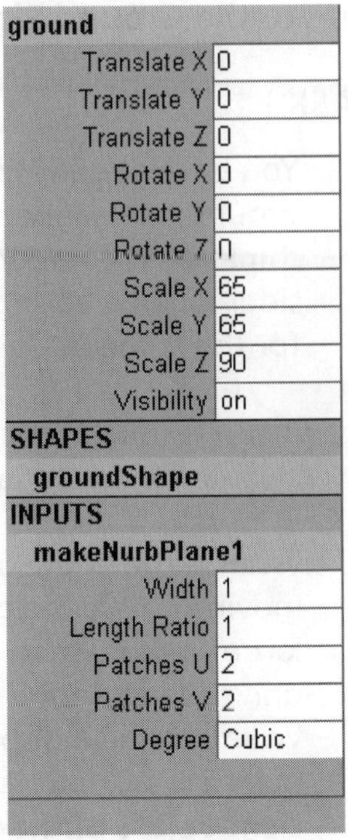

ground	
Translate X	0
Translate Y	0
Translate Z	0
Rotate X	0
Rotate Y	0
Rotate Z	0
Scale X	65
Scale Y	65
Scale Z	90
Visibility	on
SHAPES	
groundShape	
INPUTS	
makeNurbPlane1	
Width	1
Length Ratio	1
Patches U	2
Patches V	2
Degree	Cubic

FIGURE 9-7   *The channel information of the ground geometry*

Create the Dust Particles

To cover the entire ground plane with sufficient particles, it is more appropriate to use a surface emitter.

5. Create a new plane.
6. Rename the plane dust_emitter.
7. Scale the plane to a value of 27 along its X, Y, and Z axes.
8. With the plane selected, go to Particles ➤ Add Emitter -❑.
9. Set the option values as shown in Figure 9-8.

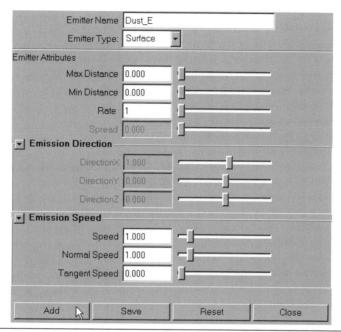

FIGURE 9-8   *The dust emitter creation options*

10. Click on Add to add the surface emitter to the plane.

Play back the animation and you should see the particles emitted from the plane.

11. Rename the default particle Dust_particles.

Create the Windy Effects

The particles need to move with turbulence as if blown by the wind. You will achieve this using a dynamic field.

12. Go to Fields ➣ Create Air -❑.

The Air Option (Create) window opens.

In Maya, there are a few default air effects that allow you to quickly create the desired air effects. They are the Wind, Wake, *and* Fan. *Refer to the Maya manual for details.*

13. Click on the Fan button to use the default fan option.
14. Set the rest of the options as shown in Figure 9-9.

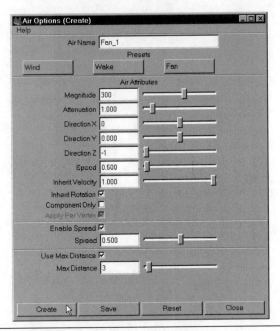

FIGURE 9-9   *Setting the Air dynamic field options to Fan*

Create more windy effects

15. Repeat the above steps and create four additional dynamic Air fields.
16. The table below shows a summary of the additional dynamic effects that you should have created.

AIR NAME	MAGNITUDE	ATTENUTATION	DIRECTION X	DIRECTION Y	DIRECTION Z
Fan_2	250	1	0	0	−1
Fan_3	200	1	0	0	−1
Fan_4	250	1	0	0	1
Fan_5	250	1	0	0	1

17. Set the rest of the parameter values the same as Fan_1.

Position all the windy effects

18. Position all the Air dynamics that you have just created as shown in the table below:

AIR DYNAMIC	FAN_1	FAN_2	FAN_3	FAN_4	FAN_5
Translate X	−3.2	2.0	8.2	−9.0	4.8
Translate Y	0.0	0.0	0.0	0.0	0.0
Translate Z	20.0	14.5	8.0	−27.0	−16.0

Connect the dynamics effects

19. Go to Window ➢ Animation Editors ➢ Dynamic Relationships… .
20. Connect the Dust_particles to each Fan_# (see Figure 9-10).

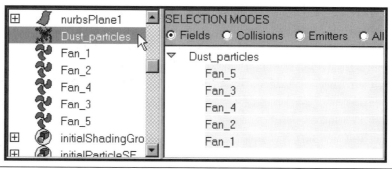

FIGURE 9-10 *Connecting the dust particles with the air dynamic fields*

Animate the Movement of the Air Dynamics

In order to create the effect in which the air appears and starts blowing upwards, you will animate the movement of the Air dynamics.

21. Select Fan_1, Fan_2, Fan_3, Fan_4, and Fan_5.
22. Highlight the Translate Z value from the Channel box.
23. While in frame 1, keyframe the Translate Z values.
24. Go to frame 60.
25. Translate the Z values according to the table below:

FAN_#	TRANSLATE Z VALUES
1	−23.0
2	−18.0
3	−11.6
4	25.5
5	11.6

26. Set the keyframe with the above values at frame 60 if the keyframes are not automatically set.

NOTE

The keyframe will be automatically set whenever you change your values at another frame. This is the default setting when you have your SetKey options set to the Current Time (see Figure 9-11).

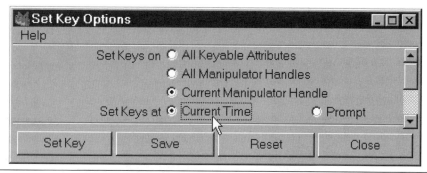

FIGURE 9-11   *With the Current Time option, keyframes are automatically set when you change the frame and values*

27. Play back the animation and you should see the particles being blown away as the dynamics fields move.

Fine-tune the Particles' Movement

To create a more natural and realistic particle movement, you will add in more dynamics to control the particles.

TASK

• Try fine-tuning the movement on your own and see what additional dynamic effects you think are needed to create a more natural and realistic effect.

You will add two more dynamic effects: *Gravity* and *Turbulence* dynamics. The gravity field will pull the particles back to the ground after they are being blown upwards by the air dynamics. The turbulence field will create more turbulence to the air particle movement.

28. Create a Gravity dynamic field.
29. Name it CG and set the parameters shown in Figure 9-12:

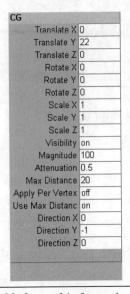

FIGURE 9-12   *The gravity dynamic field channel information*

30. Notice that the CG field is translated upwards by 22 units. In this way, given the attenuation, you will have a more gradual Gravity result based on the distance.
31. From the Dynamic Relationship Editor, link the Dust_particles with the CG dynamics.
32. Create a Turbulence dynamic field.
33. Name it Turbulence.
34. With the Turbulence selected, go to Window ➤ Expression Editor... and enter the following expression:

Turbulence.magnitude = 6*sind(10*frame);

35. This will cause the Turbulence magnitude to change its values as a function of the sine curve.
36. From the Dynamic Relationship Editor, link the Dust_particles with the Turbulence dynamics.
37. Play back the animation and you should see a general movement of the particles. Fine-tune and adjust the parameters as necessary for your animation.

SETTING THE PHYSICAL PROPERTIES OF THE PARTICLES

Now that you have created the movement, you will set the physical properties of the particles.

Set the particle properties

1. Open the Attribute Editor of Dust_particle.
2. Set its Particle Render Type to Cloud (s/w).
3. Click to add the attributes for the Current Render Type.

The default Radius, Surface Shading, and Threshold attributes are added.

4. Set the Radius to 1.0 and leave the rest of the parameters as the default values.

Now that you have created the movement, you will set the rendering of the particles.

Create a new particle Cloud Shading Group

5. From the Multilister or Hypershader, create a new Volumetric Particle Cloud.
6. Name it DustSG and its material DustM.
7. Set the Color attribute as shown in the Figure 9-13.

FIGURE 9-13   *Color values for the Color attribute of the dust shader*

8. Set the Transparency attribute as shown in the Figure 9-14.

FIGURE 9-14   *Color values for the Transparency attribute of the dust shader*

9. Map the Blob Map attribute to the Cloud texture (see Figure 9-15).

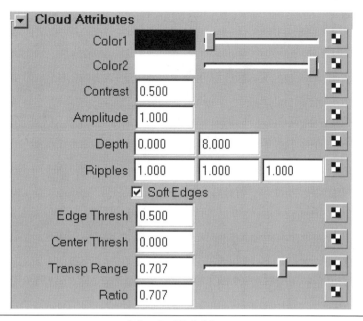

FIGURE 9-15 *Cloud texture parameters used for the Blob Map*

Texture map the ground

10. Create a Lambert shading group.
11. Name the shading group as groundSG and its material as groundM.
12. Set the Color attribute as shown in Figure 9-16.

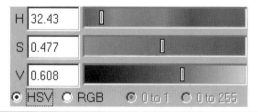

FIGURE 9-16 *Color values for the Color attribute of the ground shader*

13. Bump Map the material to a 2D Fractal as shown in Figure 9-17.

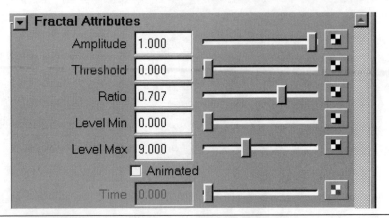

FIGURE 9-17　*Fractal material attributes used for bump mapping the ground*

14. Assign groundSG to the ground geometry.

CREATE THE SAND EFFECTS

Add Another Emitter

You will notice that the particle created is just for the dust and not for the sand. To add sand, you will duplicate and create another emitter.

15. Select the plane dust_emitter.
16. Add another particle emitter from particle ➢ Add Emitter.
17. Name this emitter as Sand_E.
18. Set its attributes the same as Dust_E.
19. Set the new particles created to the same attributes as Dust_particles, except that the Radius of the Cloud (s/w) attribute is 0.065.
20. Name the particle Sand_particles.

Create shading type for the sand

21. Create a new Particle Cloud shading group type.
22. Name the shading group SandSG and the material as SandM.
23. Set the Color attribute as shown in Figure 9-18.

FIGURE 9-18 *Color values for the Color attribute of the sand shader*

24. Set the Transparency attribute as shown in Figure 9-19.

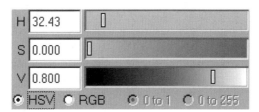

FIGURE 9-19 *Color values for the Transparency attribute of the sand shader*

25. Set the rest of the shading parameters as shown in Figure 9-20.

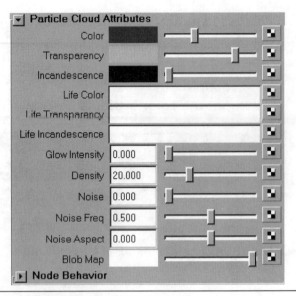

FIGURE 9-20　*Attribute values for the sand shader*

CACHING THE PARTICLE EFFECTS

In creating the dusty effects, the particles should remain on the ground like the real dust. They should not be generated as time passes. Therefore, you will now set the initial state of the particles and fix its maximum number so that no more particles are generated.

Setting the initial state

26. Unlink all the dynamic field forces from Dust_particles.
27. Unlink all the dynamic field forces from Sand_particles, if you have linked them.
28. Play back the animation.
29. Stop the playback when you are happy with the amount of particles in the scene.

30. Select Dust_particles.
31. Go to Solvers ➢ Initial State ➢ Set for Selected.

This will set the current state of the dust particles as the initial state.

32. Go to the Attribute Editor of Dust_particles.
33. Set its Max Count attribute to the same value as the Count number shown.

An example of the result that is used for this project is shown in Figure 9-21.

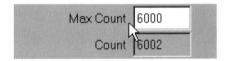

FIGURE 9-21 *Limit the number of dust particles with the Max Count parameter*

34. Select Sand_particles.
35. Go to Solvers ➢ Initial State ➢ Set for Selected.
36. This will set the current state of the sand particles as the initial state.
37. Go to the Attribute Editor of Sand_particles.
38. Set its Max Count attribute to the same value as the Count number shown.

An example of the result that is used for this project is shown in Figure 9-24.

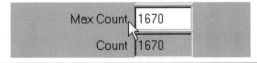

FIGURE 9-22 *Limit the number of sand particles with the Max Count parameter*

39. Link all the previous dynamic field forces back to Dust_particles and Sand_particles.

THE LIGHT

Now you will create the point light.

Create the light source

1. Press F5 to switch to the Rendering menu.
2. Go to Lights ➤ Create Point Light.

A point light source is created at the origin.

3. Name the point light lightDust.
4. Open the relationship editor from Window ➤ Relationship Editors ➤ Light Linking ➤ Light-Centric…
5. Unlink lightDust so that it does not shine on any of the objects in the scene.

Although this light is unlinked from the scene, this does not stop its opticalFX from being rendered out.

6. Close the Relationship Editor.
7. Under the Light Effects section, click on the Light Glow map button (see Figure 9-23).

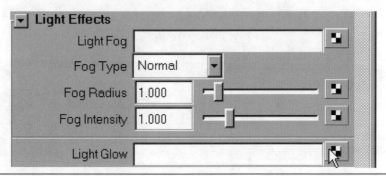

FIGURE 9-23   *Mapping the Light Glow attribute*

A default opticalFX node is created for the point light. Its attributes are shown in the Attribute Editor.

8. From the attribute editor, set the various parameters of the optical effects as shown in Figure 9-24.

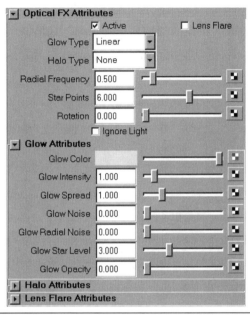

FIGURE 9-24 *Keyframe values for the Glow Intensity*

9. The Glow Color attribute is set with the values shown in Figure 9-25.

FIGURE 9-25 *Keyframe values for the Y translation values of the light source*

Animate the Light Source

You will now animate the light source. You will animate both the movement of the light source as well as the attached Glow intensity of the optical FX.

10. Keyframe the Glow Intensity of the Optical FX light source as shown in Figure 9-26.

This will ensure that the optical FX is invisible in the beginning and appears as the light moves upwards and eventually loses its intensity again.

Keys				
	Time	Value	InTan Type	OutTan Type
0	1	0	flat	flat
1	14	0	flat	flat
2	20	1	flat	flat
3	75	1	flat	flat
4	80	0	flat	flat

FIGURE 9-26   *Keyframe values for the Glow intensity*

11. Animate the Y-axis value of the light source (see Figure 9-27).

Keys				
	Time	Value	InTan Type	OutTan Type
0	15	0	spline	spline
1	75	7.5	spline	spline

FIGURE 9-27   *Keyframe values for the Y translation values of the light source*

NOTE

When you render the scene, the Optical FX glow appears to be passing through the object, you can simply select the pointlight source and scale the spherical shape to a smaller size.

THE GATE

The gate is created by simply overlaying several layers of ramp and animating the ramp position as well as the ramp color values.

Create the gate geometry

1. Create a default NURBS plane.
2. Name it gate.
3. Transform the gate to the values shown below:

TRANSFORMATION	VALUES
Translate	3.68, 5.47, –1.97
Rotate	0, 0, 90
Scale	18.48, 36.17, 28.36

Create the gate shading group

4. Create a Lambert shading group for the plane.
5. Name the shading group GateSG and its material GateM.
6. Assign the shading group to the gate geometry.

Map a Sequence of Images

In Maya, besides the normal texture map, you are able to map a sequence of images to a geometry. This allows you to easily create animation such as a video board.

In this animation, you will next map a series of images to GateM.

7. Map the Color attribute to a file texture (see Figure 9-28).

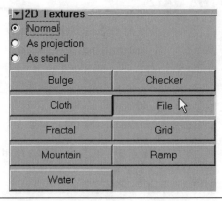

FIGURE 9-28 *Create a user input file texture*

8. Open the Attribute Editor of the file texture.
9. Change the default name of file1 texture to fileGateImages.
10. Click on the map button and load in an image of a sequence.
11. Keyframe the Frame Extension parameter to go according to your required animation.

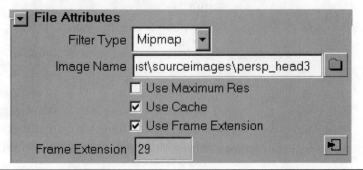

FIGURE 9-29 *Mapping a series of images by keyframing the Frame Extension parameter*

This series of images is not provided in the companion CD. You should load in any sequence of images for the purpose of this project. You may, for example, load in the images that you created from the previous projects.

An example of the animated frame extension used for the project is shown in Figure 9-30.

Keys

	Time	Value	InTan Type	OutTan Type
0	109	29	spline	spline
1	150	70	spline	spline

FIGURE 9-30 *Keyframe values for the Frame Extension parameter*

12. If the images that you loaded are not oriented correctly, simply go to the place2dtexture of the file GateImage and set appropriate values for Rotate Frame.

Create the edge of the gate

13. Open the Attribute Editor of GateM.
14. Map the Transparency attribute to a standard Fractal texture.
15. Name the fractal Trans_Fractal.
16. Set the fractal with the attributes shown in Figure 9-31.

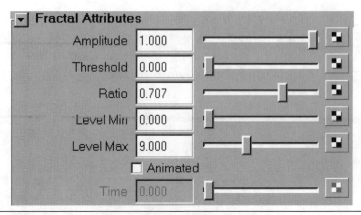

FIGURE 9-31   *Fractal attributes values used for mapping the Transparency of the Gate shader*

17. Map the Color Gain and Color Offset attributes of Trans_Fractal to a ramp texture.

The Color Gain attribute is used to create and control the round ring that serves as a frame for the file images. The Color Offset attribute is used to control the blackout area of the image so that as the ring expands, only what should be seen within the ring will be shown (see Figure 9-32).

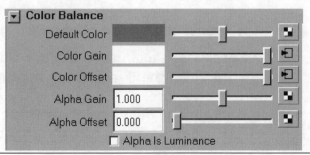

FIGURE 9-32   *Mapping the Color Gain and Color Offset attributes*

18. Name the ramp texture for the Color Gain attribute ramp_colorGain.
19. Name the ramp texture for the Color Offset attribute ramp_colorOffset.
20. For the ramp_colorGain, set the various parameters as shown in the following table and in Figures 9-33 through 9-36. Notice that the positions of the ramp entries are keyframed according to the timing for the opening of the gate.

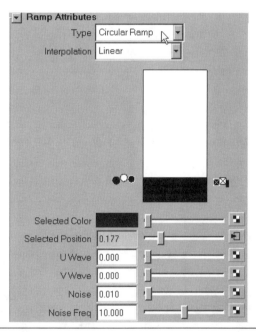

FIGURE 9-33 *Ramp texture used for the Color Gain attribute*

RAMP ENTRY	RAMP COLOR	POSITION KEYFRAMES
0	0, 0, 0	figure 09_034.tif
1	1,1,1	figure 09_035.tif
2	0,0,0	figure 09_036.tif

Keys	Time	Value	InTan Type	OutTan Type
0	75	0.01	spline	spline
1	120	0.51	spline	spline

FIGURE 9-34   *Keyframe values for the Color Gain ramp entry 0*

Keys	Time	Value	InTan Type	OutTan Type
0	75	0.02	spline	spline
1	120	0.52	spline	spline

FIGURE 9-35   *Keyframe values for the Color Gain ramp entry 1*

Keys	Time	Value	InTan Type	OutTan Type
0	75	0	spline	spline
1	120	0.5	spline	spline

FIGURE 9-36   *Keyframe values for the Color Gain ramp entry 2*

21. For the ramp_colorOffset, set the various parameters as shown in Figure 9-37.

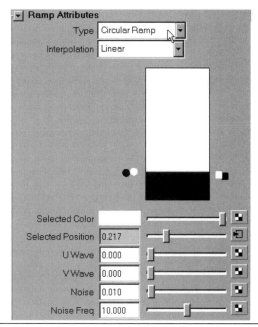

FIGURE 9-37 *Ramp texture used for the Color Offset attribute*

22. Set and animate the ramp entries as shown in the table below and in Figures 9-38 to 9-40.

RAMP ENTRY	RAMP COLOR	FIGURES
0	1,1,1	figure 09_013.tif
1	0,0,0	figure 09_014.tif

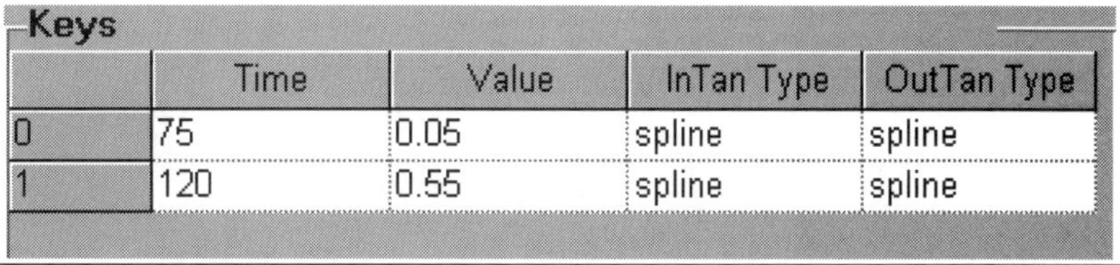

Keys		Time	Value	InTan Type	OutTan Type
0		75	0.05	spline	spline
1		120	0.55	spline	spline

FIGURE 9-38 *Keyframe values for the Color Offset ramp entry 0*

Keys				
	Time	Value	InTan Type	OutTan Type
0	75	0.04	spline	spline
1	120	0.54	spline	spline

FIGURE 9-39   *Keyframe values for the Color Offset ramp entry 1*

23. Play back the animation and you should see the movement of the rings.

You have now completed creation of the various elements of the scene. The following instructions are presented to complete the scene.

CAMERA

Set up the camera based on the given sketch.

TASK

- In the scene, the gate is facing the camera directly. In most camera settings, it is seldom the case that an object is directly facing the camera. This concept was discussed in the introductory chapters.
- You should attempt to change the view of the camera so that it may better convey the idea that the gate is opening from nowhere.

ENHANCING THE DEPTH

Load in the tree models

- Load in the tree models that you have created.

- Scale the tree models to fit into the scene.
- Create simple wood texture to texture the tree.

Add in the Fog

Most of the time, the models and scenes that you build in the CG world are not in direct proportion to the actual size of objects in the real world. Hence various tricks and methods are used to create the believability. One common method is to use fog to increase the depth of the scene.

In the previous tutorials such as the underwater scene, you have used fog to enhance the scene depth. However, what was not obvious is that fog has a tendency to flatten out the light and to reduce highlights. It also absorbs a considerable part of the light.

Thus, when you employ the use of fog in most scenes, you should try to increase the contrast and intensity of the light. For example, the file texture mapped on the gate geometry should be adjusted with greater Color Gain.

From your experience in creating the fog for the under water scene, you should be comfortable in applying the same instructions to complete the scene. Therefore the instructions are left as an exercise for you to explore.

Final Rendering

Test-render your scene. Compare the result of your rendering with the color plate 8. Open and play the movie file chpt09.mov.

The following instructions present the creation of the cloud animation. Upon completing the instructions, you should apply the cloud animation to your scene and compare your results with the movie file chpt09.mov.

Cloud Creation

In creating outdoor animation, it is almost inevitable that your camera will show part of the sky. It is possible that the sky is cloudless, however, a cloudless sky is like a wall without any decoration. It is a picture of loneliness. Having clouds in the sky will often help create a better depth. A well-presented cloud will give a better perspective and help establish the mood of the picture.

Clouds change and take many different forms. Clouds seen in the daylight, sunset, rain, summer, winter, and so on, are all different. While there are cumulus, cirrus, and stratus clouds, you should learn their artistic interpretation rather than the technical names.

There are several ways to create clouds. The following are the three main ways to create clouds. Depending on the requirements of your animation, you may be employing any one or a combination of all of them.

Procedural Cloud. In Maya, the easiest way to create a background of cloud texture is to create an environment texture map. The advantage of using the environment texture map is that, being procedural in nature, you can animate the various parameters and easily fine-tune them. For example, you can animate the movement of the cloud, and change from a daylight, sunny cloud pattern, to a golden sunset cloud. However, one disadvantage is that the cloud could tend to look flat and it is rather difficult, if not impossible, to get a great looking self-shadowing cloud from this procedural method alone.

Create a new project

1. Create a new project with the default settings.
2. Name the project Cloud_Examples.

Create an Image Plane

The common method of mapping an environment cloud texture is via the use of the *camera image plane*. Using the image plane, the environment texture will appear to move with the movement of the camera. This continuous, seamless environment movement is especially necessary if your camera animates and moves freely in an outdoor scene. Another method of, creating a plane and mapping the environment texture, has the shortfall of the plane getting different views when the camera animates.

3.   Open the attribute editor of the persp camera.
4.   Under the Environment section, click on the Create button next to the Image Plane.

An image plane is created and its Attribute Editor is opened (see Figure 9-40).

FIGURE 9-40   *Create an image plane*

Create an environment Sky texture

5.   Under the Image Plane Attributes section, click on the Map button (see Figure 9-41).

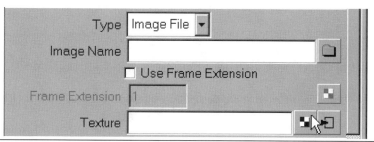

FIGURE 9-41   *Mapping a texture as an image plane*

The Create Render Node window opens.

6. From the Create Render Node window, click on the Env Sky button to create an environment sky texture (see Figure 9-42).

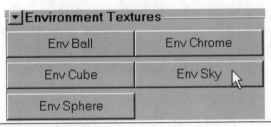

FIGURE 9-42   *Create an Environment Sky texture*

Create a Crater texture

7. Create also a Crater texture.

This texture will be used as a texture map to map the cloud texture of the Env Sky (see Figure 9-43).

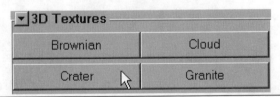

FIGURE 9-43   *Create a crater texture*

Edit the attribute of Env Sky

8. Open the Attribute Editor of Env Sky texture that you have just created.

9. Click and open the Cloud Attributes section, if it is not already available (see Figure 9-44).

FIGURE 9-44 *Turn on the Use Texture check box*

10. Turn on the checker box button Use Texture.
11. Drag and drop the Crater texture that you have just created to the Cloud Texture attribute of Env Sky (see Figure 9-45).

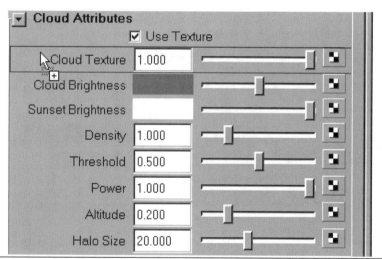

FIGURE 9-45 *Drag and drop the crater texture to the cloud texture attribute*

This would map the outAlpha value of the crater texture to the Cloud texture.

Adjust the 3D Texture node of the Env Sky

12. Do a test-render.

You will probably not see anything other than red and grey colors. This is because you need to adjust the 3D Texture of Env Sky so that the floor and sky of the texture are properly oriented

13. Select the place3dTexture of the Env Sky.
14. Adjust its rotation and scaling values to the values shown in Figure 9-46.

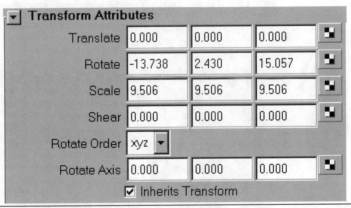

FIGURE 9-46   *Transform values of the 3D placement node of the Env Sky texture*

15. Do another test-render. You should get an image similar to that shown in Figure 9-47.

FIGURE 9-47   *A test render of the procedural cloud*

Fine-tuning the Cloud

With the cloud created, all you need to do now is fine-tune it by adjusting the various attributes of the Env Sky.

16. To change the cloud color, adjust the Cloud Brightness attributes of Env Sky (see Figure 9-48).

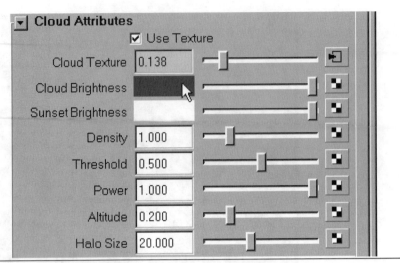

FIGURE 9-48   *Adjust the Cloud Brightness attribute to get different cloud color*

17. To adjust the sky color, adjust the Sky Brightness under the Atmospheric Settings of Env Sky (see Figure 9-49).

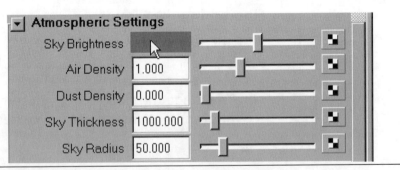

FIGURE 9-49   *Adjust the Sky Brightness attribute to get different sky color*

18. To animate and change the patterns of the cloud, adjust the place3dTexture of the Crater node.
19. To adjust the patterns and density of the cloud, adjust the Density of the Cloud attributes.

In this example, you have used Crater as the cloud texture. Good results can also be obtained using any other fractal texture such as the 2D Fractal and 3D Brownian and Solid Fractal textures.

The sky background of the sea animation (chpt06.mov) was also created using the exact same method as described here.

TASK

• Create an animation where the clouds and atmosphere change from a sunny clear sky, to a cloudy sky, and finally to a dark cloudy sky before rain.

Notice in the chpt09.mov movie file, the animation of the procedural cloud also goes from bright daylight to a dark gloomy set.

Geometrical Cloud. To have precise and direct control over every detail of the cloud such as the self-shadows, size and location of the cloud, you can choose to directly model and texture the cloud. This method is inexpensive and you can generate realistic looking clouds very quickly. However, if you were to have a large sky filled with overlapping clouds, this method may turn out to be too tedious and time-consuming.

Create the cloud geometry

1. From Create ➢ NURBS Primitive ➢ Sphere, create a few spheres.

These spheres will function as the geometry of the cloud in which appropriate textures will be applied on them.

2. Place these sphere in an overlapping position as shown in Figure 9-50.

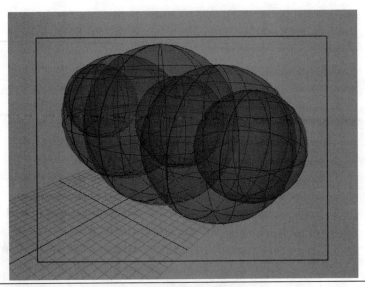

FIGURE 9-50   *Positions of the sphere geometry used for the cloud*

Create the cloud texture

3.   From the Create Render Node window, create a 3D Cloud texture (see Figure 9-51).

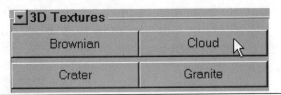

FIGURE 9-51   *Create a 3D Cloud texture*

Edit the cloud texture attribute

4.   Open the Attribute Editor of the Cloud texture that you have just created.

5.   Edit the attribute to the values shown in Figure 9-52.

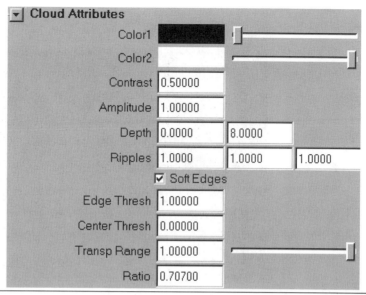

FIGURE 9-52 *The values used for the Cloud texture*

6. Drag and drop the Cloud texture to the default Lambert shading group's Color and Transparency attributes.
7. From the shading group's Special Effects section, set the Glow intensity to 0.8.
8. Click also on the Hide Source check box to set to On.
9. Set up a simple lighting.
10. Test-render the image.

You should get an image similar to the one shown in Figure 9-53.

FIGURE 9-53   *A rendered image view of the geometry cloud*

The background image used in chpt025.mov is an example of such a cloud.

Particle Cloud.   Creating clouds using particle systems is the most versatile but expensive method. As the cloud is volumetric in nature, you will be able to fly through it without noticing any edges or surfaces of the cloud, much like a real fly-through when an airplane passes through a cloud. In addition, in Maya, you can easily control the animation of the cloud using dynamic simulation. For example, if you have a scene where clouds start parting and sun rays shine through, you can easily achieve this in Maya. An example of such animation is the chpt10.mov.

When creating a particle cloud, it is very important to pay attention to the employment of light. As people are accustomed to seeing real clouds dispersing through the sunlight and casting of shadows within the clouds, a badly positioned light will result in washing out the entire mood and atmosphere otherwise created by particle clouds. There are generally at least two places where you have to position your light source: within the cloud and outside the cloud. The light position within the cloud will account for the way that real light rays are being dispersed by the cloud particles and result in the illumination of the cloud within. The external light will be the atmospheric light that shines on the cloud itself.

Create the cloud particles

1. Press F4 to go to the Dynamics menu.
2. Using Particles ≻ Particle Tool, create a set of particles.
3. From its Attribute Editor, edit the Particle Render Type from Points to Cloud (s/w) (see Figure 9-54).

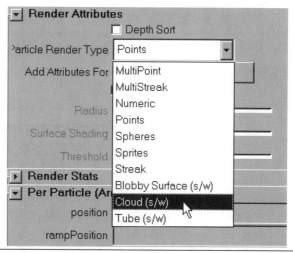

FIGURE 9-54 *Setting the Particle Render Type to Cloud*

4. Figure 9-55 shows an example of the arrangement of the cloud particle position.

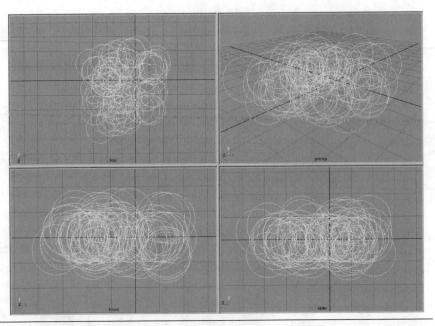

FIGURE 9-55 *Positions of the Cloud particles*

Edit the cloud particle attributes

5. Create a 3D Cloud texture node and a 2D Ramp texture node.
6. Drag and drop the Cloud texture node to the Blob Map and Color attributes of the particleCloud attribute.
7. Edit the Ramp texture node with the values as given below:

POSITION	RGB VALUES
0.0	0.97, 0.97,0.97
0.5	0.99, 0.99,0.99
1.0	0.98, 0.98,0.98

8. Drag and drop the Ramp texture node to the Transparency Map attributes of the cloud particle. Figure 9-56 shows the connection of the various nodes.

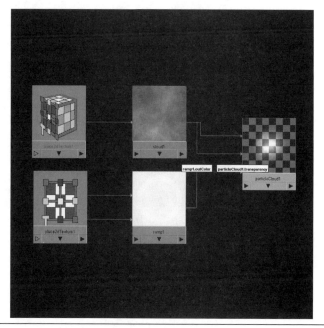

FIGURE 9-56 *Connection setup for the cloud particle node*

Lighting the internals of the particle

9. Create three point light sources.
10. Position the light sources within the particle Cloud as shown in Figure 9-57.

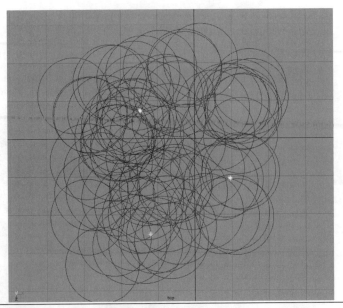

FIGURE 9-57　*Light source positions for the cloud particle*

11. From the Attribute Editor of the point light source, edit the Decay Rate of each point light source to Quadratic and leave the rest of the attributes at the default values (see Figure 9-58).

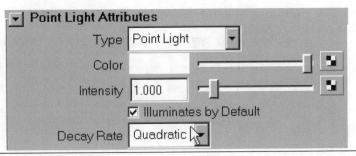

FIGURE 9-58　*Setting a high decay rate for the light source*

The three point light sources will serve as the internal illumination of the cloud. This internal illumination is the result of the dispersing and scattering of the sunlight.

Clouds are generally light, filmy, and puffy. But they can also be the opposite. So, whichever method you use, first understand he atmosphere that you want to create for the scene. Then you can research and find the best cloud to suit your needs.

Lighting the Externals of the Particle

Depending on the need of your scene, you may choose to use any type of light for lighting the external of the cloud particles. In this simple example, you will use a spot light.

12. Create a spot light.
13. Adjust the position of the light so that its cone of illumination covers the entire cloud.
14. Figure 9-59 below shows an example of position of the spot light.

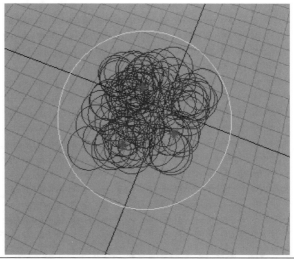

FIGURE 9-59   *Looking at the cloud particles through the spotlight view*

Test-render the scene

15. Test Test-render the scene.
16. If the image appears too dim, adjust the Color Gain of the Transparency Ramp to a lower values such as 0.95 (see Figure 9-60).

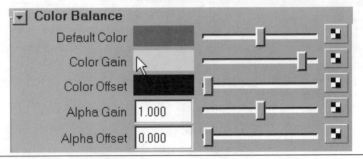

FIGURE 9-60 *Changing the color gain value to get a more balanced picture*

17. You should get an image similar to the one shown in Figure 9-61.

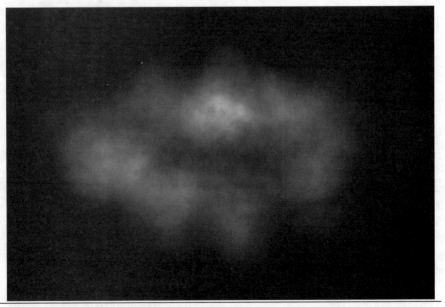

FIGURE 9-61 *A test render of the particle cloud*

Animating Particle Cloud.   Animating the cloud is most effectively done with the help of the Fields dynamics. For example, to create a sequence of clouds opening and sunlight passing through them, you can use the Radial field to slowly push open the cloud particles. The cloud movement seen in Chapter Ten's chpt10.mov is basically done using this Radial dynamic field. With the addition of the various dynamic fields, you can easily create and control various movements of the particles. The particular parameters such as the Maximum Distance and the Attenuation attributes of the dynamic fields allow you to control the flow and patterns of the movement with great ease. By animating the dynamic field attributes, other effects such as Steam and Smoke can also be created.

POST-PRODUCTION

As with most effects tutorials that you have done, you should plan how to composite your cloud and other effects. When you composite your clouds, pay particular attention to the lighting condition and the theme that you are setting for your scene. Since most cloud effects are used for outdoor shots, natural lighting will come into play. Hence, simple clues such as where the sunlight is should be carefully noted and taken into account when you set up and composite your entire scene.

CONCLUSION

This chapter will conclude the section on creating air effects. You have learned here the creation of subtle air movements in the form of dust. You have also learned how to create various types of clouds.

The techniques presented here and in the previous chapter will help you efficiently create your required air effects animation.

EXERCISE

1. Animate a shot in which a window opens and a gush of wind starts flowing into the room. The theme for the scene is mystery.

2. Create a scene where you are able to see both the sky with clouds and the green land. Animate the movement of the clouds so that as the cloud moves, the shadows they cast on the land also move. This is a common daily scene in the summer when the sky is filled with large cumulus clouds with shadows cast on the land.

10

GENERATING TERRAIN, GRASS, AND PLUG-INS

INTRODUCTION

Every single element exists in nature—from river streams, to blades of grass, from the fishes swimming in the water, to the birds flying in the sky—they all form part of the earth. Therefore, it would be a great exaggeration to say that this chapter contains a tutorial on creating the earth. Instead, we will focus on creating a large part of the earth, terrain. Terrain is something that you would have modeled and animated in one way or another during your work as a digital artist.

You have already learned in Chapter Five that there are several ways to generate terrain:

1. Model slowly using the standard available modeling tools.
2. Use a terrain generator program.
3. Write your own terrain generator.

Each approach has advantages and disadvantages. Using the first approach, the advantage is that you have precise and direct control over every single detail of the terrain. However, unless the terrain is rather flat and even, you are likely to be overwhelmed by the huge number of details needed for a realistic terrain.

The second approach of using a terrain-generating tool seems efficient and effective. Currently there are many terrain generator programs. They are generally inexpensive and some of them even exist as shareware or freeware. The main advantage of using commercially available terrain generators is that most of them support the DEM (Digital Elevation Map) format. This allows you to import real-world terrain data if, for example, creating accurate terrain is of paramount importance to you. On the other hand, if synthesizing your own terrain is more important for you, you may find that most of the terrain generated is basically alike and you do not have a lot of control over changing it. Therefore if your production requires a specific form of terrain, it may be difficult to achieve using such tools.

The last approach of rolling up your sleeves and writing your own terrain generator program is the most challenging but rewarding approach. Writing your own terrain generator program gives you precise control over the different features of the terrain such as the height and depth using procedural parameters. You are able to make changes easily and even animate the terrain without having to remodel the entire thing. In addition, using a procedural method implies that your terrain data is small and efficient since you need to store only the various parameters that control the features of the terrain. However, the obvious hurdle is that you are required to have the technical knowledge to write it, and the terrain program will only be as good as your knowledge of the terrain algorithm.

In previous chapters, you have already been introduced to generating terrain using the first approach (e.g., the seabed model). In this chapter, you will generate terrain using the third approach. In addition, a description of how to generate trees and grass, two very commonly seen representations of earth, will be presented.

WRITING YOUR OWN TERRAIN GENERATOR PLUG-IN

Many digital artists, including some who are technically trained, believe that writing tool plug-ins is reserved for experienced software engineers or CG-programmers. This is both true and not true. It is true because to write a good plug-in requires sound technical knowledge and sufficient experience and understanding of implementing algorithms. However, there is no rule that says simple and easy algorithms cannot be compiled into a plug-in! Hence, regardless of the complexity of the algorithm, writing a plug-in is really nothing more than just putting in some lines of codes and compiling them into .mll (for Maya NT) or .so (for Maya Irix) binaries.

This section will take you through a simple process of writing a terrain generator plug-in. We will focus on the relevant details and present the minimum concepts that are needed to enable you to write your first plug-in. Thus, inevitably, there will be more advanced details that will be omitted. However, as a beginner, the details presented here will be sufficient to give you a taste of writing your own plug-in. And hopefully at the end of it, you will be inspired to experiment with more algorithms and implement them yourself.

Now, first of all, what is plug-in? And why do you need to write plug-ins when there are already so many tools available to use? To understand the concept of plug-ins, let's take an example. Imagine that you are writing a simple program to draw lines on a screen, say, using a programming language such as BASIC. While writing the program to draw lines on a screen, you have written various procedures: Procedure A will draw red lines, procedure B will draw green lines, and procedure C will draw blue lines. Then, you compiled your code into an executable program. The program runs beautifully and drew three lines on the screen. Next, you decided that you would like to add more patterns to your lines. So, you change your procedures to include various parameters such as defining the length of the lines, the orientation of the lines, and the thickness of the lines. From there, the process repeats itself and you keep rewriting the procedures and improving your program. Finally, you reach the stage where you are very happy with your program and would like others to use it too. So, the natural thing to do is sell your program, or release it as a shareware or freeware.

Upon releasing your program, everyone is impressed with your line-drawing program. Many requests come in asking for new features and improvements. You are overwhelmed by the requests. Although you would like to comply with all the requests, you realize that there are simply too many to handle. However, in order to keep your product alive, you have to find ways to improve it, either by yourself, or with the users themselves. In order for the users to also contribute and add functionality to your program, you have decided to make this an open product and release the necessary information to the public. However, to protect your own interests, it is not possible for you to release your source code with your marvelous line-drawing procedures.

Therefore the next logical thing for you to do is to build your own API (Application Programming Interface). An API is a set of library routines that pertain particularly to your application, in this case your line-drawing application. In a very simple sense, to create your own API is pretty straightforward. Instead of compiling your program into an executable, you compile it into a set of library files. All users will then have access to this set of library files (API) and they can create their own additional tools on top of the library. The tools they create and essentially what we call *plug-ins* because they can literally be plugged into the application, in this case your line-drawing program, and their new features or functions will work well with your application.

Let's say you have included in your API the procedures named A, B, and C. Nobody knows how you implemented these procedures. But, they are able to write another program using the same language and just name your A, B, and C procedures and create another new set of procedures on top of them. Eventually, your product will expand and everyone will be very happy because they will be able to use a better product.

Theoretically, if you can write a simple program that calls the printf ( ) function to print "Hello World," you will be able to write your own plug-ins that call the various readily available Maya procedures. However, this time, instead of only three procedures (A, B, C) and using BASIC, you will have access to over one hundred Maya procedures using the C++ programming language.

Figures 10-1 and 10-2 show a very simple idea of what is presented here.

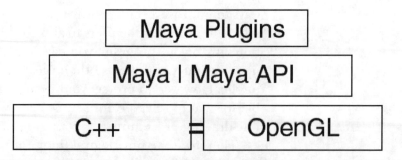

FIGURE 10-1 *A simply hierarchy structure of building a Maya plug-in*

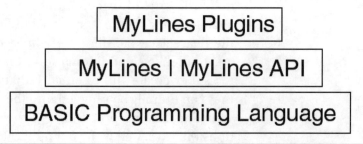

FIGURE 10-2 *A Maya plug-in is analogous to the simple line drawing plug-in example*

The advantages of learning and writing Maya plug-ins are numerous. First of all, it does not cost you anything to have access to the Maya API. Many other software companies require you to make an additional purchase of their so-called development kit. However, the Maya API comes bundled with the product. All you need is a C++ compiler (Microsoft C++ 5.0 or 6.0 for NT, or MIPS Pro 7.2 C++ on Irix), which is available in most learning environments and production or game companies. Secondly, as you get more familiar with the scripting language of Maya, you will inevitably have written your own procedures and functions. Having some experience in writing Maya API, you will be very pleased to see that your code could run many times faster than when you implement it using MEL.

There are several methods of generating terrain. You can use a subdivision method, the faulting and collaging method, or noise synthesis method. Whichever method you use, the basic idea is to generate a heightfield map. And based on the heightfield information, different parts of the terrain will be displaced above the ground.

This chapter of terrain generation will take you to two very common and fundamental methods: fractal terrain generation and the fBm (Fractional Brownian motion) terrain generation method.

FRACTALS

Modeling natural objects such as trees, plants, mountains, and clouds through geometrical means is a difficult process. With every little detail added, the geometries will easily end up highly complex and computationally heavy. In addition, you are likely to have numerous aliasing problems to address. Fractals, first introduced by Mandelbrot in 1977, provide a solution to modeling most natural objects.

What is fractal? By definition, *fractal* is a rough or frag-mented geometric shape that can be subdivided into parts, each of which is (at least approximately) a reduced-size copy of the whole. To fully understand the definition, it is best to use a simple illustration.

Say, for example, you have a one-dimensional line. You break this line into two halves and displace the join between them slightly upwards. Now you have a triangle-like structure (see Figures 10-3 and 10-4).

FIGURE 10-3 *The line before breaking*

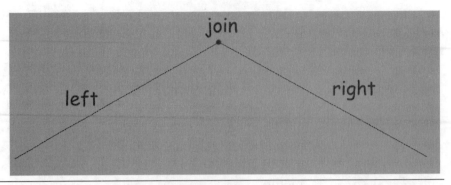

FIGURE 10-4   *The line broken into 2 parts - left and right*

You further break each left and right side into two smaller halves each and displace the joins by an arbitrary value of your choice. The proccss keeps repeating itself. At the end of several iterations, you will end up with something similar to Figure 10-5.

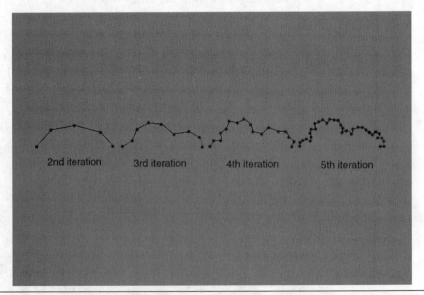

FIGURE 10-5   *Results of subdivision at various iteration stages*

Notice that the final result resembles the cross-section of a mountain. When you extend the iteration to not just a one-dimensional line, but to a two-dimensional surface, an interesting terrain pattern is immediately obvious.

Fractals exhibit the property of *scale independence*. That is to say, they are invariant under the change of scale. When any portion of fractals is magnified, it produces a fractal similar to the original fractal itself. Take a look at things around you and notice that many natural phenomena such as mountains, clouds, coastlines, trees, leaves, and crystals exhibit some form of self-similarity as described above. These objects do not correspond to normal geometrical shapes but they can be easily described using fractals. Figures 10-6 and 10-7 show a typical fern leaf that exhibits the fractal property.

FIGURE 10-6 *A fern leaf*

FIGURE 10-7   *A fern leaf that displays the fractal nature of scale independence*

Therefore, the basic principle of generating fractals involves repetitive application of a transformation function to points within a region of space. The final details of the object depend on the number of iterations performed. Hence, the traditional means of using a large number of polygons to represent many apparently complex objects has been replaced by the use of fractals. With basic functions and equations, a large amount of information could be stored and generated with ease. A term called *database amplification* has been coined to reflect this advantage of using fractal representation.

Another important concept of fractals that you are likely to encounter, is the concept of *fractal dimensionality*. You may not be aware, but the world does not exist in only three dimensions represented on the X, Y, and Z axes in the digital model world. This three-dimensional representation is known mathematically as the *Euclidean space*. Under the Euclidean space, a line is one dimension since it is a series of connected points, which you can represent with a single number, like 10 units in length or 5 km in distance. A plane is two dimensions because it is a set of two numbers, like a 2 cm by 2 cm box or 10 m by 16 m area. And volume is three dimensions because you need three numbers to present it. For example, you need to specify a coordinate (e.g., 3,4,5) to precisely locate a point in a volume of space.

Fractals, on the other hand, do not conform to the Euclidean space of three dimensions. Fractals can exists in a dimension of say, 1.456. Don't get worried now by imagining how a 1.456 dimension would look. It is really a matter of simple representation from a different view.

Another form of representing dimension is to base it on how an object changes size as the linear dimension increases. For example, when you double a one-dimensional object, say, two units in length, you get the size doubled (2^2 = 4 units). When the object exists in two dimensions, its size will be increased by a factor of 4 (($2 \times 2)^2$ = 16). When the object exists in three dimensions, its size will be increased by a factor of 8 (($2 \times 2 \times 2)^2$ = 64). Therefore, the relationship between the dimension D, the linear scaling L, and the increase in size S can be represented by the following equation:

$$S = L^D$$

Rearranging the equation, you get

$$D = log\ (S)\ /\ log(L)$$

So, using the above example,

$$1\ (dimension) = log\ (2)\ /\ log\ (2)$$
$$2\ (dimension) = log\ (4)\ /\ log\ (2)$$
$$3\ (dimension) = log\ (8)\ /\ log\ (2)$$

Now, consider a simple object such as a snowflake curve as shown in Figures 10-8 and 10-9.

FIGURE 10-8 *A line with a fixed length*

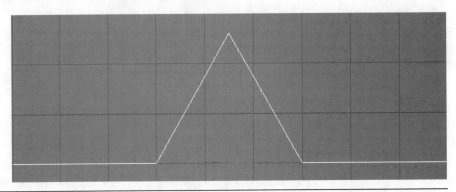

FIGURE 10-9 *A well-known snowflake curve is created with each of the segment $^1/_3$ of the original length*

Each of the four segments of the snowflake curve is one-third the length of the original curve. Consider the case of tripling the snowflake curve. The resultant size is increased by a factor of 4. Hence the dimension of the snowflake curve is:

$$D = \log (4) / \log (3) = 1.262.$$

Based on this example, the snowflake is a fractal. Figure 10-10 shows the well-known snowflake fractals.

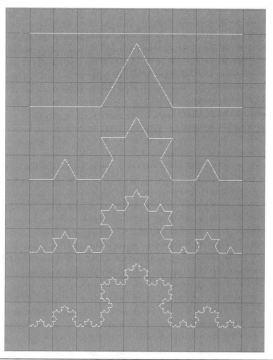

FIGURE 10-10 *The fractal nature of the snowflake curves at various iterations*

Fractals can be classified very broadly into two major types, depending on the process of their generation: deterministic fractals and random fractals. As the terms suggest, *deterministic fractals* are fractals generated through a known regular function and *random fractals* are generated through random process. Random fractals, also known as *stochastic fractals*, are more widely used to represent such elements as coastline, mountains, and clouds.

GENERATING FRACTAL TERRAIN

Fractal techniques have been widely used to generate terrain models. Among the techniques used, the easiest method is the spatial subdivision method. The idea behind *spatial sub-division* is quite straightforward. Consider a flat plane. In the first iteration, the plane is split into four parts. The vertices of each part is then perturbed in a controlled random manner. The second iteration will take each of the divided parts and further subdivide it into smaller pieces. The vertices of the smaller polygons are further perturbed but with decreasing values. This process is iterated as many times as required to generate the required terrain model (see Figure 10-11).

In a typical spatial subdivision fractal terrain generation function, the following parameters are normally available for users:

1.   A seed for the random number generator. By changing this random number generator, an entirely different terrain may be generated.

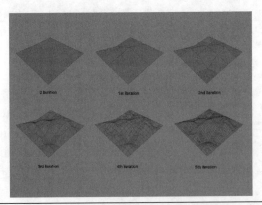

FIGURE 10-11 *Fractal terrain generated at various iteration stages using spatial subdivision*

2.   A roughness parameter that controls how much the vertices are to be influenced by the random number. The lower the value, the less the randomness and thus the smoother the terrain.

3. Maximum and minimum height parameters that control the maximum peak and minimum valley of the terrain.
4. Color map parameters that map the height of the terrain with a given color ramp. Generally the terrain generated will include the blue color that represent the rivers.
5. The number of iterations. This controls the detail and density of the terrain mesh.

Pros and Cons of Using Spatial Subdivision.   Terrain generated using the spatial subdivision method can be very fast. This is especially the case when your step size is two. The main drawback of this method is its obvious aliasing effects, which are particularly obvious when looking down from above or across. However, the aliasing could be reduced with a number of simple considerations during the setup. There is fractal literature devoted to discussion of solving this problem.

Implementing fractal terrain.   Implementing the fractal terrain is a straightforward process in Maya. Based on the concepts discussed, you can easily create a polygon and iteratively subdivide the polygon into more parts and create a simple fractal terrain. Though you can implement a plug-in that generates a fractal terrain, there is really little incentive in doing so. Instead what is more interesting and useful for you to implement is to base the plug-in on the fBm function as presented below.

FBM

In the introductory chapters, you saw the importance of chaos. In particular, we discussed the Oscar-award-winning Perlin noise function. From the Perlin noise function, several other interesting results can be derived. Among them is the well-known *fractional Brownian motion (fBm)* by F. Kenton Musgrave. The idea of fBm is similar to the concept of fractal creation. In Maya, the fBm function is known as the *3D Brownian texture function.* You can create it easily from the Create Node Window by clicking on the 3D texture Brownian.

In fractals, the details of the results are based on the number of iterations performed. This is similarly implemented in the fBm function. The general idea in fBm is to sum different Perlin noise functions from each iteration. For each Perlin noise function, the amplitude and frequency are scaled. Normally, in each iteration, the amplitude is reduced by half while the frequency is doubled. Though you have the option to scale by different values, it is almost a default practice that the value of two is used. And precisely for this reason, each iteration in an fBm function is known as an *octave*, which has the same meaning as the term octave in the musical world.

In the first iteration, a basic Perlin function is used. Figure 10-12 shows a pattern of the noise function created with the default Perlin noise function introduced earlier.

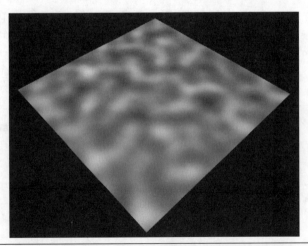

FIGURE 10-12 *A noise image based on Perlin's noise function*

In the second iteration, the frequency of the noise function is doubled while the amplitude is scaled to half its original value (see Figure 10-13).

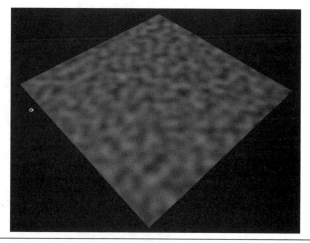

FIGURE 10-13 *The noise image created by increasing the frequency but decreasing the amplitude*

This iteration process is repeated for a finite number of times. Musgrave suggested that the number of times should be based on the following equation:

$$octaves = log_2 \ (screen.resolution) - 2$$

Therefore, for a screen resolution of 640 × 480:

$$octaves = log_2(640) - 2 = \sim7 \ octaves$$

Any iteration greater than the suggested number of times does not yield any visible difference. To create the final image of an fBm function, the results of each iteration are then summed up together (see Figure 10-14).

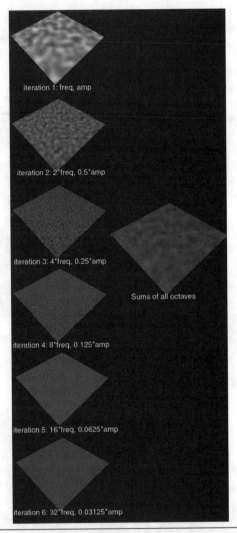

FIGURE 10-14 *Various stages of the octaves are summed up to create the fractional Browian motion image*

The concept of fBm function is of particular importance in computer graphics. Its noise-like fractal nature has made it a popular function in creating objects such as fractal shaders, as well as visualizing various different natural phenomena such as terrain and clouds.

The following instructions help you create an fBm terrain as well as your own Maya terrain plug-in.

FBM TERRAIN CREATION

Create the terrain

1. Create a nurbs plane.
2. Name the plane fBmTerrain.
3. Set the following options for the plane:

PARAMETERS	VALUES
Width	10
Length Ratio	1
Patches U	20
Patches V	20

4. Create a Brownian texture function.
5. Name the Brownian texture browianDisplacement.
6. Set the parameters as follows and leave the rest at default values:

PARAMETERS	VALUES
Lacunarity	2.0
Increment	1.2
Octaves	5.0
Weight	(1.0, 5.0, 1.0)
Alpha Gain	7.0

7. Select its place3dTexture node.
8. Scale the node by a factor of 2.35 in all its axes.
9. Map this browianDisplaement as a displacement shader to the default shading group.

10. Select the plane.
11. Go to Shading ➢ Displacement to Polygon.
12. The NURBS displacement information from fBm will be converted into a polygon.
13. You should get an image similar to the one shown in Figure 10-15.

FIGURE 10-15 *A terrain generated using fBm as the displacement map*

NOTE

In Maya 2.0, there is an added function for computing the bounding box information of displacement map for any geometry. If at times you do not appear to be getting your expected results, you should change the bounding box information for the geometry. To change the bounding box information, select the object that has been mapped with the displacement map, then from its Attribute Editor window, go to the Displacement Map section and edit the bounding box values (see Figure 10-16).

Displacement Map		
Bounding Box Scale	1.500	1.500	1.500
	Calculate Bounding Box Scale	

FIGURE 10-16 *Adjust the bounding box value of the displacement map to get a better displacement*

WRITE A MAYA TERRAIN SHADER PLUG-IN

Writing a Maya plug-in is really not a difficult process. Many artists do not realize that they can write plug-ins, even without a very strong grasp of mathematics! The key to writing any code is similar to making any animation; start simple, and stay simple (S^4). Even if you don't understand a complex algorithm, as long as you understand the overall structure of writing Maya plug-ins, you will be able to simply insert your code and start testing the various results. Before you know it, you will be on the way to writing your very first plug-in!

In the book, *Texturing and Modeling*, Musgrave has developed several methods of generating different fractal terrains using methods similar to the implementation of the fBm function. You are encouraged to refer to this and other books on the terrain generation algorithm.

The following code briefly outlines an example of implementing a modified version of Musgrave's RidgedMultifractal function. Even if you do not entirely understand the actual algorithm, you are encouraged to simply plug your own simplified code into the following example and create your first plug-in.

The plug-in presented below is a standard shader type plug-in. In Maya API, the plug-ins are classified into several types, such as Command Plug-in, Interactive Tool Plug-in, Dependency Graph Plug-in, and Device Plug-in.

Each plug-in has a unique TypeID in Maya, which is managed globally. For example, if you are using an ID of 0x80000, for your plug-in called my_first_maya_plugin, then no one in the world would be using the same ID as this. If two plug-ins are using the same ID, then you will almost definitely have problems in using any of them. In addition, once a plug-in has been created with a unique plug-in ID, it should keep the same ID throughout. If you decided to change your plug-in ID after releasing your plug-in, a problem of compatibility would surface. To obtain a set of unique IDs for your work, you must contact Alias Wavefront. However, generally, it is not necessary that you must always use an ID for every plug-in that you write. The plug-in ID is associated only with the creation of nodes in Maya. If your plug-in does not create any nodes but is just simply a command, such as to create a basic nurbs surface, you may create the plug-in without any ID. The compiled plug-in presented below is available on the CD. Remember that to use the plug-ins from the CD, you have to rename them according to the instructions on the CD:

```
// = = =
//
// Information such as author, company, date are normally presented
// at the beginning of your code
//
// Author - Maya
// Date - June 1999
//
// A brief description of the function of the plug-in is usually described
// An example is —
// DESCRIPTION:
//      A modified implementation of Ridged MultiFractal Shader of Musgrave
//      The precise codes are available from the book Texturing & Modeling
//
// The input and output of the plug-ins are briefly described
// Example is —
// Inputs:
//      pointWorld          - world space sample point
//      placementMatrix     - world to texture space transform
//      H                   - determines the highest fractal dimension
//      lacunarity          - is the gap between successive frequencies
//      octaves             - is the number of frequencies in the fBm
//      offset              - is the zero offset, which determine miltifractality
//      threshold           - threshold values
//      gain                - is for the gain of alpha
//      sharpness           - is for the smoothness of the ridgeline
//
```

```
// Outputs:
//      outColor            - output color
//      outColorR           - output color Red
//      outColorG           - output color Green
//      outColorB           - output color Blue
//      outAlpha            - output Alpha
//
// TypeId Used:             - This should be your own TypeID value
//////////////////////////////////////////////////////
// = = =
// All the #include headers
// are inserted here.
// You should refer to the Developer Kit documentations for details.
// An example (incomplete) is -
#include <math.h>
#include <maya/MPxNode.h>
// = = =
// All the #define function.
// These definition will help save you// some precious time.
// An example is -
#define PI                  3.14159265358979323846
// = = =
// Local functions
// You may have some of your own functions such as
// your own noise function.
// You may copy and insert the Perlin noise function
// here. Even if you don't fully understand the noise
// function, you will be able to compile the function easily
float Noise(float, float, float);
// = = =
// Define the class
// The attributes name are
// usually identified with a letter "a"
// However, use whatever convention you prefer.
//////////////////////////////////////////////////////
class kbRMFractal : public MPxNode
{
public:
                            kbRMFractal();
    virtual         "kbRMFractal();
    virtual MStatus compute( const MPlug&, MDataBlock& );
    virtual void    postConstructor();
    static  void *  creator();
    static  MStatus initialize();
    static  MTypeId id;
// You have all your inputs defined here.
// inputs
    static MObject  aPointWorld;
    static MObject  aPointWorldX;
    static MObject  aPointWorldY;
    static MObject  aPointWorldZ;
    static MObject  aPointObject;
```

```
    static MObject   aPointObjectX;
    static MObject   aPointObjectY;
    static MObject   aPointObjectZ;
    static MObject   aPlacementMatrix;

    static MObject   aH;
    static MObject   alacunarity;
    static MObject   aoctaves;
    static MObject   aoffset;
    static MObject   athreshold;
    static MObject   again;
    static MObject   asharpness;
// What goes in, must come out, on way or another.
// outputs
    static MObject   aOutAlpha;
    static MObject   aOutColor;
    static MObject   aOutColorR;
    static MObject   aOutColorG;
    static MObject   aOutColorB;
};
// Id must be unique.
// However, if you are testing for your
// own use. You may try any value that
// are beyond those that are currently in use
///////////////////////////////////////////////////
MTypeId kbRMFractal::id(InsertYourTypeID);
void kbRMFractal::postConstructor( )
{
setMPSafe(true);
}
//
// Attributes
///////////////////////////////////////////////////
MObject   kbRMFractal::aPointWorld;
MObject   kbRMFractal::aPointWorldX;
MObject   kbRMFractal::aPointWorldY;
MObject   kbRMFractal::aPointWorldZ;
MObject   kbRMFractal::aPointObject;
MObject   kbRMFractal::aPointObjectX;
MObject   kbRMFractal::aPointObjectY;
MObject   kbRMFractal::aPointObjectZ;
MObject   kbRMFractal::aPlacementMatrix;
MObject   kbRMFractal::aH;
MObject   kbRMFractal::alacunarity;
MObject   kbRMFractal::aoctaves;
MObject   kbRMFractal::aoffset;
MObject   kbRMFractal::athreshold;
MObject   kbRMFractal::again;
MObject   kbRMFractal::asharpness;
MObject   kbRMFractal::aOutAlpha;
MObject   kbRMFractal::aOutColor;
MObject   kbRMFractal::aOutColorR;
```

```
MObject   kbRMFractal::aOutColorG;
MObject   kbRMFractal::aOutColorB;
//
// Functions
///////////////////////////////////////////////////////
kbRMFractal::kbRMFractal()
{
}
kbRMFractal::~kbRMFractal()
{
}
//
// Create
///////////////////////////////////////////////////////
void * kbRMFractal::creator()
{
    return new kbRMFractal();
}


//
// initialize
///////////////////////////////////////////////////////
MStatus kbRMFractal::initialize()
{
    MFnNumericAttribute nAttr;
// Create input attributes.
//  You can set the attributes default
//  vales, etc.
//  You need to define every input and output attributes
//   The examples (incomplete. samples only) are as follow -
    aPointWorldX = nAttr.create( "pointWorldX", "pwx", MFnNumericData::kFloat);
    nAttr.setStorable(false);
    nAttr.setReadable(true);
    nAttr.setWritable(true);
    nAttr.setHidden(true);
    aPointWorldY = nAttr.create( "pointWorldY", "pwy", MFnNumericData::kFloat);
    nAttr.setStorable(false);
    nAttr.setReadable(true);
    nAttr.setWritable(true);
    nAttr.setHidden(true);
    aPointWorldZ = nAttr.create( "pointWorldZ", "pwz", MFnNumericData::kFloat);
    nAttr.setStorable(false);
    nAttr.setReadable(true);
    nAttr.setWritable(true);
    nAttr.setHidden(true);
    aPointWorld = nAttr.create( "pointWorld", "pw", aPointWorldX, aPointWorldY,

aPointWorldZ);
    nAttr.setStorable(false);
    nAttr.setReadable(true);
    nAttr.setWritable(true);
    nAttr.setHidden(true);
```

```
    MFnMatrixAttribute mAttr;
    aPlacementMatrix = mAttr.create( "placementMatrix", "pm",
                                                    MFnMatrixAttribute::kFloat);
    mAttr.setStorable(false);
    mAttr.setReadable(true);
    mAttr.setWritable(true);
    mAttr.setHidden(false);
// Your own attributes
//
    alacunarity = nAttr.create( "Lacunarity", "lac", MFnNumericData::kFloat);
    nAttr.setDefault(1.0f);
    nAttr.setMin(0.0f);
    nAttr.setMax(10.0f);
    nAttr.setStorable(true);
    nAttr.setReadable(true);
    nAttr.setWritable(true);
    aoctaves = nAttr.create( "Octaves", "oct", MFnNumericData::kFloat);
    nAttr.setDefault(2.0f);
    nAttr.setMin(0.0f);
    nAttr.setMax(10.0f);
    nAttr.setStorable(true);
    nAttr.setReadable(true);
    nAttr.setWritable(true);
// …Continue for the rest of all your attributes …
//


// Outputs
// Examples are -

    aOutColorR = nAttr.create( "outColorR", "ocr", MFnNumericData::kFloat);
    aOutColorG = nAttr.create( "outColorG", "ocg", MFnNumericData::kFloat);
    aOutColorB = nAttr.create( "outColorB", "ocb", MFnNumericData::kFloat);
    aOutColor  = nAttr.create( "outColor",  "oc" , aOutColorR, aOutColorG, aOutColorB);
    nAttr.setStorable(false);
    nAttr.setHidden(false);
    nAttr.setReadable(true);
    nAttr.setWritable(false);
    aOutAlpha = nAttr.create( "outAlpha", "oa", MFnNumericData::kFloat);
    nAttr.setStorable(false);
    nAttr.setReadable(true);
    nAttr.setWritable(false);
// Add the attrubutes here
// Examples -
    addAttribute(aPointWorld);
    addAttribute(aPointWorldX);
    addAttribute(aPointWorldY);
    addAttribute(aPointWorldZ);
    addAttribute(aPointObject);
    addAttribute(aPointObjectX);
    addAttribute(aPointObjectY);
    addAttribute(aPointObjectZ);
    addAttribute(aPlacementMatrix);
```

```
        addAttribute(aH);
        addAttribute(alacunarity);
        addAttribute(aoctaves);
        addAttribute(aoffset);
        addAttribute(athreshold);
        addAttribute(again);
        addAttribute(asharpness);
        addAttribute(aOutAlpha);
        addAttribute(aOutColor);
        addAttribute(aOutColorR);
        addAttribute(aOutColorG);
        addAttribute(aOutColorB);
// Affects
//
        attributeAffects (aPointWorld, aOutColor);
        attributeAffects (aPointWorldX, aOutColor);
        attributeAffects (aPointWorldY, aOutColor);
        attributeAffects (aPointWorldZ, aOutColor);
        attributeAffects (aPointObject, aOutColor);
        attributeAffects (aPointObjectX, aOutColor);
        attributeAffects (aPointObjectY, aOutColor);
        attributeAffects (aPointObjectZ, aOutColor);
        attributeAffects (aPlacementMatrix, aOutColor);
        attributeAffects(aH, aOutColor);
        attributeAffects(alacunarity, aOutColor);
        attributeAffects(aoctaves, aOutColor);
        attributeAffects(aoffset, aOutColor);
        attributeAffects(athreshold, aOutColor);
        attributeAffects(again, aOutColor);
        attributeAffects(asharpness, aOutColor);
        attributeAffects (aPointWorld, aOutAlpha);
        attributeAffects (aPointWorldX, aOutAlpha);
        attributeAffects (aPointWorldY, aOutAlpha);
        attributeAffects (aPointWorldZ, aOutAlpha);
        attributeAffects (aPointObject, aOutAlpha);
        attributeAffects (aPointObjectX, aOutAlpha);
        attributeAffects (aPointObjectY, aOutAlpha);
        attributeAffects (aPointObjectZ, aOutAlpha);
        attributeAffects (aPlacementMatrix, aOutAlpha);
        attributeAffects(aH, aOutAlpha);
        attributeAffects(alacunarity, aOutAlpha);
        attributeAffects(aoctaves, aOutAlpha);
        attributeAffects(aoffset, aOutAlpha);
        attributeAffects(athreshold, aOutAlpha);
        attributeAffects(again, aOutAlpha);
        attributeAffects(asharpness, aOutAlpha);
return MS::kSuccess;
}


// Compute is the core of the plug-in.
//   This is where you will add in your own
//   ideas, codes etc. to try out different algorithm
```

```
//
//////////////////////////////////////////////////////
MStatus kbRMFractal::compute(const MPlug& plug, MDataBlock& block)
{

if ( !(plug == aOutColor) &&
 !(plug == aOutColorR) &&
 !(plug == aOutColorG) &&
 !(plug == aOutColorB) &&
  !(plug == aOutAlpha)
   )
        return MS::kUnknownParameter;
// Connect the variables with the input values
//
    const MFloatVector& p = block.inputValue( aPointObject ).asFloatVector();
    const MFloatMatrix& m = block.inputValue( aPlacementMatrix ).asFloatMatrix();
    const float H = block.inputValue( aH ).asFloat();
    const float lacunarity = block.inputValue( alacunarity ).asFloat();
    const float octaves = block.inputValue( aoctaves ).asFloat();
    const float offset = block.inputValue( aoffset ).asFloat();
    const float threshold = block.inputValue( athreshold ).asFloat();
    const float gain = block.inputValue( again ).asFloat();
    const float sharpness = block.inputValue( asharpness ).asFloat();
//
//
    MFloatVector q = p * m;
// The point variable below is the sample point to create
//   the texture
//
    MFloatVector point = q;
    MFloatVector resultColor;
//  Declare any local variables
//
    double result;
    int i;
for( i=0; i<octaves; i++ ) {
//  Codes insertion.
//   For copyright reason, the modified codes of Musgrave's
//   Ridged Multifractal are not inserted here. However,
//   the exact algorithm is not the main idea here. The idea is to
//   comprehen the structure of writing Maya shader plug-ins
//   and start exploring and writing your own plug-ins with the understanding
//   of the fractal concepts.
//   In anycase, you should be able to simply plug the codes of other
//   functions such as
//   Perlin noise function, etc.
//   and compile without much problem
//
//   A simple example is -
//
result += Noise( point.x, point.y, point.z );
}
```

```
    MDataHandle outHandle = block.outputValue( aOutColor );
    MFloatVector & outColor = outHandle.asFloatVector();
    resultColor = (result, result, result); //You can change the color output
    // by putting some offset values to result
    outColor = resultColor;
    outHandle.setClean();
    outHandle = block.outputValue(aOutAlpha);
    float alpha = result*gain;
    outHandle.asFloat() = alpha;
    outHandle.setClean();
    return MS::kSuccess;
}
// Initialize the plug-in
// This part is pretty standard
////////////////////////////////////////////////////////////////////
extern "C" MStatus initializePlugin( MObject obj )
{
    const MString UserClassify( "texture/3d" );
    MString command(
        "if( `window -exists createRenderNodeWindow` ) "
        "{refreshCreateRenderNodeWindow(\""
            );
    MFnPlugin plug-in( obj, "Kian Bee Ng", "2.0", "Any" );
    plugin.registerNode( "kbRMFractal", kbRMFractal::id,
    kbRMFractal::creator, kbRMFractal::initialize,
    MPxNode::kDependNode, &UserClassify
        );
    command += UserClassify;
    command += "\");}\n";
    MGlobal::executeCommand(command);
    Noise_init();

    return MS::kSuccess;
}
// Uninitalize and unplug
// This part is pretty standard
/////////////////////////////////////////////////////////
extern "C" MStatus uninitializePlugin( MObject obj )
{
    const MString UserClassify( "texture/3d" );
    MString command(
    "if( 'window -exists createRenderNodeWindow' ) "
    "{refreshCreateRenderNodeWindow(\""
    );
    MFnPlugin plug-in( obj );
    plugin.deregisterNode( kbRMFractal::id );
    command += UserClassify;
    command += "\");}\n";
    MGlobal::executeCommand(command);
    return MS::kSuccess;
}
```

Playback the movie file chpt10.mov from the CD. The terrain seen in the file is generated using the terrain plug-in in the CD, which is based on a modified form of Ridged-MultiFractal terrain shader.

CREATING TREES

There are several approaches to creating scenes with a large number of trees and leaves:

- Model by hand.
- Use the L-system.
- Use texture mapping.

MODEL BY HAND

In the military world, it is known that there is nothing that the infantry troops cannot overcome. There is a limit where the tanks can go, the choppers can fly, the bombers can arrive, but there is no one place on earth that the infantry troops cannot cross. Similarly, theoretically, there is nothing that you cannot create with your basic modeling tool. However, the question is whether the approach is efficient and productive. Modeling scenes with trees and leaves by hand is a poor man's solution. Though it is possible, it requires a great deal of time and patience. The advantage of modeling trees and leaves by hand is that you can totally control the details. However, a scene with great detailing of trees, branches, and leaves will easily become a nightmare for any modeler.

USING THE L-SYSTEM

The L-system was introduced by Astrid Lindenmayer in 1968. It is essentially a string-like method that is particularly useful in describing the growth of self-similar structures over time. The self-replacing grammar of the L-system is central to creating the self-similar structures.

Since its introduction, the L-system has been the central idea in modeling trees, leaves, and many other types of structures that exhibit self-similarity. Take the fern, for example. A fern consists of a leaf, which is itself made up of many smaller, similar leaves. And each small leaf is in turn made of even smaller leaves. Hence, using the L-system, the structure of the fern leaves can be easily described with just a few lines of codes. There are many structures in nature that exhibit self-similarity. Therefore, using the L-system, most of them can be described and created. (See the previous Figures 10-6 and 10-7).

It is beyond the scope of this book to describe the implementation of an L-system. Several books are available that give very good descriptions of the implementation of an L-system. You are encouraged to read up and hopefully implement one for yourself. One of the recommended books is called *The Algorithmic Beauty of Plants* written by P. Prusinkiewicz and A. Lindenmayer.

TEXTURE MAPPING

The easiest method for most animators to create scenes with trees and leaves is to snapshot the real objects. The advantage of this approach is that not only can you choose different details to present, you are also able to choose different types of trees, plants, and leaves.

From there, you are able to simply create a plane or other primitive and texture map the image onto it, though most likely you will need to touch-up the image captured. This method of pasting the real object onto a simple primitive is also a common trick used in real-time visualization.

A common question about this method is what happens when your camera moves in the scene? The solution to this problem is pretty simple. All you need to do is create a script that will ensure that the plane is always facing the camera no matter how and where the camera moves. The expression below shows an implementation of making sure that the plane primitive always follow the rotation of the perspective camera.

```
$offset1 = 45.0;
$offset2 = 135.0;
nurbsPlane1.rotateY = $offset1 + persp.rotateY;
nurbsPlane2.rotateY = $offset2 + persp.rotateY;
```

You will notice in the expression above that 2 primitive planes are used to represent a tree. This is because to create a more convincing look of the trees from all angles, it is better to use two planes to create a cross object instead of simply using a single plane. The result is as shown in Figures 10-17 and 10-18.

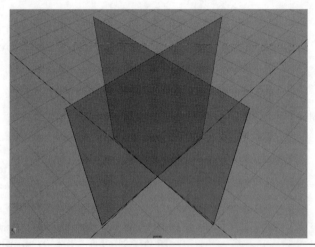

FIGURE 10-17 *Create an efficient and convincing looking tree with 2 crossing planes*

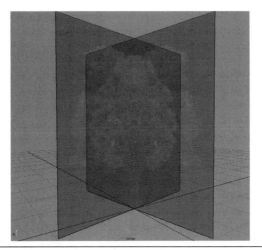

FIGURE 10-18 *Using 2 primitive planes to represent a tree*

CREATING GRASS USING PARTICLES

There are several approaches to creating convincing looking grass in Maya. One method is to create a strain of grass and simply instance or copy it as many times as needed for your scene.

TASK

• What is the difference between instancing and copying an object?

The advantages of using this approach is similar to that of creating trees. You have direct control over the shading and various surface details of the grass.

The other approach to creating grass is with the help of the particle system. If you have the Fur Module of Maya (which comes with the Maya Unlimited package), you will be able to create convincing-looking grass. However, even without the Fur Module, you are able to grow good-looking grass. The following section will show the methods of creating grass using the standard particle system.

Creating grass in Maya can be achieved using the hardware render type. With careful control over the life span and radius of the particles, you can create grass of any length and thickness. In addition, with the help of the dynamic forces, you can easily control the animation of the grass.

You will attempt to create a simple patch of grass in this example

Create the grass surface patch

1.   Create a default NURBS plane.
2.   Name the plane grasspatch.

Set grasspatch to the parameters shown below.

You can deform and alter the plane to any size and shape according to your required terrain.

PARAMETERS	VALUES
Width	2
Length Ratio	1
Patches U	4
Patches V	4

3.   Name the plane grasspatch.

Create the grass emitter

4.   Go to Pick Component Select mode.
5.   Make sure that you are able to pick the Edit Points (see Figure 10-19).

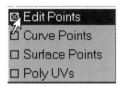

FIGURE 10-19 *Pick components with Edit Point selection*

6. Select the Edit Points that you want to emit the particles.

    If there are not enough edit points, increase the UV patch.

7. Go to Particles ➣ Add Emitter ➣ -❑.
8. Set the parameters shown in Figure 10-20 and add the particles.

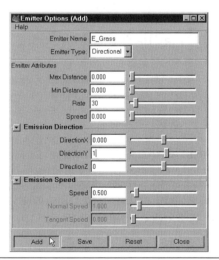

FIGURE 10-20 *Create the grass emitter options*

9. Play back your animation.

You should see a steady stream of particles coming from the selected edit points.

The rate of 30.0 was set based on the calculation of one particle emitted from each edit point per frame. So, if you want to have 1 particle every 5 frames instead, then your emission rate is 30 fps/5 = 6. And if your run time is different than 30 fps, you may want to change the values.

10. Name the particle created particleGrass.
11. Open the Attribute Editor of particleGrass.
12. Set the Particle Render Type to Tube (s/w).
13. Click on the Current Render Type button to add the default attributes for the Tube render type.
14. Set the Radius 0 and Radius 1 attributes to 0.05.
15. Leave the tail size at the default value of 1.0.
16. Add a Lifespan Per Object attribute.
17. Set the lifespan to 0.5.
18. Play back the animation.

You should see that the grass is straight up and that the length is controlled by the life span of the particles.

Animating the grass

19. Select particleGrass.
20. Add a Uniform Field with the options shown in Figure 10-21.

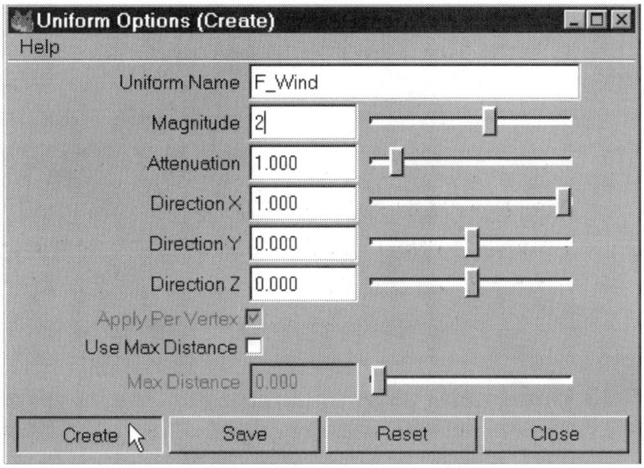

FIGURE 10-21 *Create the Uniform dynamic field to function as wind*

21. Play back the animation.

You should now see that the grass is swaying towards the X-axis.

22. To make the grass swing and dance, simply enter a varying magnitude of the Uniform field.

An example of the expression that varies the magnitude the Uniform field is given below:

```
F_wind.magnitude = sin(5*time)*2.0;
```

23. Create a particle shading group and map a greenery color to the particles grass (see Figure 10-22).

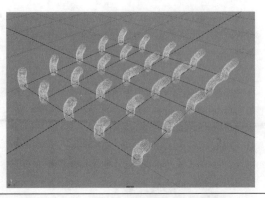

FIGURE 10-22 *Grass created under the influence of the dynamic field*

Alternative Hardware Grass

In Maya, besides the usual software render, the hardware render feature also provides very good-looking results.

24. Select particleGrass.
25. From its Attribute Editor, change the render type to Multistreak.
26. Set the rest of the attribute as shown in Figure 10-23.

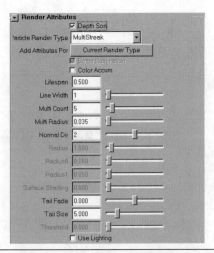

FIGURE 10-23 *Setting the various render attributes for the grass*

27. To test-render the scene, go to Window ➢ Rendering Editors ➢ Hardware Render Buffer....

The hardware render buffer window opens as shown in Figure 10-24.

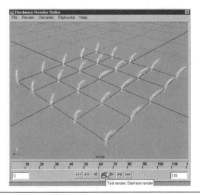

FIGURE 10-24 *Grass created under the influence of the dynamic field*

28. To color-map the hardware particles, simply add color attributes on a per object or per particles basis.

Figure 10-25 shows an example of the hardware-rendered grass.

FIGURE 10-25 *Hardware rendered look of the grass*

Maya's Fur module is one of the advanced tools that allows you to create scenes with hair, fur, etc. Creating and animating patches of grass is a series of simple steps using the Fur module. Maya Fur even allows you to render the fur information as a separate pass for use in composition. Figures 10-26 and 10-27 below shows the creation of a character with the help of Maya Fur.

FIGURE 10-26 *A character with realistic looking fur*

FIGURE 10-27 *Fur created in Maya for a character*

CONCLUSION

In this chapter, you have learned the theory and practice of various fundamental concepts, such as fractals, and fBm. You have also created your own plug-in to generate a terrain model. Though the plug-in topic has been focused on generating terrain, the knowledge that you gain in writing this Maya plug-in is applicable to creating other plug-ins. With some research and trial and error, you will be able to create various plug-ins of your own. And before you know it, you will be generating various shaders of your own.

Remember, there are no rules that say a plug-in must be complicated and include bleeding edge technology or concepts. As long as the plug-in works well and helps increase your productivity, you have done a great job.

And remember also that creating terrain is like any other modeling process—you need texture, bump mapping, and lighting. Therefore, whenever you are required to create terrain, do not rely exclusively on one method. A hybrid of methods is the best approach.

EXERCISE

1. With the code outlined above, write your own plug-in to output color of shader based on the returned values of the Perlin noise function.
2. Create a mountain terrain using your own fractal method. With the terrain created, generate patches of grass on the mountain terrain.

11

SOFT AND RIGID BODY DYNAMICS

INTRODUCTION

There are generally two ways of creating three-dimensional computer animations. One is the physics approach and the other is the entertainment approach. The *physics approach* corresponds to simulation methods based on the various laws of physics, such as the law of gravity. The *entertainment approach* is the way that traditional animation has been created. Each method is applicable under different circumstances. For example, using the simulation approach, you are able to create accurate and realistic animation. This is often required in scientific and medical visualizations. On the other hand, the main objective of the entertainment approach is to entertain. Thus, exaggerated motions are acceptable and often desired in such animation.

Take the bouncing ball animation as an example. Using a simulation approach, you can create a realistic bouncing ball animation based on the laws of mechanics such as Newton's laws and quantum conservation. Using the entertainment approach, you will typically apply the principles of traditional Disney animation such as squash and stretch and overlap. Though the squashing and stretching may be exaggerated, they do give the impression that the ball is bouncy, and depending on how much it deforms when bounced, the idea of the ball material is conveyed whether it is a rubber ball or plastic ball.

Each method of animation is appropriate for different scenes. The simulation method is often mathematically complex to implement. And it almost always takes a relatively long time to play in real time. The entertainment approach is easier to implement and does not require a great deal of mathematics. However, it does not accurately depict what we see in real life. So, most of the time, simulation methods are required for science and accurate visualization while entertainment methods are used to convey an idea, motion, and even emotion. However, with faster computers available now, simulation has found its way to the desktop. The line between simulation animation and entertainment animation has become blurred. In fact, at times it is easier to use simulation to do animation for the entertainment.

In recent years, another approach to animation has been introduced: *motion capture animation*. Motion capture employs the use of 3D technology to capture the motion of an actor. The targeted motion could be a normal walk cycle, or facial animation, or any action that can be performed by an actor. The actor employed is usually a human, though any conceivable object could be used as an actor. The actor is usually tagged with sensors at various key points. The action is then performed under a controlled environment where the sensor data are captured. This captured data is fed into a process of filtering, editing, and eventually plugged into a software application where a digitally modeled object is able to perform the same action with all the captured details.

Motion capture animation is useful when both the entertainment and simulation approaches fall short. For example, in creating facial animation, there are hundreds of detailed muscles to control in order to convey any facial expression. Though it is often possible to reduce the number of controls to an order of ten, it still takes a good animator a considerable amount of time to set up each new facial expression for all new requirements. On the other hand, it would be equally difficult, if not impossible, to create an accurate facial simulation system to achieve the animation desired. In this case, the motion capture system will come into play and allow facial data to be generated relatively quickly and applied with great ease.

Although you are able to generate very believable animation relatively quickly and easily, it would be a mistake if an animator relied solely on the advantage of technology to create animation. Just as having the world's most advanced machine guns won't make you the best soldier, relying on advanced technology, be it software or hardware, without knowing the fundamentals is as good as building a castle on sand. Your castle may stand today, but it probably won't tomorrow.

In this chapter, you will create a simple animation using the soft and rigid body dynamics in Maya. In addition, a brief description of Maya's *Cloth Simulation* module is presented.

PRE-PRODUCTION

SCENARIOS AND TASKS

In this scenario, you are required to create an animation that has less to do with the four elements of nature. Instead, you are required to create the animation that is closer to home. The scene in this animation is set with a birthday celebration. This cut begins with everyone singing "Happy Birthday To You" to the three-year-old birthday girl. The handycam is zooming around the hall, recording the beautiful faces of the birthday girl and the cake, and so on. The beat changes when a baseball comes through the window and smashes into the cake. What follows after this is a series of "Oh, my God!" exclamations.

You are required to design and model the birthday cake. In addition, you are to create the animation of the cake getting smashed by the baseball. No sketch is given to you for this animation. You are required to propose and make your own sketch.

ANALYZE THE PICTURE

TASK

- Ponder how you would approach the design and model of the birthday cake.
- What are the considerations when creating the animation of the cake getting smashed?
- How might you create the candle flame?
- How many layers will you use to complete the animation?

APPROACHES

The scene is divided into the following individual parts. You will attempt to create the individual parts separately and integrate them into the final scene for rendering.

- Create the candle flame.
- Model the cake.
- Create the smashing animation.
- Integrate the scene and set up the lighting.

PRODUCTION AND TESTING

Create a new project

1.   Create a new project with the default settings.
2.   Name the project Dynamics.

Create the Candle

You will first attempt to create the candle animation separately as a test. After successfully creating the candle, integrating and creating a similar candle in the scene will be easy.

3.   Create a simple cylinder to be used as a stand-in candle.

You will create a proper candle model in the later stage.

Create the candle particle

4.   Create a directional emitter.
5.   Name it E_Candle.
6.   Set the parameters of the emitter as shown in Figure 11-1.

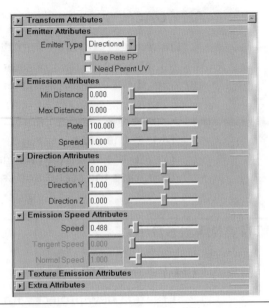

FIGURE 11-1   *Create the candle emitter*

7. Name the particles particleCandle.
8. Set the Render Type of particleCandle to Cloud (s/w).
9. Add a per particle life span attribute for particleCandle.
10. Open the Expression Editor and enter the following as the Creation Expression for particleCandle:

    ParticleShape1.lifespanPP = rand(2.0,2.7);

11. Add a radiusPP attribute to particleCandle.
12. From the Attribute Editor of particleCandle, create and map a ramp to radiusPP (see Figure 11-2).

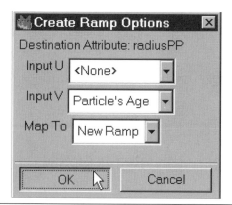

FIGURE 11-2 *Mapping a ramp texture to the radiusPP attribute*

13. Name the ramp ramp_radiusPP.
14. Edit the ramp to the following attributes (see Figure 11-3):

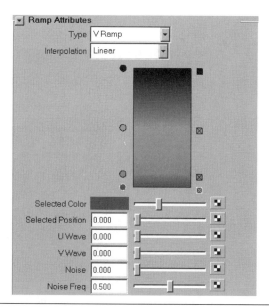

FIGURE 11-3 *Setting the various ramp attributes for the radiusPP*

POSITION	RGB VALUES
0.0	0.325, 0.325, 0.325
0.110	0.592, 0.592, 0.592
0.5	0.654, 0.654, 0.654
1.0	0.0, 0.0, 0.0

Animate the Candle

To form the candle flame, you will need the help of the dynamic field.

TASK

- Think about a good dynamic field to use.

15. Create a dynamic Radial field.
16. Name the radial field F_candle.
17. Set the parameter values as shown in Figure 11-4.

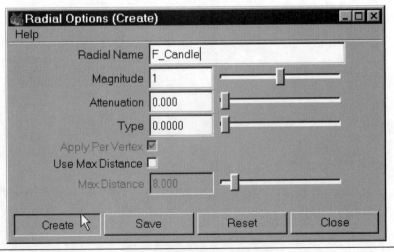

FIGURE 11-4   *Create a radial dynamic field to control the candle particles*

18. Play back the animation.
19. Interactively position F_candle.
20. You should get a result similar to the one shown in Figure 11-5.

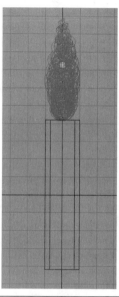

FIGURE 11-5 *Particle movement as a result of the dynamic field*

Shading the candle

21. Create a new particle shading group.
22. Name the shading group particleCandleSG and its material particleM.
23. Map the Life Color attribute of particleM to a ramp texture.
24. Name the ramp ramp_LifeColor.
25. Set the ramp with the following attributes (see Figure 11-6):

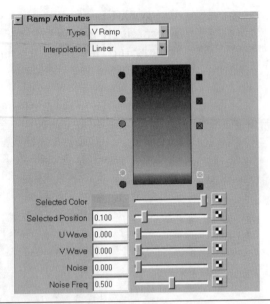

FIGURE 11-6 *Setting the ramp parameters for the Life Color attribute of the candle shader*

POSITION	VALUES
0.0	0.058, 0.193, 0.495
0.1	1.0, 0.638, 0.0
0.510	1.0, 0.192, 0.0
0.720	0.357, 0.157, 0.0
0.92	0.0, 0.0, 0.0

26. Map the Life Incandescence attribute of particleM to a ramp texture.
27. Name the ramp ramp_LifeIncand.
28. Set the ramp with the following attributes (see Figure 11-7):

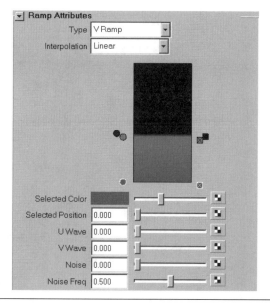

FIGURE 11-7 *Setting the ramp parameters for the Life Incandansance attribute of the candle shader*

POSITION	VALUES
0	0.357, 0.357, 0.357
0.380	0.486, 0.486, 0.486
0.410	0.0, 0.0, 0.0

29. Map the Life Transparency attribute of particleM to a ramp texture.
30. Name the ramp ramp_LifeTransp.
31. Set the ramp with the following attributes (see Figure 11-8):

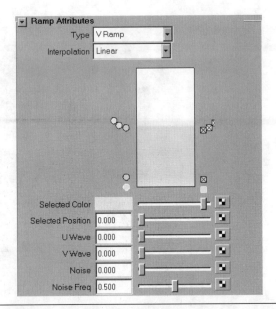

FIGURE 11-8 *Setting the ramp parameters for the Life Transparency attribute of the candle shader*

POSITION	RGB VALUES
0.0	0.95, 0.95, 0.95
0.085	0.910, 0.91, 0.91
0.5	0.9, 0.9, 0.9
0.52	0.98, 0.98, 0.98
0.56	1.0, 1.0, 1.0

32. Set the rest of the particleM attributes as follows:

ATTRIBUTES	VALUES
Glow Intensity	0.293
Density	0.8
Noise	0.374
Noise Freq	0.5
Noise Aspect	0.0

Test-render

33. Test-render your candle.

You should get an image similar to the one shown in Figure 11-9.

FIGURE 11-9 *A render image of the candle*

TASK

•   What parameters do you need to change to create a flickering candle such as what you would see when the wind blows at a candle?

Create the Cake Model

The cake designed is a typical creamy, chocolate cake. This will probably be highly suitable because the birthday celebration is for a three-year old kid. You should consider your own choice of design, color, and type of cake.

Creating the cake model is not really a piece of cake. There are many accessories and considerations that you should have considered and planned before starting to model it.

The following instructions will take you through the creation of several parts of the cake.

Create the main cake model

1.   Create a curve similar to the one shown in Figure 11-10.

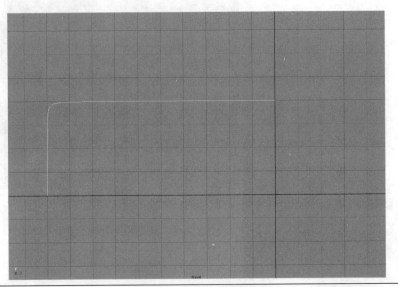

FIGURE 11-10 *Profile curve of the cake model*

2.   Using the Revolve Tool, create a revolved surface.
3.   Name the surface Cake.
4.   Create a Blinn shading model.

This will be used as the shading model for the cake.

5. Name it CakeSG and its materials CakeM.
6. Assign this CakeSG to Cake.
7. From the Attribute Editor, set the Color attribute of the CakeM as RGB (0.992, 0.992, 0.792).
8. From the Color Chooser window, store this value.

You will subsequently be using this color attribute value (see Figure 11-11).

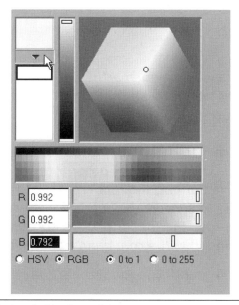

FIGURE 11-11 *Storing the color information for subsequent use*

Mapping the Cake Model

A main part of the cake is the image design that you use on it. Depending on how you design your cake, you should source for or create your own image. The important idea to remember is that the picture need not be highly detailed since it is supposed to be an image created by the baker using the normal baking devices, which will naturally be crude and irregular.

The image used in this animation was based on a typical cute Japanese anime girl. The image was created with very low resolution of 128 × 128 pixels. The image, when scaled, will appear to be rather crude and thus more convincingly appear that it is drawn with a human hand.

9. With the help of a photo-touching tool, create an image that you would use as your cake design.
10. Save your image.
11. Convert the image to cake.iff using the imgcvt command.

As a well-rounded artist, you should be able to use at least one type of photo-touching tool, such as PhotoShop or Alias Eclipse. Touching up images is a basic skill that you should master. Though Maya supports various file formats, it is important to always try to use the format native to Maya. The native formats are .iff and .sgi. Any other formats in Maya will have to be converted during the rendering process. Therefore, it is always advisable to convert the image you created to Maya .iff or .sgi to improve the speed. You are encouraged to refer to the Maya manual on the command options for imgcvt.

12. Open the attribute editor of CakeM.
13. Click on the Color Attribute Map button.

You will now override the color value and map a projection texture.

14. Create a Project File texture (see Figure 11-12).

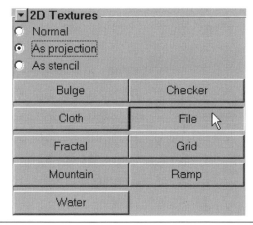

FIGURE 11-12 *Create a file project texture*

15. Name the project node cakeProjection and the file texture cakeFile.
16. Open the Attribute Editor of cakeFile and load in the cake.iff that you have created as the image for the file texture (see Figure 11-13).

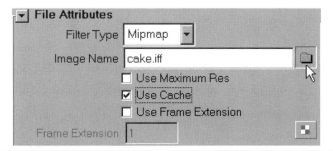

FIGURE 11-13 *Load a cake texture image for your model*

Loading the image with the Use Cache option will allow you to improve your rendering speed since the image will be cached.

NOTE

17. Open the Attribute Editor of cakeProjection.
18. Click on the Fit to Bbox button.

The placement 3D node of cakeProjection will fit to the cake.

19. Rotate the placement 3D node by –90 degrees about the X-axis.
20. Set the Warp checkbox of the placement 3D node to off if you do not want the image to be repeated (see Figure 11-14).

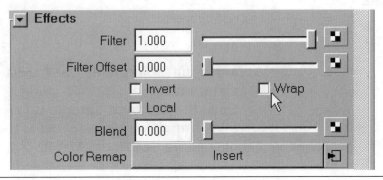

FIGURE 11-14 *Turning off the warp attribute*

21. Under the Color Balance section, set the Default Color attribute to the sameRGB values as above (RGB – 0.992, 0.992, 0.792). This is the stored value. So, if you have stored the color according to the instructions above, you will be able to just click to use the color.
22. Adjust the placement so that the image will fit nicely on the cake.
23. Set up a simple light source.
24. Test-render your image (see Figure 11-15).

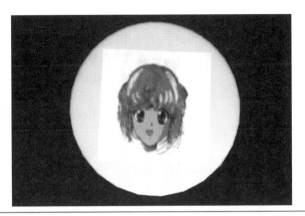

FIGURE 11-15 *A test render image of the cake*

From the rendered image, you will notice that the background of the image is also rendered out as a white area. Furthermore, the image itself is rather flat and uninteresting. You will now attempt to solve these two problems with the help of the Stencil and Bump Mapping tool.

Stencil the image

25. From the Multilister, create a stencil file texture (see Figure 11-16).

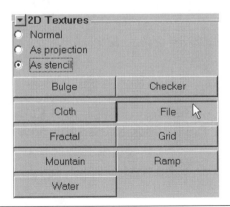

FIGURE 11-16 *Create a stencil file texture*

26. Name this stencil cakeStencil.
27. Name the file cakeStencilMask.
28. Click and drag the same cake.iff file to the Image
    attribute of the Stencil texture.

This will replace the cakeStencilMask texture you have created just now.

To cover up the white area of the cake.iff file, you have the option of either masking off a selected area using the Mask Color Map or creating a mask pattern of your choice and applying it to the Color Key attribute. Using the first approach is efficient but could easily create aliasing edges on the image. The second approach is preferred in this case.

It is always advisable to create a texture image with a plain white or plain black background. This will save you valuable time when you need to mask off the image background.

29. Go back to your photo creation tool and create the
    same image but this time with just the alpha outline
    (see Figure 11-17).

FIGURE 11-17 *Alpha image of the cake texture*

30. Name this image Cakemask.iff.
31. Click to load this new image, Cakemask.iff, to the
    cakeStencilMask texture node.

32. Drag and drop cakeStencilMask to the Color Key
     attribute of the cakeStencil.
33. Set the rest of the cakeStencil attributes as shown in
     Figure 11-18.

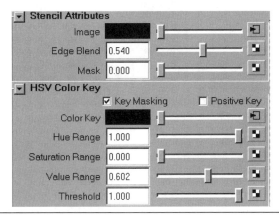

FIGURE 11-18 *Mapping the Color Key and setting the other attributes of the Stencil texture*

You should adjust the values based on your own image.
Refer to the Maya manual for a detailed explanation of the
various stencil attributes.

34. Similar to the Projection attributes done earlier, set
     the Default Color attributes of the stencil to the RGB
     values (0.992, 0.992, 0.792). Or just click on the stored
     value.
35. Drag and drop this cakeStencil to the Image attribute
     of the cakeProjection node.
36. Test-render the image.

You should get a figure similar to the one shown in Figure
11-19.

FIGURE 11-19 *A test render image of the cake with the background of the image texture removed*

Bump Map the Image

To create better depth for the image, you will bump map cakeSG.

37. Select the cakeProjection texture node.
38. Drag and drop the texture node onto the Bump Mapping attribute of the cakeSG.

This will create a default bump map for the mapping.

39. Set a higher value of the bump map, such as 3.0 (see Figure 11-20).

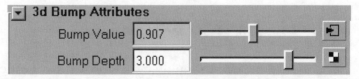

FIGURE 11-20 *Set a higher bump depth value*

40. Test-render your image. You should get an image similar to the one shown in Figure 11-21.

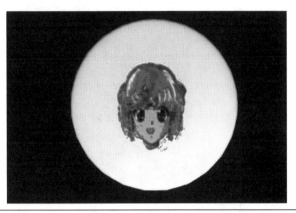

FIGURE 11-21 *A test render image of the cake with the addition of the bump map*

Layer Shader

As you smash the cake, it is important that the details inside the cake be seen to have a different texture. This will emphasize the volume of the cake. To accomplish this, you will create a layer shader that will layer two shading materials to the cake. One of them is the image shader group that you have just created. This shader maps the image from the top. The other layered shader will be mapped from the side of the cake.

You will first create the side shader.

41. Create a new shader.
42. Name the shader CakeSideSG and its material cakeSideM.
43. Using the method from above, map a project texture to the side of the cake (see Figure 11-22).

FIGURE 11-22 *Project mapping of the cake model*

44. Map the Color attribute of cakeSideM to a ramp texture.
45. Name the ramp ramp_cakeInside.
46. Set the ramp entries similar to the ones shown in Figure 11-23.

The ramp is used to create the layers of cream and chocolate of the cake. You are free to map different methods to the various attributes of the shader.

47. Set the ramp's placement2d node with a V noise of 0.03. This will create a more natural look to the cake.

You will now create the layer shader.

48. Create a layer shader.
49. Name the shader cakeLayerSG.
50. Drag and drop cakeSG to the layer attribute.
51. Drag and drop cakeSideSG to the layer attribute (see Figure 11-24).

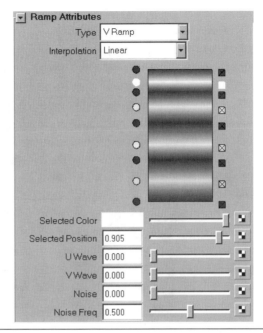

FIGURE 11-23 *A ramp texture used for mapping the Color Attribute of the sideCake shader*

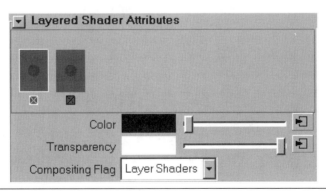

FIGURE 11-24 *Layer shading the cake model*

52. Assign cakeLayerSG to cake.
53. Your overall shading network should resemble the Figure 11-25.

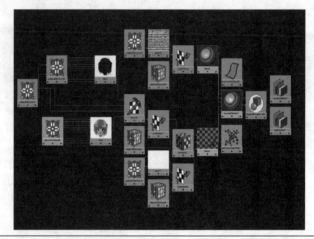

FIGURE 11-25 *Overall shading network of the cake model*

When you test-render your scene, you will notice that the side of the cake is visible. This is undesirable since you want only the inside to be visible when the cake gets smashed. Therefore, you will detach the cake into two parts: the top surface of the cake and the side surface of the cake.

54. Select Cake.
55. Detach the cake into the top surface and the bottom surface.
56. Name the top detached surface CakeTop.
57. Name the lower detached surface CakeLow.
58. Assign the cakeLayerSG to the CakeTop.
59. Create a Blinn shader.
60. Name the shader CakeLowSG and its material CakeLowM.
61. Assign CakeLowSG to CakeLow.

62. Set the shading Color attributes using the stored color that you stored earlier.

TASK

- Think about how to show the volume of the cake. Is this approach of layering the shader the only solution? Can you not create a texture map and try using a cubic or tri-planer or other method to get your desired results?

Create the Candle

You will attempt to create a simple candle with a spiral pattern.

1. Create a default circle primitive.
2. From the Create ➤ CV Curve Tool, create an eight-sided curve.
3. Duplicate six copies of the eight sided curve.

When duplicating, translate and rotate the curve along the Y-axis (see Figure 11-26).

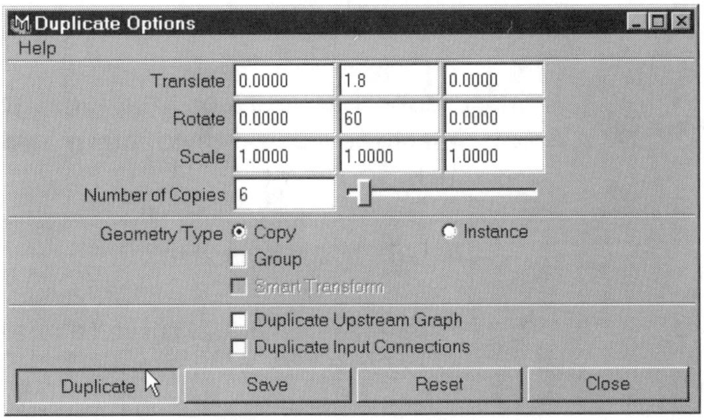

FIGURE 11-26 *Transform while duplicating the object*

4. Create another circle primitive and place it at the top of the rest of the curve.

You should get an image similar to the one shown in Figure 11-27.

FIGURE 11-27 *Building the candle using simple circular curves*

5. Ensure that your Construction History is ON.
6. Select the curve individually in order and go to Surfaces ➤ Loft.

A lofted surface is created.

7. Scale each individual curve to get the desired candle model (see Figure 11-28).

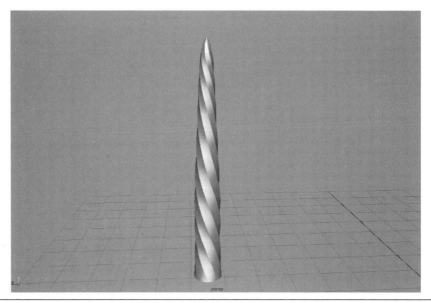

FIGURE 11-28 *A simple spiral candle is created by just lofting the curves*

CREATE THE ACCESSORIES

Star Shapes

Though Maya comes with various intuitive and powerful tools, many modeling tasks in production do not require that you use all these tools. In the simple cake model, you are able to create the various patterns such as the star and the flower shape of the cake very easily by simply using the nurbs primitives.

To create the star shape of the cake:

8. Create a default NURBS sphere.
9. From the top view, select each of the alternative outer CV points.
10. Scale the points to the size that you want.
11. You should get a star shape similar to the one shown in Figure 11-29.

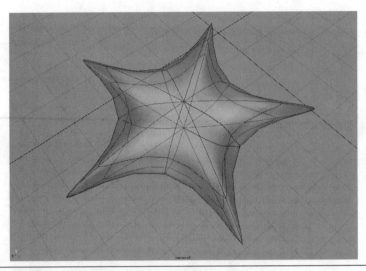

FIGURE 11-29 *A star geometry created with simple scaling of CVs*

12. The other shapes used in the animation are created in a similar way, simply by picking the CV points and scaling them. Figures 11-30 and 11-31 should give you some ideas to try out.

FIGURE 11-30 *A flower-like shape is similarly created*

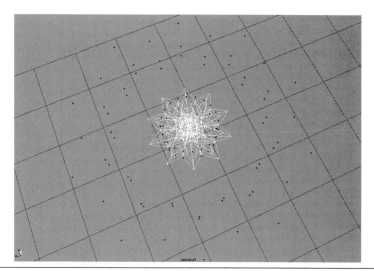

FIGURE 11-31 *Selectively scaling the CVs for the flower shape*

Birthday Words

Creating text is a basic operation in Maya. In addition to creating text, Maya's various deformation tools allow you to deform the text to many different forms. The following instructions describe how to create a bevel text and how to bend a given text.

13. Go to Create ➣ Text.
14. Enter the text (see Figure 11-32).

FIGURE 11-32 *Create a text*

Deforming the text

15. With the text selected, go to Deform ➤ Create NonLinear ➤ Bend.

This will create the Bend Deformation for the text.

16. Edit the Curvature values to any values you want.

You should get an image similar to the one shown in Figure 11-33.

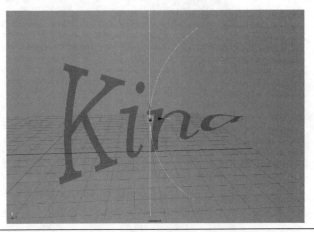

FIGURE 11-33 *Non-linear shape deformation using Bend tool*

17. By rotating and adjusting the Bend Deformation node, adjust the text until it is similar to Figure 11-34. This text will be the name on the cake model.

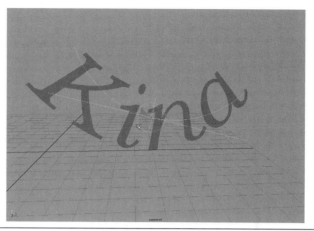

FIGURE 11-34 *Text adjusted by changing the parameters of the Bend tool*

Bevel the Text

In Maya, you can easily bevel the text by using various functions. In this case, you will attempt to create beveled text using simple curves and offset.

18. Go to Create ➣ Text.
19. Enter the text as shown in Figures 11-35 and 11-36.

Note that this time, you will create the text as curves instead of directly as surfaces.

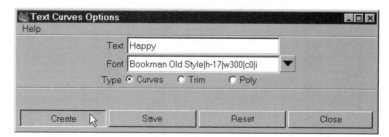

FIGURE 11-35 *Create text as curves*

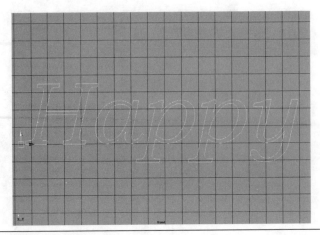

FIGURE 11-36 *Text created with only curves geometry and not surface*

20. Select the created text curve.
21. Go to Edit Curves ➤ Offset.
22. Set the options shown in Figure 11-37.

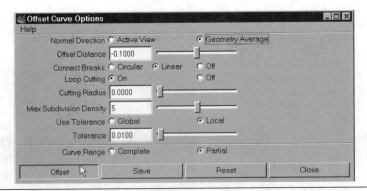

FIGURE 11-37 *Offset curve options*

23. Click Create to create the offset text (see Figure 11-38).

FIGURE 11-38 *Offset text curves created using the Offset Curve Tool*

With the offset text, you can easily create the beveled text by using a surface tool such as Loft.

Create the Other Patterns

Creating the rest of the patterns such as the nuts, chocolate chips, etc. is a simple task of duplicating a deformed sphere.

Integrating the Scene

In the introductory chapters, you learned the basics of lighting. You will now attempt to light up the cake using these concepts. Your lighting should make the cake looks as delicious as possible.

Lighting the scene

1. Create four spot lights.
2. Name them front, sideL, sideR, and back.
3. Set the four spotlights with the values shown in Figures 11-39 through 11-42.

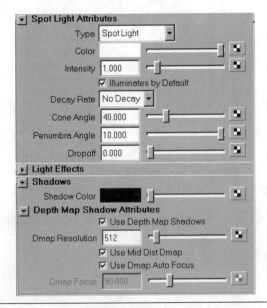

FIGURE 11-39 *Attributes setting for the front spot light*

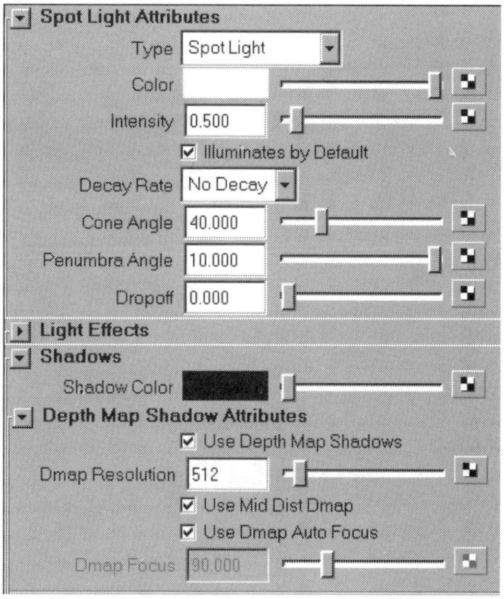

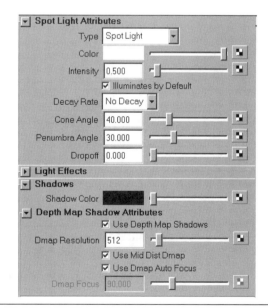

FIGURE 11-40 *Attributes setting for the back spot light*

FIGURE 11-41 *Attributes setting for the left-side spot light*

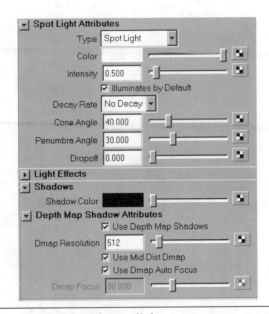

FIGURE 11-42 *Attributes setting for the right-side spot light*

4.   The spotlights were transformed with the following values but your values may differ slightly:

TRANSFORMATION	FRONT LIGHT	SIDE L LIGHT	SIDE R LIGHT	BACK LIGHT
Translate	32.53, 19.4, 0.336	8.81, 27.84, 45.39	19.24, 30.14, -33.6	-32.29, 30.18, -0.881
Rotate	-30.6, 88.4, 0	-29.4, 6.8, 0.0	-38.7, 154.4, 0.0	-42.6,-91.2,0
Scale	1,1,1	1, 1, 1	1,1,1	1,1,1

5.   The effects of the individual light can be seen from color plate 15.
6.   Test render the scene and you should get an image similar to the one shown in color plate 15.

ANIMATE THE SMASHING OF THE CAKE MODEL

Another challenging part of this animation is the smashing of the cake. You will attempt to create this animation using soft and rigid body dynamics. You will first create the baseball and make it a rigid body. Subsequently you will create the cake as a soft body.

Create a Baseball

The baseball geometry consists of two parts. The first part is the body and the second part of the ball is the liner on it. To create the liner on the body, you will need to create curves on the surface. In Maya, you can very easily create curves on objects. One typical way that is implemented in most software is to create a curve and do a projection of the curve onto the object. Another way is to use a one-click Live solution as shown below.

1. Create a sphere.
2. With the sphere selected, click the Make Live button located at the top of the main window (see Figure 11-43).

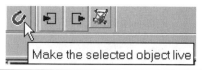

FIGURE 11-43 *Make an object "live"*

3. The sphere will turn light-green.

With the sphere set to Live, you can simply create a curve in the usual way that you create it in the world space.

4. Create a curve on the baseball body.
5. When finished, click back on the Make Live button again.

With the curve on surface, you can simply extrude a circle on the surface curve to create the liner bump or you can simply detach the surface into two parts and assign appropriate shadings to each of them. This step is left as an exercise.

Make the Baseball a Rigid Body

You will now create another sphere to function as the actual rigid body. This rigid body will be templated so that it would not be rendered but will still function with the dynamic movements. This sphere will be grouped with the actual baseball and animate with the baseball movement.

6. Create a NURBS sphere.
7. Template this sphere.
8. Group this sphere with the baseball geometry.
9. Select this sphere and go to Bodies ➤ Create Active Rigid Body.
10. Set the parameters as shown in Figure 11-44.

You can switch the active rigid object to a passive rigid body easily from the Attribute Editor.

Animate the Baseball

To animate the baseball, simply keyframe the ball so that it hits the cake and gets bounced off.

The keyframe curve for the baseball is as shown in Figure 11-45.

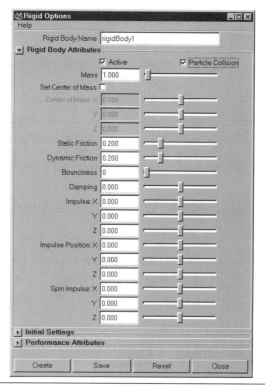

FIGURE 11-44 *Setting various parameters for the rigid body*

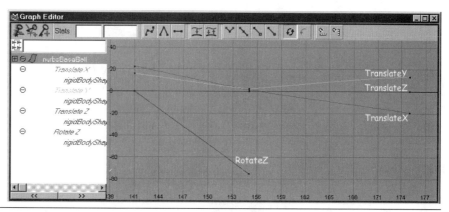

FIGURE 11-45 *Keyframe curves for the movement of the baseball*

TASK

- Attempt to animate the movement of the baseball group using the dynamic solver. Compare the difference in the result.

Make the Text as Rigid Body

When the baseball hits the chocolate words "happy birthday," it will fly off. To accomplish this, you must make the "happy birthday" words a passive rigid body.

11. Select the HappyBirthday word.
12. Go to Bodies ➤ Create Passive Rigid Body.
13. Test-run the animation and you should see that the ball will hit the text and send it flying off.

TASK

- What is the difference between an active and a rigid body in Maya? Can you convert one to the other easily?

Create the Smashing Soft Body

In Maya, the soft body and rigid body dynamics are implemented with the help of particle dynamics. Thus each individual part of the soft or rigid body may be controlled the way that a normal particle system controls objects. You are able to easily make a body deform and change shape and volume and yet remain integrated as a whole geometry. This is very useful for creating organic animations such as making a fish swim with all the parts of the fish moving seamlessly under the influence of the water medium.

Since the lower part of the cake will not be smashed, you will make only the upper part of the body a soft body.

14. Select CakeTop.
15. Go to Create ➢ Softbody.
16. Set the parameters shown in Figure 11-46.

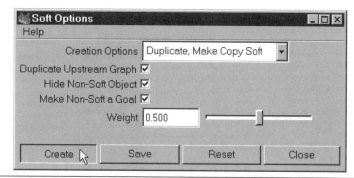

FIGURE 11-46 *Making the cake model a soft body object*

17. If you are using an older version of Maya, set the options as shown in Figure 11-47.

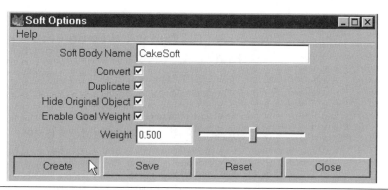

FIGURE 11-47 *Making softbody option window for older version of Maya*

18. Name the soft body particleCake.
19. From the Attribute Editor, set the parameters as shown in Figure 11-48.

Expressions After	off
Is Dynamic	on
Dynamics Weight	1
Forces In World	on
Conserve	1
Emission In Worl	on
Max Count	-1
Inherit Factor	0
Current Time	1
Start Frame	1
Input Geometry S	Geometry
Enforce Count Fr	on
Target Geometry	Particle Lo
Goal Smoothness	3
Goal Weight[0]	0.05
Goal Active[0]	on
Cache Data	off
Trace Depth	1
Collision Resilien	1
Collision Friction[	0
Particle Render T	Points

FIGURE 11-48 *The various channel information for the softbody cake*

20. From the Dynamic Relationship Editor, link the rigid body with the soft body.
21. Now, play back the animation.

You should see the movement of the smashing.

The softbody control in Maya is easy and straightforward. You should attempt to try out the various parameter values such as the conserve value of the particle body and the weight of the rigid body. Figures 11-49 and 11-50 show the results with the corresponding parameters changed.

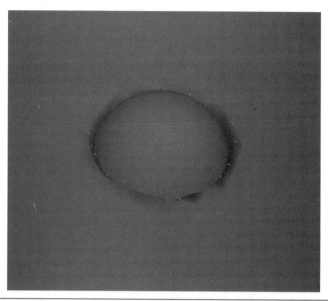

FIGURE 11-49 *Different results obtained by varying the soft and rigid body dynamics parameters*

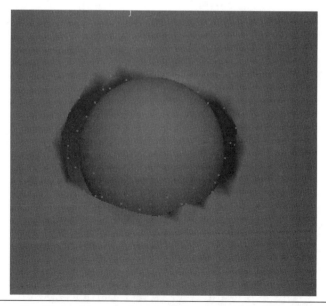

FIGURE 11-50 *Different results obtained by varying the soft and rigid body dynamics parameters*

Fine-tune the Smashing

When particleCake gets smashed, the particles that flew up must come down under the influence of the force of gravity.

TASK

• What is the dynamic field that you would use to create the falling down ?

One way to control the falling down movement of the cake is to use the dynamic field Gravity. However, in Maya a dynamic field is applied to an entire body. If this were done, instead of just a part of the particleCake, the entire particelCake would start to collapse. A way to solve this problem is to restrict the influence of the dynamic forces. However, a better approach is to control the movement of individual particles, using expressions. In Maya, you are able to control the position, velocity, and acceleration at the per particle level. Hence, you will use a simple expression to allow the required particles to fall freely as if under the influence of gravity.

22. Select particleCake.
23. Enter the following expression for its RunTime Expression.

```
vector $pos = particleCake.position;
vector $accel = particleCake.acceleration;
$tempy = $pos.y;
if ($tempy > 4.50) // 4.50 is the height value
  {
$pos = particleCake.position;
$accX = $accel.x;
$accY = $accel.y - 30.0*clamp(1.0, 20.0,($pos.y - 4.50));
$accZ = $accel.z;
particelCake.acceleration = <<$accX, $accY, $accZ>>;
  }
```

This expression queries each particle's position and acceleration values. Based on its position in world space, if they are above a certain height of the cake, then a negative acceleration is applied. This negative acceleration function is the force of gravity. However, to prevent the particles from falling under the level of the current cake height, a clamp value is used to control the acceleration. The height value used here may be different from yours depending on the thickness of your cake model. You are also encouraged to try out different values other than the 4.50 value.

TASK

- Modify the given expression so that you are able to introduce more randomness to the falling of the particles. The particles should fall with some randomness so that they do not form a nice layer on top of the cake.

Animating the camera

24. Create a new two-node camera.
25. Set the camera as the default camera view in the persp camera window.
26. Animate the camera using the techniques explained in the introductory chapter.

POST-PRODUCTION

To render this animation, you should have the following layers:

The main cake and other non-animating accessories

When dealing with complex softbody animation, you should always bake your softbody once you are happy with the simulation. Once you bake your animation, the movement will be recorded as keyframes. This will save you a lot of time during rendering since there is no need to run the simulation anymore.

The Rigid Body Words for "Happy Birthday"

These rigid body words are rendered separately so that if the words need to be changed, you are able to do it easily. For example, if it is decided that the font used should be of a different type, you are able to replace the model and simply regenerate the animation without affecting the rest of the model.

The Background Layer

The background layer in this example refers to the cardboard, the table, and any other objects in the background. You should be aware of the advantages in rendering backgrounds as separate layers. What is particularly important in this background is the overlaying of the cake cardboard and the table. Because the objects are closely overlapping, you may encounter some unpleasant shading results due to the computational round-off. Figure 11-51 shows exaggerated results.

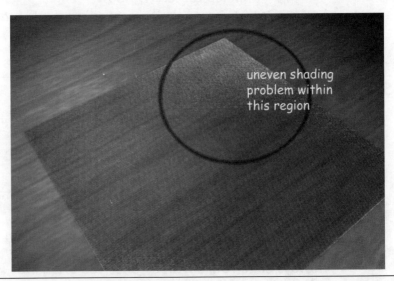

FIGURE 11-51 *Image rendered with problem of aliasing*

To solve this problem, you may increase the distance between the table and cardboard. However, doing so may create an "in the air" feeling for the cardboard. Another simple way to solve this problem is to render the cardboard and the table as separate layers. This approach however will require more storage space for your images (see Figure 11-52).

FIGURE 11-52 *A correct rendered image*

The Candles Layer

Having the candles created in different layers will allow you to add more candles and animate the flames separately.

In addition to rendering in layers, you should have the animation rendered with motion blur in order to emphasize the fast movement of the baseball (see Figure 11-53).

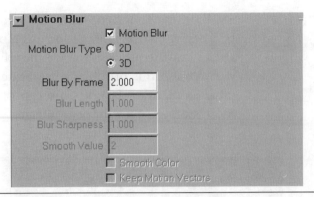

FIGURE 11-53 *The motion blur options*

Maya 2.0 comes with 2D and 3D motion blur techniques. You are encouraged to try them out. For unknown reasons, the motion blur implementation in Maya has traditionally been rather problematic. In order to avoid any frustrations that you may encounter, you are strongly encouraged to read the manual for more details.

Play back the animation chpt11.mov from the CDROM. Your results should be similar to the one shown in this movie file.

Maya Cloth

Simulating cloth has always been one of the toughest animations to create. Maya's *Cloth Simulation module* (bundled with Maya Unlimited) features a set of powerful and easy-to-use tools. You are able to very quickly create simple cloth, as well as complex shirts and pants. With the Cloth module, it is possible for your characters to have clothes that move in a more natural manner.

The challenge in creating cloth simulation lies in making the cloth move smoothly and seamlessly under the influence of various factors. The factors to be considered include the following:

- The mass of the fabric, such as silk and cotton.
- The fictional component between the fabric and its medium, such as human flesh and glass table.
- External dynamics, such as wind and gravity.
- Collision with other objects and within itself, such as cloth to cloth collision.

These factors should also be taken into account when you create scenes where characters are clothed. The following is the creation of a simple animation to test how Maya Cloth reacts to a shape-changing animation. The Maya Cloth module comes with several complete tutorials. You are encouraged to visit the tutorials for more examples.

In the animation, the type of cloth simulated is similar to silk—smooth and with a little weight. The shapes used range from a simple sphere to a sharp-edged object. From there, you will have an idea how well Maya Cloth can be used with your different forms of characters.

Create the Shapes

The shapes used in this example are a set of simple primitive shapes. However, these shape primitives are all created from a single primitive and thus are of a single topology. With the shape primitives, a blend shape animation is created.

The shape primitives created are all created from a plug-in called *kbCube*. This plugin is available from the CD. Before using the plug-in, you must copy the plug-in to your harddisk and rename it to kbCube.mll. The original default name in the CD is called KBCUBE.MLL. Since Maya commands are all case sensitive, you must ensure that the plug-in name is also of the same case letter. For the other plug-in that you plan to use, you should also rename them before you use them. KBTORUS.MLL must be renamed to kbTorus.mll and KBRM-FRAC.MLL must be renamed to kbRMFractal.mll.

1. Load the kbCube.mll plug-in (see Figure 11-54).

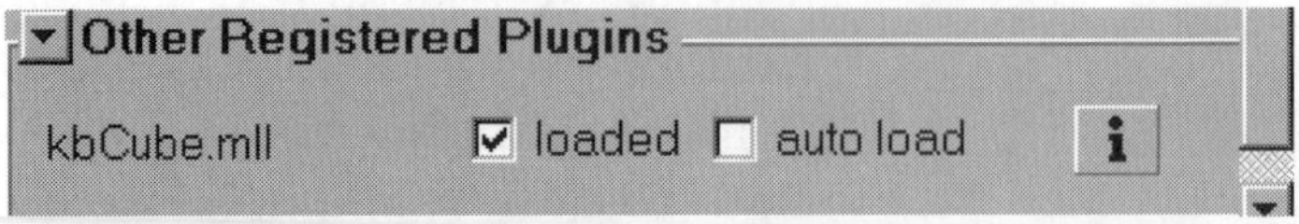

Other Registered Plugins

kbCube.mll ☑ loaded ☐ auto load ⓘ

FIGURE 11-54 *Load the kbCube.mll plug-in*

2. From the Script Editor enter the following commands with the syntax given below (see Figure 11-55):

    kbCube <roundness1> <roundness2> <radiusx> <radiusy> <radiusz>

    Each time you enter the command with different arguments, it will create a type of primitive. The primitives created are all of the same topology (i.e., same number of CVs, EPs, and isoparms). The range of values for <roundness1> and <roundness2> used in this animation are from 0.0 to 5.0. Enter as many times as you like to create different shapes.

FIGURE 11-55 *Various different geometry of the same topology created using kbCube plug-in*

3.   After all the primitives are created, select all of them and assign any given shader. If you do not assign a shader, when you render you will not see them being rendered.

4.   The primitives created are not of the right orientation. Select all the kbCube primitives and rotate them by –90 degrees about the X-axis.

Animate the shapes

5.   Select each kbCube primitive in the order that you want them to be used in the blend shape. The final primitive selected will be the targeted blendshape.

The target shape used in this example animation is the default round-edged cube. However, you are encouraged to choose any target shape you prefer.

6.   From the Animation menu, Go to Deform ➤ Create Blend Shape- ➤.

The Option window opens.

7.   Enter Table as the name of BlendShape (see Figure 11-56).

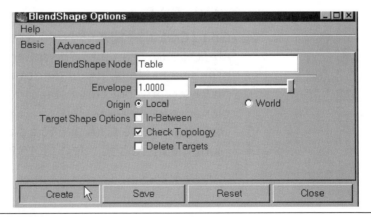

FIGURE 11-56 *The BlendShape option window*

8. Click to create the Blend Shape node.
9. Open the Blend Shape window from Window ➤ Animation Editors ➤ Blend Shape... .
10. From here, simply go to the different frames where you would like to create the various shapes and click on the Key button (see Figure 11-57).

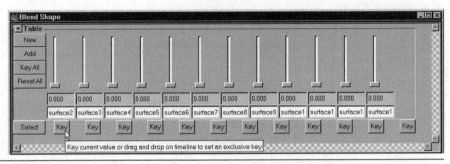

FIGURE 11-57 *Keyframe the blendshape to create a blend shape animation*

11. Scale the target shape to a value of 5 for all its X, Y, Z values.
12. Name the target blendshape blendTarget.
13. Hide the rest of the kbCube primitives.

Create the cloth

14. Go to Create ➤ NURBS Primitives ➤ Square and create a square primitive. The square primitive is a new primitive in Maya. If you do not have this primitive, simply create four curves that form the shape of a planar square.
15. Scale the square primitive to a size of 16 times.
16. From the menu set, select Cloth (see Figure 11-58).

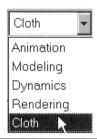

FIGURE 11-58 *Changing to the cloth set-menu*

17. Translate the square primitive vertically by 6 units so that it is slightly above the blendTarget shape.
18. Select the square primitive curves and go to Cloth ➢ Create Garment.

A polygonal-shaped cloth and a panel are created (see Figure 11-59).

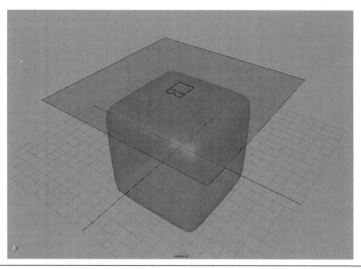

FIGURE 11-59 *A cloth object created with the panel*

19. Select panel1.
20. From the Channel box, change the cpStitcher 's base value to 400.

This high value of 400 is based on the anticipated sharp edges that the cloth will have on blendTarget. You are encouraged to change to lower or higher values later.

21. From the Channel box, change the cpSolver1 and set the values as shown in Figure 11-60.

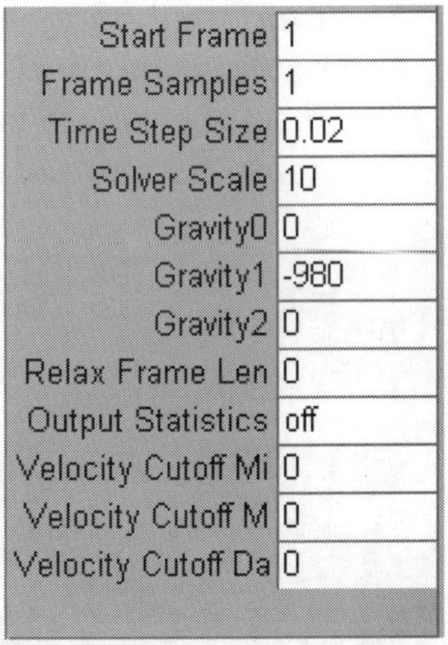

Start Frame	1
Frame Samples	1
Time Step Size	0.02
Solver Scale	10
Gravity0	0
Gravity1	-980
Gravity2	0
Relax Frame Len	0
Output Statistics	off
Velocity Cutoff Mi	0
Velocity Cutoff M	0
Velocity Cutoff Da	0

FIGURE 11-60 *Setting the various attributes of the cloth solver*

22. With the panel still selected, go to Simulation ➤ Properties ➤ Create Property.

A cpProperty is created.

23. Go to Simulation ➤ Properties ➤ cpProperty -❏.
24. Set the property to the values shown in Figure 11-61.

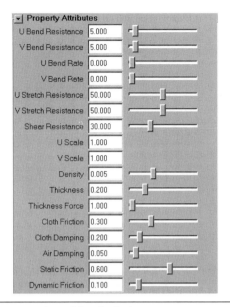

FIGURE 11-61 *Setting the various properties of the cloth*

Make the collision

25. Select blendTarget.
26. Go to Cloth ≻ Create Collision Object.
27. From its channel box, set the values as shown in Figure 11-62.

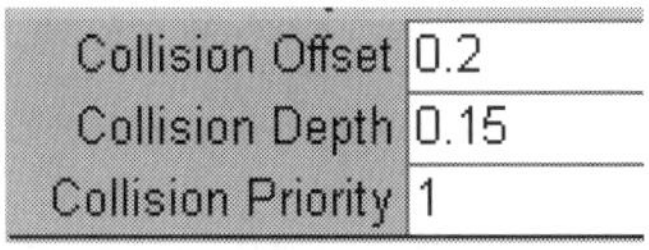

Collision Offset	0.2
Collision Depth	0.15
Collision Priority	1

FIGURE 11-62 *Setting the collision properties for the object to collide with the cloth*

Run the simulation

28. Play back the animation.

You should see the cloth dropping and colliding with the cube.

29. Play back the chpt11_cloth.mov animation from the CD.

This is the result that you should obtain for the movement of the cloth.

NOTE

Maya Cloth allows you to cache the cloth simulation. However, the cache file could be rather large at times. Therefore, you should always delete the cache for your file if you do not need it. Maya Cloth is display-bound, which means that when you are running the Maya Cloth simulation, you are unable to switch to another display. This is similar to the way playblast works for your animation. To simulate Maya Cloth more efficiently, you should use the command: cpRunBatch <startframe> <endframe>. cpRunBatch is a MEL file that allows you to solve a cloth animation and create the cache file without having to run Maya graphically.

CONCLUSION

In this chapter, you have learned how to create animation through the use of accurate simulation; in particular, the soft body and rigid body dynamic simulation. Remember when creating animation, the point is not whether to use the simulation or motion capture tool, but to remain open to all technology and methods. And often, what is most important in animation creation is the content of your story and the personality of your characters—not which bleeding-edge tool you use.

EXERCISE

1. Create a model of a Mars or Snickers chocolate bar. Place it on top of a wooden table. Animate the melting of the chocolate bar. As the chocolate bar melts, allow some of the melted chocolate to flow through the cracks between the wooden table. If you are creating a Snickers bar, ensure that the nuts slowly become visible as the candy melts.
2. Create a snooker-playing animation. Attempt to approach the animation from both the simulation method as well as the keyframing method.

12

GROUP
BEHAVIORAL
CONTROL
SYSTEM

INTRODUCTION

In the previous chapter, we explored the use of dynamic simulation in Maya. As you no doubt noticed, creating simulation via software can be pretty slow. In this chapter, instead of doing another dynamic simulation, you will take an even more challenging but rewarding step: developing your own simulation system. To be more precise, you will write a group behavioral control system. Do not be taken aback by the thought of writing your own control system. It is not rocket science. Let me explain a little on what do I mean by group behavioral control system.

A *control system* is analogous to a procedural function. You control everything that you desire essentially with a few parameters. In this case, what you will control is a group of objects, namely, fish. The behavior of the group of fish—how they swim, how they move about and twist their bodies—is all within the system that you develop and control. Another type of system you will use is *simulation*. A simulation system, strictly speaking, is supposed to be precise and scientifically correct. Ideally, it is a duplication of a real-world observation. However, in this case, you need not be concerned with such accuracy. What matters in the entertainment production environment is the final imagery. As long as your control system allows you to produce the final imagery that looks convincing, you have achieved your goal.

The main advantage of writing your own control system is that you will be able to control a large number of objects efficiently. For example, when doing a crowd scene, it is nearly impossible for you to individually keyframe every object of the scene. If there are 1000 objects, the amount of data that you need to keyframe and animate is prohibitively large. With a control system, you will be able to easily offset different parameters and achieve your desired animation.

A note of warning: the rest of this chapter requires familiarity with vector mathematics. If at any time you find that the vector mathematics parts are too complicated and that you simply cannot understand them, you can safely skip those parts and just get an idea of what the steps are trying to achieve. The methods are not hard and fast rules for writing a control system. What is most important is the idea of achieving it. When you have gained enough skills to digest the mathematics part of the implementation, you will find that the entire system is really very simple and straightforward.

PRE-PRODUCTION

SCENARIOS AND TASKS

Given the sketch below you are told that what is required of this scene is a school of fish swimming in any desired direction. The exact number of fish where are they going, etc. and has not been determined yet. You are to research and develop a method to control the fish animation for possible production use. Take note that the camera view will be above the water surface. The school of fish will be jumping around and moving in a desired direction. The camera may cut to underwater. That is of secondary importance at this time. Your main task is to take care of the above-the-water animation. (see Figure 12-1)

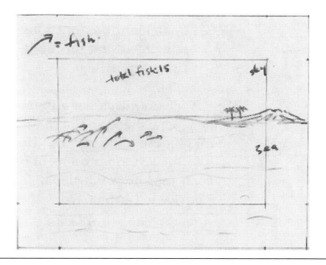

FIGURE 12-1 *Sketch*

ANALYZE THE PICTURE

When creating a control system for users, it is of paramount importance that you spend enough time thinking about how the users will want to control the objects. Flexibility is one priority. There is little point in developing a control system that fails to provide enough flexibility to control the objects. And it is also of little use if it does not allow new functions and parameters to be created for any unforeseen need. However, you will be able to avoid a lot of rewriting of code and scripts if you understood the requirements of the animation well in advance.

TASK

- Consider the parameters that are likely to be useful and needed for any artist, not just yourself, to control the movement of the school of fish.

APPROACHES

In Maya, to implement your own functions or expressions, you have essentially two options:

- Implement the functions in C++ as a plug-in.
- Implement the functions in MEL (Maya Embedded Language).

Each approach has advantages and disadvantages. Using the programming approach will allow you to have precise control over every single detail. However, for this reason, you are likely to need to write a lot of basic functions such as the commonly used noise function in Maya. You have already seen this approach in Chapter Ten.

Using the MEL approach you will have direct access to many pre-defined functions. These same functions that build up a large part of Maya and its user interface. As MEL is a high-level scripting language, the speed of execution will definitely be slower than the same function implemented using the low-level programming approach. However, unless your production needs require real-time execution and feedback of your functions, the performance of MEL is more than sufficient for implementing a good control system. Hence, you will approach the implementation of the control system using MEL.

In implementing a group control system, there are two main aspects to consider:

- The group behavior
- The individual member's behavior

The *group behavior* represents the behavior exhibited by the entire group as a whole. For example, in the school of fish, the entire movement of the school of fish is its group behavior. However, while moving as a group, each individual fish will, for example, be jumping at a different height and moving at a different speed. Such individual characteristics constitute its *individual behavior*. Another common example is a crowd control system. The crowd movement as a whole is the group behavior, whereas the individual members of the crowd exhibit their own distinct behavior.

Thus, to implement the group control system, you will have to implement it considering both the group as well as the individual member's behavior.

The table following table shows the different parameters that you will implement to control the school of fish.

GROUP BEHAVIORAL CONTROL SYSTEM

Parameter Name	Functions
Group	
Start Position	Random starting position
Number	User input's number of fish
Direction	User input's direction of the group
Individual	
Height	Individual fish's jump height
Speed	Individual fish's speed
Direction	Individual fish's direction
Tweaking	Individual fish's body twisting when in air
Advanced Control	
Collision Avoidance	Collision avoidance of individual fish
Splashing	Splashes of water as a fish enters and leaves the water surface

TASK

- Compare the table above with the list of parameters that you have written down in the previous section.
- Think about how you would start to implement the system. Will you start with the group behavior or with the individual member's behavior?

WHERE TO START

With the general framework in mind, the next question is: How should you start implementing the system? There are no rules that say you should start implementing a system from the top-down or bottom-up approach. Much is dependent on how comfortable and familiar you are with the various functions that you need to implement. In general, thinking through the framework and functions, you should identify the most challenging and difficult part and start from there. It is much like building a character for animation; you would study the different movements required and build the skeleton of your character that is able to handle the most extreme position. If, during the process of setting up, you realize that it is impossible for you to accomplish the extreme requirement, you are then able to identify alternative solutions at the earliest stage. This saves you a lot of last-minute work and stress. Similarly, when implementing the control system, try tackling the most difficult part at the earliest stage. You are more likely to gain confidence and be able to handle the requirements and deadlines. However, for inexperienced users, starting from the most difficult part could prove to be too discouraging. Hence, it is then advisable for you to start implementing the system with the most comfortable function. From there, you will start growing the other functions.

TASK

- Think about which function is the most challenging part for you to start.
- From there, think about what mathematical equations or algorithms will be best used to describe your function.

For easy presentation, you will start the implementation of the system with the focus on the movement of the fish jumping above the water.

THE FIRST STEP

From your early days of physics study, you probably know that the movement of any object in air, other than free a fall, is a form of trajectory path. Just like the missiles that you see flying on TV and the big screen, the path is generally trajectory in nature (see Figure 12-2).

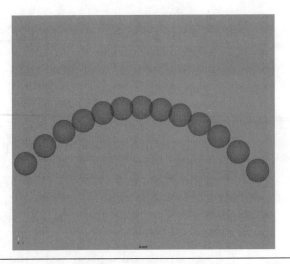

FIGURE 12-2 *A typical trajectory path of an object under the influence of gravity*

A typical trajectory path can be described using a simple mathematical equation:

$$S = ut + \frac{1}{2}\,at^2,$$

where
S is the displacement of the object

u is the initial velocity of the object

t is the time of flight

and **a** is the acceleration, which in this case is the force of gravity.

Assuming that the air resistance is negligible, this equation is appropriate to model the movement of the fish in the air, with **S** and **u** being vector quantities. Since MEL provides a complete set of vector functions, you will be able to implement this equation very easily. However, what determines whether a function is useful or appropriate in modeling a system is not merely its accuracy in producing real-world results, it is also the ease of implementation and flexibility. Remember that in the entertainment production environment, realistic simulation is of secondary importance to the flexibility and extensibility of the functions.

In most control systems, there are three basic qualities of flexibility that you need to implement under almost all circumstances:

- Amplitude control, which allows you to vary the magnitude that the function returns.
- Frequency control, which allows you to vary the frequency of the function returns.
- Phase or offset control, which allows you to offset and create variations from the original default values.

The importance of these three basic parameters is evident in the implementation of most fractal related functions. For example, in the Browian Shader of Maya, you have control over the amplitude of the output (indirectly via the Alpha or Color Gain), the frequency of the function (indirectly via the Lacunarity control), and the offset of the function (indirectly via the Increment that controls the ratio of the fractal noise).

Looking at the above trajectory function, you will realize that it may turn out to be quite unnecessarily complex and troublesome to build in the three controls for the motion of the fish. An alternative to the trajectory function is the very simple and versatile trigonometry functions, sine and cosine. In fact, a study of several computer graphics related algorithms will show that sine and cosine functions are the building blocks of many wonderful algorithms. If you are an artist who is still not familiar with sine and cosine functions, I strongly recommend that you pick up a trigonometry book and spend some time studying them. It will be time well spent.

Although sine and cosine functions will not produce the exact path that we expect of a trajectory function, with some modification and appropriate changes of values, you will be able to achieve rather convincing results. Remember that in entertainment production animation is not precise simulation; rather it involves substitution of that convincing animation model you have in mind.

PRODUCTION AND TESTING

When building your control system, you should always start with simple geometry that serves as a stand-in for your actual model. Once the core of your system is completed, then you can substitute the stand-in geometry with your detailed model.

Create a new project

1. Create a new project with the default settings.
2. Name the project GroupControlSystem.

Create the Stand-in Model

Nothing is better than using the basic primitives as the stand-in model.

3. Create a default Cone primitive.
4. Name it fish1.

Basic Movement

In the control system, you will use the X-axis as the forward facing direction and the Y-axis as the height of the jump.

5. Open the Expression Editor.
6. Enter fish as the default object.
7. Enter the following expression:

```
fish1.translateX = time;
fish1.translateY = sin(time);
```

NOTE

By now you should know that time is a built-in definition in Maya and that it is measured in seconds.

8. Name the expression ControlSystem.
9. Play back the animation.

You will notice that fish1 is moving slowly in a sine function path.

Control the Speed

TASK

- How do you modify the sine function to increase the speed of movement?

10. Edit the ControlSystem expression to the following:

```
float $speed_ctrl;
$speed_ctrl = 3.0;
fish1.translateX = time;
fish1.translateY = sin($speed_ctrl*time);
```

Now, by varying the $speed_ctrl value, you are able to control how fast fish1 moves in the sine function. Of course, what you have done mathematically is simply increase the frequency of the sine function and strictly speaking it is not increasing the speed of movement of fish1. However, for the purpose of building a control system, the output is more important than being mathematically or scientifically correct.

Control the Upwards Jump Movement

You can guess now that the way to control the height of the fish movement is through the amplitude of the sine function.

11. Edit the following lines in the ControlSystem
    expression:

```
float $height_ctrl;
$height_ctrl = 1.5;
fish1.translateY = $height_ctrl*sin($speed_ctrl*time);
```

Add More Fish

You will now attempt to add a few more fish to help build
up your system.

12. Select fish1.
13. Duplicate five more copies of fish 1 (see Figure 12-3).

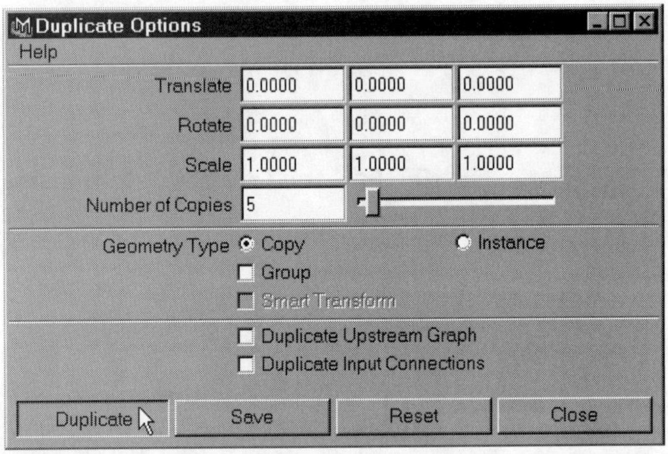

FIGURE 12-3 *Duplicating the fish geometry*

Control All the Fish

You will now edit the expression to control all the fish.
When you duplicate the fish, they are all automatically named
in an increasing order. This makes your naming and selection
of the fish very easy. You can simply use a loop to cycle
through the list of fish.

14. Edit the ControlSystem expression.
15. Your expression should now be as follows:

```
float $t = time;
float $speed_ctrl[];
float $height_ctrl[];
int $num; // number of fish
string $object = "fish";
$num = 6;
 for ($i = 1; $i <= $num; $i++)
 {
  $posx = $t;
  $posy = ($height_ctrl[$i]*sin($speed_ctrl[$i]*time));
  setAttr ($object + $i + ".translateX") $posx;
  setAttr ($object + $i + ".translateY") $posy;
}
```

You will notice that there are a few basic changes to the expression:

- A new variable $object is created so that you are able to change the name of the fish to another name.
- A new variable, $t, is created that replaces the direct use of the built-in name, time. If you attempt to use the time variable directly in the setAttr function, the time variable may not be recognized.
- A variable $num is used so that you can restrict the simulation to a chosen number of fish.
- The list of fish names is cycled within the loop. However, the assignment of the values is done through the setAttr command instead of the normal =assignment. If you attempt to use the = assignment, the expression will not work.

Create the Randomness

When you play back the animation, you will notice that all the fish start from the same position and move in the same manner. Therefore, you will now add a random factor to compensate for this.

The idea behind randomness includes the following:

- Set up individual fish positions randomly within a defined area.
- Include randomness in the speed and height control so that each fish will end up jumping at a slightly different height and moving at a slightly different speed.

The new expression should be as follows:

```
float $t = time;
float $speed_ctrl[];
float $height_ctrl[];
int $num; // number of fish
vector $position_start[];
string $object = "fish";
$num = 6;
for ($i = 1; $i <= $num; $i++)
{
 if (frame = = 1)
 {
  $position_start[$i] = abs (sphrand (<<float ($num),0.0,float ($num)>>));
  $speed_ctrl[$i] = rand(3.0,4.0);
  $height_ctrl[$i] = rand(1.5,1.5);
 }
  vector $temp;
  float $posx, $posy, $posz;
  $temp = $position_start[$i];
  $posx = $temp.x + $t;
  $posy = $temp.y + ($height_ctrl[$i]*sin($speed_ctrl[$i]*time));
  $posz = $temp.z;
  setAttr ($object + $i + ".translateX") $posx;
  setAttr ($object + $i + ".translateY") $posy;
  setAttr ($object + $i + ".translateZ") $posz;
}
```

For easy control, the positions set up for the fish are all positive values. This is achieved with the use of the abs( ) function.

Rotation control

16. Play back the animation.

You will notice that so far the fish have been facing upwards, regardless of where they are going and at which stage of movement. You will now make the fish rotate in the direction that they are moving.

To achieve this, you will use a cosine function to approximate their rotation values.

17. Edit the expression ControlSystem to include the following lines:

```
float $rotz;
  $rotz = -90+50*cos($speed_ctrl[$i]*time);
  setAttr ($object + $I + ".rotateZ") $rotz;
```

Direction Control

So far the fish have been moving in the forward X-axis direction. Now, what happens if you need fish to move in the other direction, such as on a diagonal axis? You must be able to control the direction that the fish are going. To accomplish this, you will supply a vector that directs the fish to the desired orientation.

18. Edit the following lines in the expression:

```
vector $heading[];
$heading[$i] = <<1.0, 0.0, 1.0>>;
$temp2 = $heading[$i];
$posx = $temp.x + $t*$temp2.x;
$posz = $temp.z + $t*$temp2.z;
```

The $heading vector allows you to enter any direction that you want the fish to be moving.

Further Rotation Control

When you play back the animation with the heading direction set to the diagonal, you will realize that the fish are moving in the right direction. However, they are not orientated in the direction they are moving. Therefore, you must add a further control for the rotation.

19. Edit the expression to include the following lines:

```
float $roty;
float $RTOD = 57.29578;
float $theta;
$theta = $RTOD*angle(<<1.0,0.0,0.0>>,$temp2);
$normal = cross(<<1.0,0.0,0.0>>,$temp2);
if ($normal.y > 0.0)
 $roty = $theta;
else
 $roty = (360-$theta);
setAttr ($object + $i + ".rotateY") $roty;
```

The lines above make use of two pre-defined vector functions in Maya. The idea is to first find the angle between the direction vector and the forward facing vector. The direction vector is assigned as $temp2 in the earlier expression. The forward facing vector is simply the X-axis and is defined as the unit vector (1.0, 0.0., 0.0).

The function angle returns values in radians. Convert these to degree values by multiplying the RTOD (radian to degree variable).

The next tricky part is to manage the direction when it is in a negative direction. That is to say, the rotation must be able to take care of all directions that the fish may face. To handle this, you will make use of the cross product of the heading direction and the forward facing direction. Based on the result of the cross product, you will set the direction as computed or take a complement of the angle values.

20. Play back the animation with different heading values.

You will notice that the orientation is still not in the expected direction. This is because the order of the rotation for the fish is different from the order that the expression is executed. Recall that transformation multiplication matrices are non-commutative. That is to say, a rotation of X followed by Y will yield different results than if the operation is a rotation of Y followed by X.

In Maya, the default order of matrix multiplication is always X, Y, Z. In the implementation above, the order of multiplication should have the Z rotation first. Hence, you will adjust the order of the matrix.

21. Select the geometry of each fish.
22. Open the Attribute Editor of the fish geometry.
23. Set the Rotate Order to Z, Y, X (see Figure 12-4).

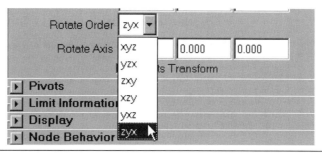

FIGURE 12-4 *Changing the rotation order of the geometry*

Play back the animation now and you will see that the fish are oriented in the direction that they move.

User Direction Control

So far the direction has been hardcoded into the expression. The direction that the fish are moving is always fixed at the beginning of the expression. You will now edit the expression to allow the user to interactively control the direction of the fish.

The fish should change direction while they are in the water. While they are jumping in the air, they will not be able to turn and change direction. Therefore, your expression should allow the fish to change direction while in the water.

As indicated in the requirement, the required shots are all above the surface. Therefore, this reduces the constraint imposed on your implementation for the changing of direction. You need not be concerned with fish changing direction in an unnatural way while underwater.

24. Go to Create ➤ Locator.

The locator will be the node used to control the direction of the fish.

25. Edit the entire expression to the following results:

```
float $t = time;
float $speed_ctrl[];
float $height_ctrl[];
int $num; // number of fish
vector $position_start[];
vector $heading[];
float $current_t[];
string $object = "fish";
$num = 6;
for ($i = 1; $i <= $num; $i++)
{
 // Initial position
 //
 if (frame == 1)
 {
  $position_start[$I] = abs (sphrand (<<float ($num),0.0,float ($num)>>));
  $speed_ctrl[$i] = rand(3.0,4.0);
  $height_ctrl[$i] = rand(1.5,1.5);
  $current_t[$i] = time;
  $heading[$i] = <<locator1.translateX, 0.0, locator1.translateZ>>;
 }
 // Direction control
 //
 int $lowest_point = 141.37167/$speed_ctrl[$i];
 int $cycle = 188.49556/$speed_ctrl[$i];
 if (((frame + $cycle)%($cycle)) == $lowest_point)
 {
 $heading[$i] = <<locator1.translateX, 0.0, locator1.translateZ>>;
 float $temp3x;
 float $temp3z;
```

```
vector $temp_heading;
$temp3x = getAttr ($object + $i + ".translateX");
$temp3z = getAttr ($object + $i + ".translateZ");
$current_t[$i] = time;
$temp_heading = $heading[$i] - <<$temp3x, 0.0, $temp3z>>;
$heading[$i] = $temp_heading;
$position_start[$i] = <<$temp3x,0.0,$temp3z>>;
}
// Position control
//
vector $temp;
float $posx, $posy, $posz;
$temp = $position_start[$i];
$temp2 = $heading[$i];
$posx = $temp.x + ($t-$current_t[$i])*$temp2.x*0.15;
$posy = $temp.y + ($height_ctrl[$i]*sin($speed_ctrl[$i]*time));
$posz = $temp.z + ($t-$current_t[$i])*$temp2.z*0.15;
setAttr ($object + $i + ".translateX") $posx;
setAttr ($object + $i + ".translateY") $posy;
setAttr ($object + $i + ".translateZ") $posz;
// Rotation control
//
float $rotz;
$rotz = -90+50*cos($speed_ctrl[$i]*time);
setAttr ($object + $i + ".rotateZ") $rotz;
// Further Rotation control
//
float $roty;
float $RTOD = 57.29578;
float $theta;
$theta = $RTOD*angle(<<1.0,0.0,0.0>>,$temp2);
$normal = cross(<<1.0,0.0,0.0>>,$temp2);
if ($normal.y > 0.0)
 $roty = $theta;
else
 $roty = (360-$theta);
setAttr ($object + $i + ".rotateY") $roty;
}
```

26. Set your playback slider range to a large value, such as 500.
27. Play back the animation.
28. While the animation is playing back, select and move the locator to different locations and observe how the fish react to it.

The animation now appears to be rather interesting. The fish seem to already have some life of their own. You will notice that the movement of the fish follows the *rule of diminishing returns*. That is, they will pass the locator position but eventually get closer and closer to the locator.

There are two main parts of the expression that deserve more explanation. The first part is deriving the change of direction based on the locator position. The second part is the occurrence of the change at the lowest point under the sea.

Direction Change

The idea of direction control is fairly straightforward. You first sample the location of the locator. Then, looking at the current fish position and the new position, you derive a new direction for the fish. The computation of the direction is essentially basic positional vectors.

To implement the change of direction, simply note the current time when you sample the locator's position. From there, it is essentially like resetting the vector direction and taking the sampled current time as the beginning of the movement. Figure 12-5 depicts this part of the implementation.

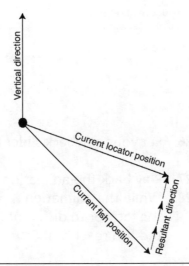

FIGURE 12-5 *Changing the direction with the help of vectors*

Time for Direction Change

In order to ensure that the changing of the direction occurs within the water and is not visible to the audience, the expression above implements the changing of direction at the lowest point of the fish movement.

To understand this part of the expression, recall that the movement of the fish is essentially a sine function. In a sine function, the lowest point occurs at the value of $3\pi/2$ where π is the standard mathematical notation of PI (3.14159). Therefore, the equation is written as follows:

$$3\pi/2 = speed\_ctrl \times time$$

and since time is 30 fps, the equation becomes:

$$3\pi/2 = speed\_ctrl \times 1/30 \times frame$$
$$frame = (3\pi/2) \times 30/speed\_ctrl$$
$$\therefore frame = 141.37167/speed\_ctrl \text{———} eq(a)$$

This takes care of the first occurrence of the lowest point. However, because the movement is a cyclic function, the expression must handle subsequent occurrences. Since the sine function cycles every 2π, the expression can be achieved by taking the modulus of the result:

$$2\pi = speed\_ctrl \times 1/30 \times frame$$
$$frame = 2\pi \times 30/speed\_ctrl$$
$$\therefore frame = 188.49556/speed\_ctrl \text{———} eq(b)$$

Combining conditions from eq(a) and eq(b), you will get the following expression:

```
int $lowest_point = 141.37167/$speed_ctrl[$i];
int $cycle = 188.49556/$speed_ctrl[$i];
if (((frame + $cycle)%($cycle)) = = $lowest_point)
{
...
}
```

TASK

• Try changing this part of the expression to a simplified form, such as the following:

```
if (sin($speed_ctrl[$i]*time) < 0.8)
{
...
}
```

• Can you explain the results?

Fine-tune the Movement

You will notice that the movement of the fish is proportional to the difference between the current position and the sampled locator position. In addition, the fish appear to eventually converge to a single point. You will now edit the expression to take care of this problem.

Fine-tune the Speed

To control the speed movement, you will include some offset variables. You are encouraged to change the values to best suit your needs.

29. Edit the expression to include the following:

```
float $offsetx, $offsetz;
$offsetx = 0.15;
$offsetz = 0.15;
$posx = $temp.x + ($t-$current_t[$i])*$temp2.x*$offsetx;
$posz = $temp.z + ($t-$current_t[$i])*$temp2.z*$offsetz;
```

Randomize the Individual Direction

To ensure that the fish do not converge towards a single point, simply change the direction that each is heading in, offset by a slightly random value.

You should edit the expression to include the following lines:

```
$temp_heading = $heading[$i] - <<$temp3x, 0.0, $temp3z>>;
$temp_heading = <<$temp_heading.x + rand(-$num,$num),$temp_heading.y,$temp_heading.z +
rand(-$num,$num)>>;\
$heading[$i] = $temp_heading;\
```

When you play back the animation, you will get a more interesting group movement now.

TASK

- How do you randomize the height values so that each fish jumps at a different height?

Individual Behavior

You may have noticed that in the expression, you have already added controls for the individual as well as group behavior. For group behavior, you have controls that allow you to direct where the entire school of fish is going. For individual behavior, you have controls over the individual's height, speed, and heading direction.

Referring back to the table, you have completed the implementation of most of the controls. What is left is to control the individual tweaking of the fish movement. That is, when a fish is up in the air, although it cannot change its direction, it can tweak its body as if doing a performance jump.

The approach of tweaking the fish is to first build the anatomy of the fish. This is similar to setting up a character for animation in which you decide about the bones, the control to the skeleton, etc. Once the structure of the fish is decided, all that is left is simply animating these controls to the structures.

The biggest question now is how to control the various parts of the fish so that they will work with your expression. At first thought, this may seem quite daunting. However, if you simplify the anatomy of the fish, it is really pretty simple to control.

Figure 12-6 illustrates the simple structure that I adopt to control the tweaking of the fish. It is a four-part structure: the head, the body, the lower body, and the tail.

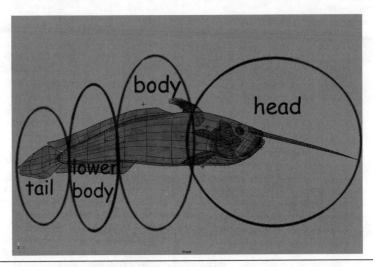

FIGURE 12-6   *The anatomy structure used for the fish model*

The model of the fish that you use will probably be different. However, regardless of whether you are using a simple geometry such as the cone or a complex fish model, the concept of the structure setup is essentially the same.

In normal character setup, the control of a character is usually achieved with the use of the skeleton joints. In this project, you will not use the skeleton setup. Instead, you will achieve the controls through the use of *clusters*.

In Maya, a cluster is a group of selected points of a geometry. Loosely speaking, the skeleton joints and clusters are the same thing with a different flavor. Essentially they just group the points of your geometry and allow you to control them in a different way.

In creating clusters, the points can be from the same geometry or different geometry. They can belong exclusively to one cluster or be shared among different clusters. In addition, the cluster points can have different weight values that allow you to control how much it will be influenced by the transformation of the cluster geometry.

For the fish model, though you have a four-part structure, you will be forming the clusters only for the body, lower body, and the tail part. The tweaking of the fish will then be created with the rotation of the clusters. In the movement, the head of the fish is taken care of by the rotation of the entire geometry. The following instructions show you how to create the clusters for the fish.

NOTE

Before you move farther, it is advisable to copy the expression text and save it to a separate text file. It is always a good practice to keep a backup copy of your program code, scripts, expressions, scene files, etc. You never know what will go wrong and if things go wrong, it's hard to remember all the details you have added to your work.

30. Delete all the fish geometry except the fish1 geometry.
31. Reset all the rotation and translation values to zero.
32. From its Channel box, change the Number of Spans to 20.

This will ensure that you have enough surface points to be grouped into various parts for the clusters (see Figure 12-7).

makeNurbCone1	
Radius	1
Start Sweep	0
End Sweep	360
Degree	Cubic
Sections	8
Spans	20
Height Ratio	2

FIGURE 12-7 *Increase the spans for more control over the deformation of the geometry*

33. Scale the cone to the X, Y, Z values: 0.3, 1.0, 0.3.
34. Go to Select Component mode by pressing F8.
35. Select the middle part of the points that you want to be used as the body cluster (see Figure 12-8).

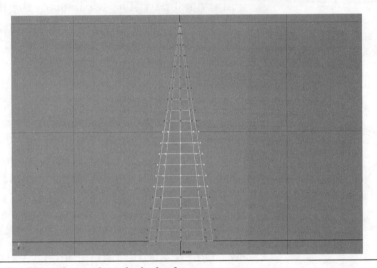

FIGURE 12-8   *Select the CVs to be used as the body clusters*

36. Press F2 to switch to the Animation menu set.
37. Go to Deform ➤ Create Cluster.

A default cluster is created.

38. Repeat the steps of selecting the points and creating clusters to create the lower body and the tail cluster of the fish.
39. Name the cluster body1, lowerbody1, and tail1, respectively (see Figures 12-9 and 12-10).

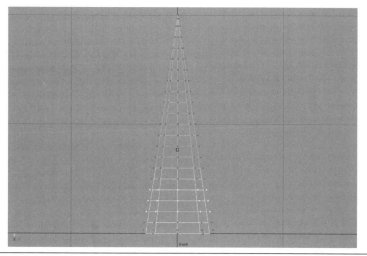

FIGURE 12-9 *Select the CVs to be used as the lower body clusters*

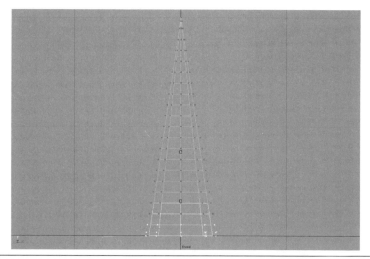

FIGURE 12-10 *Select the CVs to be used as the tail clusters*

You will now set all the pivot points of the cluster to the origin.

40. Select all the clusters and press the Insert Key on your keyboard.
41. Translate the pivot point to the origin.
42. Press the Insert Key again to switch back to the normal mode.
43. Select the clusters and test their rotation movement.

You should see each cluster of fish and be able rotate them independently. Now, to have a nice tweaking of the fish, is simply a matter of coordinating the rotation values of each of the clusters. However, before that, you must adjust the weight of the cluster so that the overall rotations result in a smooth curvature.

The concept of 3D painting in Maya has been extended beyond the mere sculpting of geometry. You can now even paint to add or remove memberships from a set or cluster. In addition, you can paint weights, and various other attributes using the paint tool. Alternatively, to adjust the membership of the clusters, you can go to Deform ➤ Membership Tool. With a cluster selected, you can add or remove any point from the cluster with the Shift or Ctrl left-mouse button click. Refer to the Maya manual for more details. You are encouraged to try out the different methods of adding and removing memberships using these tools.

44. Select the fish.
45. Press 5 to go into the shading mode.
46. Go to Deform ➤ Paint Weights Tool -❑.

The Paint Weight Tools window opens (see Figures 12-11 and 12-12).

FIGURE 12-11 *Using the paint weight tool*

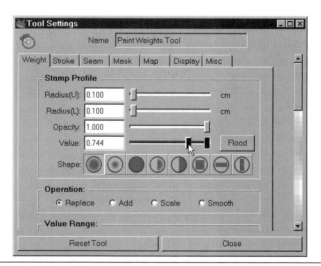

FIGURE 12-12 *Adjust the Value parameter to paint as the weight of the CVs*

47. Open the outliner window.
48. Click on the different clusterHandle nodes and you should see that the screen is updated whenever you change to different clusters.

When painting the cluster weights, a full white implies that the weight is 1.0 and the dimmer the color, the lower the cluster weights.

49. Select the cluster that you want to edit.
50. Adjust the Value parameter (from the Paint Weight Tool window) to a weight value that you desire.
51. Paint on the fish to effect your weight change (see Figure 12-13).

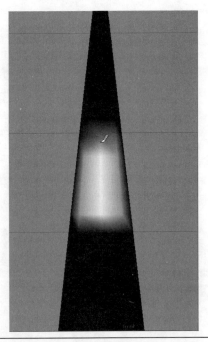

FIGURE 12-13 *Useful visual feedback when using the paint weight tool*

One simple way to adjust the weight of an object so that the movement is smooth is to move or deform the object to the extreme position and from there, using the paint weight tool adjust the weight so that the final look is smooth.

You will control the tweaking of the fish with the help of the expression. The idea behind the tweaking of the fish is similar to the movement of the fish. You will set the rotation of the clusters based on the cycle of the sine and cosine functions.

52. Edit the expression with the following lines:

```
$num = 1;
$clusterswing[$j] = rand(-1.2,1.2); //put this line in the initial position section
// Tweakings
//
//body
  setAttr ("body" + $i + ".rotateZ") (3.76*abs(cos (3.0*time))+$clusterupswing[$i]);
//lower body
  setAttr ("lowerbody" + $i + ".rotateZ") (5.86*abs(cos (3.0*time))+$clusterupswing[$i]);
//tail
  setAttr ("tail" + $i + ".rotateZ") (15.26*abs(cos(3.0*time))+$clusterupswing[$i]);
```

The value 3.76 obtained for the body cluster is the extreme rotation value when the fish bends while rotating. The values of 5.86 and 15.26 are similarly recorded. You are likely to be using different values depending on how much tweaking you would like to have. You can also include the swinging of the fish to the side when they jump. This would create an even more interesting movement.

In addition, to allow each fish to tweak in its own characteristic manner, the variable $clusterswing is assigned a random value for each fish.

You will now test the movement of the fish as a group.

53. Select fish1.
54. Go to Edit ➤ Duplicate -❑.
55. Set the option as shown in Figure 12-14.

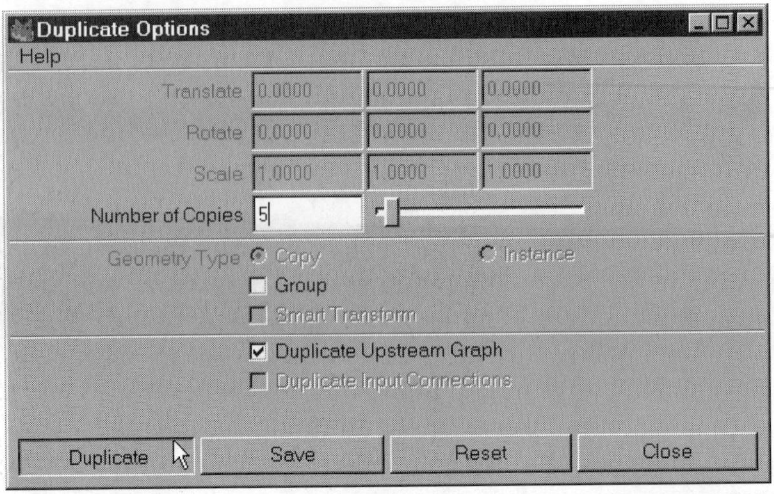

FIGURE 12-14 *A stand-in cone used for the exact fish model*

This will duplicate the fish and the clusters.

56. Update the expression to set the $num variable to 6.
57. Play back the animation.

Replace the Fish Model

The control system model that you have created is applicable to any form of the fish model. You can easily replace the simplified cone-fish model with any other model.

You may now load from the CD-ROM a fish model or create your own fish model. Figure 12-15 shows you the fish model that I use.

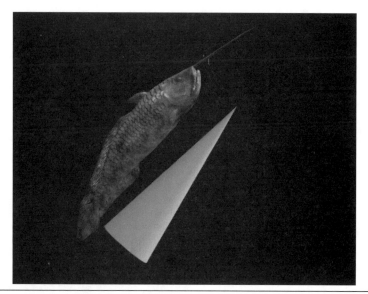

FIGURE 12-15 *A stand-in cone used for the exact fish model*

User Interface Control

In Maya, you have a pre-defined set of MEL scripts to create various types of user interface. These MEL scripts allow you to write your own functions such as this control system and yet hide the complexity from the user and allow them to use the system without worrying about the underlying details.

Before you write the user interfaces, you should think about how you want the user to use your system. Below is a simple example of the set of controls that you can create. You should feel free to come up with your own list of control variables.

INDIVIDUAL	GROUP
Max jump height	Number of fish
Maximum Speed	Group Unity

You will create a new node to serve as the link between the expression values and the user interface.

58. Create a locator.
59. Name it interfaceCtrl.
60. With interfaceCtrl selected, go to Modify ➤ Add Attribute… (see Figure 12-16).

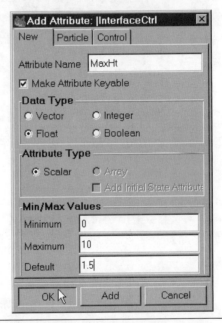

FIGURE 12-16 *Adding new dynamic attributes*

61. From the Add Attribute window, add each of the following attributes.

As you add in the attributes, you should see them being updated in the Channel Box window.

ATTRIBUTE NAME	DATA TYPE	MIN	MAX	DEFAULT
Number	Float	0	100	1
MaxHt	Float	0	10	1.5
MaxSp	Float	0	1.0	0.15
GrpUnity	Float	0	1	0.5

By default, a new Transformation node is always created with ten keyable attributes, three for each translation, rotation, and scaling, and one for visibility. Since you do not need the rest of the Transformation nodes, you can make them unkeyable and not appear in the Channel Box.

62. With interfaceCtrl selected, go to Window ≻ General Editors ≻ Channel Control… .
63. Remove all the Transformation nodes except the newly created attributes and the Visibility Channel (see Figure 12-17).

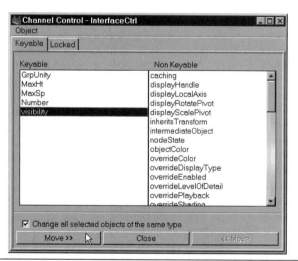

FIGURE 12-17 *Controlling what is keyable from the channel control box*

64. Open the Attribute Editor of interfaceCtrl.
65. Go to the Extra Attributes section.

You should see that the newly created attributes are available under the section (see Figure 12-18).

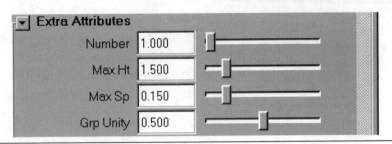

FIGURE 12-18 *The extra new dynamic attributes*

With the extra attributes available from the Attribute Editor, you are able to control the movement of the fish. However, it is more desirable to create a new window with customized interface for your user to use the control system.

66. Open a new text editor such as jot, vi, or notepad.
67. Enter the following lines into the text editor:

```
global proc kbGCS()
{
    waitCursor -state on;
    string $window = "kbGCSWindow";
    string $object = "InterfaceCtrl";
    if (!`window -exists $window`)
        makekbGCSWin($window, $object);
    showWindow $window;
    waitCursor -state off;
} // kbGCS //
//
//
global proc makekbGCSWin(string $window, string $object)
{
    window
        -title "kb Group Control System"
        -iconName "kbGCS"
        -titleBar true
```

```
        -minimizeButton true
        -maximizeButton false
        -sizeable true
        $window;
formLayout kbGCSForm;
textFieldGrp
        -l "Group Leader Name"
        -en 0
        -tx "locator1" leaderName_ft;
attrFieldSliderGrp
        -l "Number of Members"
        -at ($object + ".Number")
        -pre 0 numberMember_sf;
checkBoxGrp
        -l "Collision Avoidance"
        -ll ""
        -en 0
        -v1 true Collision_bc;
separator -style "in" sep1;
text -l "Individual:" individual_t;
textFieldGrp
        -l "Member Name"
        -en 0
        -tx "fish" memberName_ft;
attrFieldSliderGrp
        -l "Maximum Height"
        -at ($object + ".MaxHt")
        -pre 2 maximumHeight_sf;
attrFieldSliderGrp
        -l "Maximum Speed"
        -at ($object + ".MaxSp")
        -pre 2 maximumSpeed_sf;
separator -style "in" sep2;
text -l "Group:" group_t;
attrFieldSliderGrp
        -l "Group Unity"
        -at ($object + ".GrpUnity")
        -pre 2 groupUnity_sf;
separator -style "in" sep3;
button
        -l "Close"
        -c ( "window -e -vis 0 " + $window ) close_b;
formLayout -e
      -af leaderName_ft top 10
      -af leaderName_ft left 10
      -ac numberMember_sf top 10 leaderName_ft
      -af numberMember_sf left 10
      -ac Collision_bc top 10 numberMember_sf
      -af Collision_bc left 10
      -ac sep1 top 10 Collision_bc
      -af sep1 left 0
      -af sep1 right 0
      -ac individual_t top 10 sep1
      -af individual_t left 10
```

```
    -ac memberName_ft top 10 individual_t
    -af memberName_ft left 10
    -ac maximumHeight_sf top 10 memberName_ft
    -af maximumHeight_sf left 10
    -ac maximumSpeed_sf top 10 maximumHeight_sf
    -af maximumSpeed_sf left 10
    -ac sep2 top 10 maximumSpeed_sf
    -af sep2 left 0
    -af sep2 right 0
    -ac group_t top 10 sep2
    -af group_t left 10
    -ac groupUnity_sf top 10 group_t
    -af groupUnity_sf left 10
    -ac close_b top 10 groupUnity_sf
    -af close_b left 15
    -af close_b right 15
    kbGCSForm;
} // makekbGCSWin //
```

These lines of code create various buttons such as sliders and buttons using the standard MEL script commands. They are straightforward to understand from the MEL manuals.

In the above interface, an additional function, *Collision detection*, is created but is ghosted at the present moment. This will remind you or the user that this collision detection function will be implemented subsequently. This collision detection function is left as an exercise for you. It can be implemented easily using simple vector mathematics again.

68. Save the text file with the name kbGCS.mel in your default MEL directory.
69. To quickly test the result of the MEL scripts, simply enter the text into the script editor.
70. Enter kbGCS to run the script.

You should get a window similar to the one shown in Figure 12-19.

To complete the control system, you will now edit the expression to connect the link between the system and the interface.

71. Edit the expression as follows:

```
$num = InterfaceCtrl.Number;
$offsetx = InterfaceCtrl.MaxSp;
$offsetz = InterfaceCtrl.MaxSp;
$height_ctrl[$i] = rand(InterfaceCtrl.MaxHt,InterfaceCtrl.MaxHt);
float $unity = InterfaceCtrl.GrpUnity*$num;
$temp_heading = <<$temp_heading.x + rand(-$unity,$unity),$temp_heading.y,$temp_heading.z
+ rand(-$unity,$unity)>>;
```

FIGURE 12-19 *The user create interface for the control system*

72. Play back the animation.

You are now able to interactively control the system through the interface, while the animation is playing. A complete listing of the expression Control System is available in Appendix B.

CONCLUSION

In this chapter, you have developed a very straightforward group behavior control system. There are many different ways to improve and refine your system, such as building in some form of artificial intelligence where the fish exhibit some self-learning capability. For example, the fish would be able to find their own way without the user defining the path from one location to another. Or you could refine the system so that more complex animation could be built on top of this system. For example, there could be a subsystem that controls the pattern of the way individual fish twist their bodies. And with the combination of the individual subsystems, you could build a library of an almost infinite set of different animations.

This chapter has introduced to you a rather complete, challenging, and yet manageable control system. You have also learned how to use MEL to create a user interface to control your system. Hopefully, this chapter will encourage you to do further research and to implement your own control system.

Play back the animation chpt12.mov from the CD. This is the result that you should get when you have the control system implemented with the other parts of the scene. Also play back the animation chpt12_O.mov from the CD. This animation is similarly created with a collision detection implemented. The sperm-like organism changes its direction abruptly when it hits the boundary of the cell.

EXERCISE

1. Design and develop a control system using MEL that allows users to create and control a set of flying objects. The set of flying objects could be a flock of birds or a squadron of fighter jets. Include the necessary controls that you think are useful for any artist. These controls should include the following:
   • User-defined number of objects
   • User-defined flight path
   • Six degrees of freedom for the individual object. That is, in addition to moving along the path as a group, an individual object should be able to move along its local X, Y, and Z axes and be able to roll, pitch, and yaw.
2. Design and implement a complete user interface for the control system in (1).

FADE OUT

I once saw the most beautiful sunset while I was up on top of a snowy mountain. When I was back at the foot and tried to describe it to others, I was frustrated because its beauty defied words. When I tried looking through various books and encyclopedias in search of a description, I was disappointed. What the books provided were interesting but cold facts-of the scientific description of sunsets.

Having theoretical, abstract knowledge of sunsets is one thing; experiencing their beauty is another. The same goes with doing effects animation. Having a Ph.D. does not make you an expert in creating digital effects animation. Though theoretical knowledge is always good to have, the successful effects animator or TD does not rely solely on theories. Instead, they observe, experience, and creatively transfer the beauty into their own creation.

This book has taken you from theory to the practice of creating digital effects animation. I have introduced as much as possible the problem-solving elements. Betty Edwards mentioned that when drawing, draw what you see and not what you think you see. Similarly, when creating animation, do not be limited by what you believe you know or what your software can do. Rather, let your creativity flow and invent your own solutions to problems. Don't stop at what you learned here. And don't be limited by what you know about Maya. Remember, Maya is just a tool, nature is your teacher. Good luck!

APPENDIX A: A BRIEF WALK-THROUGH OF THE PAST AND FUTURE OF VISUAL EFFECTS

Motion pictures were first invented in the 1890s. Within a short span of time, special effects have taken its place as a necessary gag in all movies. During those days, special effects were done with the help of, for example, miniatures, stop-motion animation, camera multiple exposure, camera matte, glass shots, animatronics (mechanical puppets), and the revolutionary optical printer. Many wonderful movies were created, among them: The Lost World (1925), Metropolis (1927), Frankenstein (1931), King Kong (1933), Mighty Joe Young (1945), The Ten Commandments (1956), Cleopatra (1963), 2001: A Space Odyssey (1966), and the all time popular Star Wars (1977).

In the 1980s, the world saw a new turning chapter in the making of cinematic movies: the use of computer graphic effects. However, as computer graphics research was still in its infancy at that time, plus the extremely high-priced hardware, most filmmakers remained comfortable with their usual film making toys. However, enter 1990s, the potential of computer graphics started to set in with the release of several visually stunning movies, among them: Terminator II: Judgment Day (1991), Jurassic Park (1993), the first fully CG cinematic animation Toy Story (1995), and the highest-grossing movie of all time, Titanic (1997).

While nobody knows what new CG inventions will come past the millennium, one thing for sure is many schools are gearing up to prepare students for this prominent shift of paradigm. Though the decades old way of creating special effects are still irreplaceable, the potential that one day digital effects can replace the old ways are simply too prominent to be ignored.

Many schools have started to introduce courses specifically aimed at teaching students the theory and practice of creating digital effects. Looking at these courses, it is not hard to notice that most of them require you to have substantial prior experience in doing computer animation itself. This is not surprising as many digital effects are potentially complex animation that simulates the natural phenomenon. For example, it is still a challenge to provide realistic clothing, hairstyles, and human skin to the digital characters. And it is still difficult to create convincing fire, explosion, water splashes etc. that interact freely with the digital characters.

Digital effects is a highly specialized area of filmmaking. While this book may not cover everything you need to prepare yourself for this new paradigm, it will hopefully inspire you to venture further and eventually be a successful visual effects artist.

APPENDIX B: SAMPLE MEL AND UNIX SCRIPTS MEL

COMPLETE GROUP BEHAVIORAL CONTROL SYSTEM MEL SCRIPT

```
float $t = time;
float $speed_ctrl[];
float $height_ctrl[];
int $num; // number of fish
vector $position_start[];
vector $heading[];
float $current_t[];

float $clusterswing[];
float $clusterupswing[];

string $object = "fish";

$num = InterfaceCtrl.Number;

for ($i = 1; $i <= $num; $i++)
{

 // Initial position
 //
 if (frame == 1)
 {
  $position_start[$i] = abs (sphrand (<<float ($num),0.0,float ($num)>>));
  $speed_ctrl[$i] = rand(3.0,4.0);
  $height_ctrl[$i] = rand(InterfaceCtrl.MaxHt,InterfaceCtrl.MaxHt);

  $current_t[$i] = time;
  $heading[$i] = <<locator1.translateX, 0.0, locator1.translateZ>>;
  $clusterswing[$i] = rand(0.0,0.0);
  $clusterupswing[$i] = rand(0.0,0.0);

 }
```

```
// Direction control
//
int $lowest_point = 141.37167/$speed_ctrl[$i];
int $cycle = 188.49556/$speed_ctrl[$i];
if (((frame + $cycle)%($cycle)) == $lowest_point)
{
$heading[$i] = <<locator1.translateX, 0.0, locator1.translateZ>>;

float $temp3x;
float $temp3z;
vector $temp_heading;

$temp3x = getAttr ($object + $i + ".translateX");
$temp3z = getAttr ($object + $i + ".translateZ");
$current_t[$i] = time;

$temp_heading = $heading[$i] - <<$temp3x, 0.0, $temp3z>>;

float $unity = InterfaceCtrl.GrpUnity*$num;
$temp_heading = <<$temp_heading.x + rand(-$unity, $unity), $temp_heading.y, \\
                                $temp_heading.z + rand(-$unity,$unity)>>;
$heading[$i] = $temp_heading;

$position_start[$i] = <<$temp3x,0.0,$temp3z>>;

}


// Position control
//
vector $temp;
float $posx, $posy, $posz;

$temp = $position_start[$i];
$temp2 = $heading[$i];

float $offsetx, $offsetz;
$offsetx = InterfaceCtrl.MaxSp;
$offsetz = InterfaceCtrl.MaxSp;

$posx = $temp.x + ($t-$current_t[$i])*$temp2.x*$offsetx;
$posy = $temp.y + ($height_ctrl[$i]*sin($speed_ctrl[$i]*time));
$posz = $temp.z + ($t-$current_t[$i])*$temp2.z*$offsetz;

setAttr ($object + $i + ".translateX") $posx;
setAttr ($object + $i + ".translateY") $posy;
setAttr ($object + $i + ".translateZ") $posz;

// Rotation control
//
float $rotz;
$rotz = -90+50*cos($speed_ctrl[$i]*time);
setAttr ($object + $i + ".rotateZ") $rotz;
```

```
// Further Rotation control
//
float $roty;
float $RTOD = 57.29578;
float $theta;

$theta = $RTOD*angle(<<1.0,0.0,0.0>>,$temp2);
$normal = cross(<<1.0,0.0,0.0>>,$temp2);

if ($normal.y > 0.0)
 $roty = $theta;
else
 $roty = (360-$theta);

setAttr ($object + $i + ".rotateY") $roty;

// Further Rotation control
//
//body
  setAttr ("body" + $i + ".rotateZ") (3.76*abs(cos (3.0*time))+$clusterupswing[$i]);
//lower body
  setAttr ("lowerbody" + $i + ".rotateZ") (5.86*abs(cos (3.0*time)) + \\
                                           $clusterupswing[$i]);
//tail
  setAttr ("tail" + $i + ".rotateZ") (15.26*abs(cos(3.0*time))+$clusterupswing[$i]);
}
```

UNIX

Whether you are a Unix or an NT user, you must be able to write MEL scripts and command scripts to perform simple operations such as renaming or converting a series of images.

For Unix users who find it hard to switch to the NT platform, there are a series of Unix clone tools available, such as the vi editor and the t-shell. I've found them to be indispensable while working on NT.

You can download them from the Internet.

Using the t-shell on NT, I've been able to run almost all the scripts that I used to run on the Irix. Below are some of the scripts that I believe will be useful for both Unix users as well as NT users running Unix clone tools.

RENAMING A SEQUENCE OF IMAGES

If your files end with a three-digit extension, such as picture.005, picture.006, etc. and you want to rename them to picture.5, picture.6, etc., use the following script:

```csh
#!/bin/csh
@ count = 1;
@ count1 = 0;
  while ($count1 <= 9)
  @ count2 = 0;
    while ($count2 <= 9)
    @ count3 = 0;
      while ($count3 <= 9)
      echo Renaming $count1$count2$count3;
      mv picture.$count1$count2$count3 picture.$count;
      @ count++;
      @ count3++;
      end;
    @ count2++;
  end
@ count1++;
end
```

If your files are a sequence of images, such as picture.1.iff, picture.2.iff, picture.3.iff etc., and you want to rename them to picture.iff.1, picture.iff.2, picture.iff.3, etc., use the following script:

```csh
#!/bin/csh
@ count1 = 1;
while ($count1 <= 99)
  echo Renaming $count1;
  mv picture.$count1.iff picture.iff.$count1;
@ count1++;
end
```

If you prefer to be prompted for filenames, frame numbers, offset, etc., use the following script:

```csh
#!/bin/csh
echo -n "Original Image Name>>>>>"
set name = $<
echo -n "New Image Name>>>>>"
set newname = $<
echo -n "Image start No>>>"
@ i = $< #Start no
echo -n "Image end No>>>>>"
```

```
@ e = $< #End no
echo -n "Frame Offset No>>>>>"
@ d = $< #Frame Offset
while ( $i <= $e )
@ x = $I + $d
  mv $name.$x.iff $newname.iff.$x
  @ i++
end
```

With a little change in the execution line (e.g., mv picture.$count1$count2$count3 picture.$count;), you can also convert, for example, a series of tga files with names such as picture.005.tga to the maya iff files, e.g. picture.iff.005.

The shell commands on the Unix platform are very powerful. There are many commands that allow you to control your system efficiently. Though you may find them rather tedious to learn, once you get used to the various commands, you will find that working without them is like working on Maya without using any hotkeys.